THE PHENOMENON OF DEATH

Faces of Mortality

the text of this book is printed on 100% recycled paper

THE PHENOMENON OF DEATH

Faces of Mortality

Edited by EDITH WYSCHOGROD

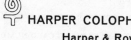
HARPER COLOPHON BOOKS
Harper & Row, Publishers
New York, Evanston, San Francisco, London

A hardcover edition of this book is published by Harper & Row.

FIRST EDITION: HARPER COLOPHON BOOKS 1973

LIBRARY OF CONGRESS CATALOG CARD NUMBER: 72–85778

STANDARD BOOK NUMBER: 06–090317–1

Designed by C. Linda Dingler

Contents

Preface

It has often been maintained that the refusal to talk about death represents psychological resistance to the most painful and universal reality of human existence. Epicurus, the ancient dispeller of mysteries, observes that when the person exists, death is absent, and that when death is, the person ceases to be. Thus in effect Epicurus alleges that there can be no *experience* of death since the two, self and death, can never coexist. What cause then can there be for fear? But few have found comfort in this argument, for it is precisely the loss of personal identity—our not being when death is—that terrifies and alarms. To utter the tautology "When death is, I am not" not only fails to allay our anxieties but is rather a precise expression of their source. In addition to the loss of the self in death there is added the fear of pain and suffering which usually accompanies the process of dying. For some the concern for an afterlife in which rewards and punishments may be meted out is an additional source of fear.

Yet the rejection of death as a theme for discussion cannot be attributed exclusively to psychological repression, to the taboos associated with what is painful. In the last analysis the question remains: What is there to say about death? Is it not a terminus, a boundary, a limiting line beyond which there are no longer any experiences at all, or at best any experiences which can be spoken of? Does it not set the limits of discourse, as it were, on the farther side of which there are no events, no states of affairs, and on the hither side of which we must designate experienced events as properly belonging to life? Furthermore, can we even know where the line which bounds life really begins, since to know it already presumes the knowledge of what lies beyond it? Is not dying itself an ongoing expression of life, and that which lies beyond appropriately designated by silence? Does not this silence have an ontological root, for can one properly say anything about that which is neither a fact nor a state of affairs?

An affirmative reply to these questions—a reply which silences their urgency—assumes the homogeneity of all facts and events and thus fails to do justice to the complexity of the observed world. It is to assume that a human life is a set of neutral events whose *terminus ad quem* is death or the cessation of these events, when, in fact, death provides a standpoint in terms of which these events may be radically reinterpreted. No interpretation of a human life can be considered "correct" in the same sense as one could assume "correctness" when asserting that Smith either was or was not in London on Tuesday. Can one deny the transformative power of death in the process of interpreting life if one considers the way in which a dying man reviews his life? The dying person who remembers the birth of a child discerns not only an event which can be universally affirmed or denied, but in addition experiences a loss of relation to the future, a loss —symbolized in the person of the child—of all ongoing relationships with the human community. After all the facts are in, the question of death opens new vistas for their interpretation.

To the survivor as well as the dying person the moment of death creates a hiatus between all experiences that preceded it and death itself. The point is poignantly illustrated in the account of a man's loss of his father quoted by Elisabeth Ross in her contribution to this volume. Death has more than ever enforced the son's need to perceive the father as a person. Yet in the passage of status from person to thing the funeral director is able to alter the appearance of the corpse so that it is no longer recognizable as the father whom the son knew and loved. "They had my Papa looking like he was fifty-two. Cotton stuffed in his cheeks had erased the best wrinkles. Makeup powder and rouge plastered his face way up into his hair and around the neck and ears. His lips were painted. He . . . looked ready to step before the footlights of the matinee performance." The son insists upon the removal of these disguises so that "in the end the man in the coffin became my Papa." The dissembling here is twofold: the artifice of the funeral director who aims to please by tricking out the man of ninety-two so that he seems to have regained his lost youth and the deeper dissembling of the son who by restoring the marks of age to the corpse seems to have regained his father. As philosophers such as Heidegger, Marcel, and Jaspers have observed, death is not separable from life; if accepted, death provides the standpoint in terms of which life can be lived authentically; if evaded it turns life into a charade, a game of lies. To deny that death is that toward which man lives is to treat man as a thing; things merely change, men die.

It would be both absurd and cruel for the psychotherapist who counsels dying patients or bereaved families to raise questions of general philosophical import during moments of personal crisis. The point is (as Ross and LeShan show) that the patient himself raises the question of death by asking, "What has been the meaning of my life?" in the context of the moment of his own imminent dying. The new interest in death has in fact arisen as a result of the observations of those who have counseled the dying and who have observed the reluctance of physicians and families to permit the dying patient to raise this question or to express his feelings about his impending death. The patient faces the loss not of one or several loved persons but of the totality of all that is loved and of all meaningful contexts. The breakdown of older structures of consolation for many and the isolation of the dying in the impersonal setting of the hospital, often accompanied by the paraphernalia of the hospital's intensive care unit, divest him of the last vestiges of humanity. The setting becomes the visible symbol of his passage from the status of person to that of thing. Much of the new literature on the psychology of the dying patient deals with the development of procedures which would enable people to die in a more humane, less isolated way. Some advocate the removal of life-support measures, raising problems of the gravest ethical concern. All advocate opportunities for the free expression of feelings. Three articles in this volume (LeShan, Kutscher, Ross) are devoted to these questions.

Much of the new interest in dying has been concerned with the problem from the individual's standpoint and that of his immediate community—his biopsychological processes, his impact upon the well-being of family and community, the cost of his care, the disposal of his remains. One purpose of this volume is to suggest that the context in which the phenomenon of death is to be explored is a wider one in which the apocalyptic events of the last three decades must be taken into account. During this period whole peoples were exterminated, willfully, ruthlessly, arbitrarily. Cultures of doom were created in the death camps of Nazi Germany and in the slave labor camps of the Soviet Union, transforming life into death. If life in this sense is the complex of conditions making possible the minimal requirements for human satiety, then death is the negation of these conditions. Hunger, cold, disease, the infliction of pain on enormous masses, undermining their status as persons, has inaugurated a new psychology of death. In this context not only the individual is exterminated, but his world. The possibility of the loss of the *totality* of one's world is introduced for the first time through the presence of nuclear weapons. Thus there is a realistic basis for apprehension, not only for the loss of self, of one's people and culture, but of the biological continuity of man and of all cultures. Atomic conflagration as total calamity— personal, historical, cosmic—has already been experienced. The carefully documented study of the survivors of Hiroshima by

Robert Lifton examines the radical change in human perspectives created by the experience of the bomb. Lifton's study reveals that mass death is not to be interpreted as the simple addition of many units to one, that is, of one death multiplied many times over, but as a phenomenon in which magnitude alters reality, thus requiring interpretation as a phenomenon *sui generis*.

Equally neglected in the current interest in death is the far more subtle issue of the disintegration of civilizations, for these, like persons, can be said to have an organic unity, to be fragile, subject to strain and pressure, in short, to be as mortal as the men who devise them. I have already noted that cultures of death have been created overnight; there is, however, a subtler process, less visible and equally omnipresent, the dying of civilizations. The expressive gestures of such civilizations, their death agonies, tend to sublate rational procedures in a quest for direct experience, valuing fluid affective structures over and against intellectual or jurisprudential structures. This process is viewed negatively by Benjamin Nelson, positively by Ralph Sleeper, and neutrally in relation to sport in my own article. The civilizational encounter with death is seen by Maurice Friedman as a preoccupation with the absurdity and meaninglessness of life as revealed in contemporary literature.

Yet there is no *general* picture of the world given by modern art or modern literature, since in the last analysis all such composites are built upon individual angles of vision: there are only individual pictures bearing individual signatures, those of Sartre or Camus, of Bergman or Fellini, of Godard or Truffaut, of Genet or Ionesco. Thus, starting from one of these, it is possible to "read off" the meaning of a civilization in its totality as one can sometimes "read off" the character of ancient communities—their level of artistic development, their technology, their views of life and death—from a single significant shard. It is not because the shard is true to type, a universal, that this is so, but rather because it gives expression to a psychosociological complex. For example, Rosette Lamont's discussion of Ionesco provides us not only with the meaning of life and death in the work of Ionesco but enables us to read from Ionesco's clues the meaning of life and death in our civilization.

All the contributions to this volume reflect the concerns of a colloquium on death conducted at Queens College during the spring and fall of 1971. The phenomenon of death was explored not only as a matter of pragmatic concern—how one can diminish the suffering of the dying person in an age lacking paradigms for healing and making whole—but, as has been suggested, in its very foundations. For this reason invitations were extended to psychiatrists, philosophers, historians of culture, literary critics, legal experts, and medical examiners, as well as to those concerned with the day-to-day business of dying, funeral directors and morticians. The papers collected in this volume reveal a representative selection of the issues raised. Some bear the marks of oral discourse and were left virtually intact as offering the most representative presentation of the speaker's views. Other papers, derived from elsewhere in the speaker's own work, present a more complete view than his oral presentation. Still others are papers written for the occasion. All contributors to this volume were participants in the colloquium. I should like to express my appreciation to those who supported the colloquium and helped to make it possible, to the President of Queens College, Joseph Murphy; to the Dean of Faculty, Nathaniel Siegel; to Darrell Taylor, Director of the Honors Program, without whose encouragement, patience, and vision the colloquium could never have come into being; to Florence Barry and Ruth Kurke, who handled the innumerable administrative details with efficiency and good humor; to Shirley Liebowitz and Susan Beck for assistance with the typing of the manuscript.

EDITH WYSCHOGROD

THE DYING PERSON
AND HIS WORLD

1 Psychotherapy and the Patient with a Limited Life Span

LAWRENCE LESHAN AND EDA LESHAN

A patient said to her psychotherapist, "I know that I'm intelligent, I have courage, and my opinions are as good as anyone else's. Just knowing this has made a big difference in my whole life. I can see the good things I've given my children, not just the bad things. I think I even love them and my husband a lot more now." Another patient said, "You know, Doc, for the first time in my life, I like myself. I'm not half so bad a guy as I always felt I was." A shy girl had written poems all her life; they represented her ego ideal, her hopes and her dreams, but she could not believe in herself enough to let others see them. With much anxiety she showed some of them to her therapist. At his response—they were of very high caliber—she began to accept her own value as a person and to talk hopefully about publishing her poetry. A brilliant woman with special skills in theoretical research had been blocked completely for nine years in her ability to do work in her field and was filled with self-doubt and self-dislike. One

Lawrence LeShan is a practicing psychotherapist currently at work for the Ayer Foundation. He has written extensively on the problems of the dying in such journals as *Psychiatry, American Journal of Psychotherapy,* and *Psychiatric Quarterly.* Eda LeShan is a psychotherapist whose work with children has been the subject of her contributions to the *New York Times Magazine.* Reprinted from *Psychiatry—Journal for the Study of Interpersonal Processes,* 1610 New Hampshire Avenue, N.W., Washington, D.C., Volume 24, Number 4 (November 1961). Copyright 1961 by The William Alanson White Psychiatric Foundation, Inc.

day she said with triumph and joy, "I started work on an article last night. I have it mapped out and the first two pages written. I think it's going to be pretty good." A thirty-nine-year-old woman who had never had a love relationship told her therapist one Monday morning of her wonderful weekend at the beach with a man she had met six months previously. As they had watched the sun go down, she had felt inside like the colors of the sunset. The affair begun that night was one of deep meaning to both of them, and she was able to give and receive the kind of love she had never known existed.

Each one of these patients was dying from cancer. None of them lived more than one year after the reported incident, and three died within four months.

In the course of a research project into the relationships between personality and neoplastic disease, these patients and others were given the opportunity of intensive psychotherapy after their cancers had been diagnosed. More than 5,000 hours of therapy with these patients brought their needs and what psychotherapy can hope to accomplish in such conditions into sharp focus.

There can be great value to the patient in the fact of someone's believing in him enough to really work to help him toward greater self-understanding and inner growth at a time when he cannot "repay" by a long period of adequate functioning—cannot "do as I tell you to and grow up to be a big, strong, successful man." His *being* is cared for unconditionally, and so he cares for it himself. The presence of the therapist affirms the importance of the here and now. Life no longer primarily seems to have the quality of something that is fading away, but takes on new meaning and validity. In the search for himself, in the adventure of overcoming his psychic handicaps and crippling, the patient may find a meaning in life that he never had found before. If the psychotherapy focuses on his strengths and positive qualities and what has blocked their full expression, the patient may come more and more to value and to accept himself, and to accept his universe and his fate.

Frequently the patient who is dying has lost his cathexes, by the natural attrition of life, by inner neurotic dictates, by an attempt on his part and on the part of those closest to him to "spare" each other from discussion of their mutual knowledge, or sometimes by a partial withdrawal in a magical attempt to ease the pain of the final parting. He is therefore very much alone and isolated in a universe which, because of his isolation, seems hostile and uncaring—as Pascal said, "The eternal silence of these infinite spaces frightens me."[1] The therapist, by his presence and by his real interest, can give the patient meaning through warm human contact, can, by providing the opportunity for a strong cathexis, give him an anchor rope to the world and to others, so that, with Bruno and Goethe, he can feel that "out of this world we cannot fall."[2] Or, like Camus's "stranger," when he had asserted, in the only way he knew, his oneness with humanity and was close to death, the patient can lay his ear "upon the benignly indifferent universe" and feel how like himself, "how warm, friendly, and brotherly" it is.[3] With contact and connectedness returned, and with the focus on life rather than on death, the patient's fear of death seems to diminish considerably.

In inexorable reality situations, the fear of death—and with it guilt and self-reproach—seems usually to be related to a sense of never having lived fully in one's own way, of never having sung the unique song of one's own personality. Thus it is by the quest for one's own essence—by finding and engaging in one's own type of relationships and activities—that the fear of death may, perhaps, be most successfully eased. This view was em-

1. Blaise Pascal, *The Thoughts of Blaise Pascal* (London: J. M. Dent, 1904), p. 85.
2. G. Bruno, *On the Immeasurable and Countless Worlds,* quoted by H. A. Hoffding, *A History of Modern Philosophy* (London: Macmillan, 1900), p. 124.
3. Albert Camus, *The Stranger* (New York: Knopf, 1946).

pirically developed in this research, but it is not new; it was advanced by Montaigne,[4] and perhaps it is only a restatement of Epicurus's "Where life is, death is not."[5]

Psychotherapy, for the patient who is aware that "time's winged chariot" is hurrying him on, cannot deal only with the technical aspects of personality as they are found in the textbooks. The larger questions are too pressing, too imminent. Values *must* be explored. As one patient put it, "Once the big questions are asked, you can't forget them. You can only ignore them as long as no one raises them." Death, the figure in the background, asks the questions, and the therapist must join in the search for answers which are meaningful to the patient. In our experience, this can be done most effectively by a search for the values most natural and syntonic to the patient—in terms of who he is, what kind of person he is, and what type of relationship would make the most sense and be the most rewarding and satisfying to him. Certainly if the patient has serious theological convictions, including some concept of afterlife, it is not the function of the therapist to attempt to disturb them; yet such convictions seldom —for who is not a child of his age?—obviate the patient's need to explore himself and his relationships with others. Thus today it is often the psychotherapist also who must try to help the person who lives in the shadow of death—to find his answers to the three questions which, according to Kant, it is the endeavor of philosophy to answer: What can I know? What ought I to do? What may I hope?[6]

A common basic assumption of psychotherapy is that the psychotherapist works with a patient to increase the value of his long-term productivity and his long-term relationships with

4. M. E. Montaigne, *The Essays of Montaigne* (New York: Oxford University Press, 1941).

5. C. Bailey, *The Greek Atomists and Epicurus* (Oxford: Clarendon, 1928), p. 401.

6. Immanuel Kant, *The Critique of Pure Reason* (Chicago: Encyclopaedia Britannica Press, 1955).

others, and, perhaps, to better his adjustment to his environment. Clearly these are not valid goals for the patient with a fatal illness. But are there other goals which therapists are committed to, or believe to be part of their responsibility? Heidegger has suggested that the age of man should not be reckoned only in terms of how long he has lived, but also of how long he has to live.[7] Within this frame of reference, it is of major importance what the person *is* and *does* during his remaining life span—that is, what it encompasses, rather than how long it is in chronological time. Perhaps life can be seen more validly as an extension in values than as an extension in time. Here may be an approach to a philosophy of therapy that does not differentiate patients according to the length of life left to them—an evaluation which can never be more than a guess, since the universe gives no one guarantees. If a person has one hour to live and discovers himself and his life in that hour, is not this a valid and important growth? There are no deadlines on living, none on what one may do or feel as long as one is alive.

Thus our point of view in therapy is that it is important—and indeed it is all that is possible—for the therapist to help the patient at whatever point he touches the patient's life. Psychotherapy has generally taken the approach of trying to help the patient shape his life in the future, and taken the pragmatic view that results measurable in time are the only basis on which to judge success. Our view here is rather in terms of the patient's life, and respect for it, whatever its time limit.

The patient with a limited life span has needs which psychotherapy can potentially fill. Unfortunately, however, very little therapy has been done, or is being done, with these patients. This paradox raises certain basic questions. For example, one might well ask if the more than 5,000 therapy hours, out of which the material presented here was derived, should have been

7. Martin Heidegger, *Existence and Being* (Chicago: Regnery, 1947).

given to these patients. Was the work worth doing, since 45 out of 47 of them died during the course of treatment? In view of the limited number of psychotherapists available, should this time have been given instead to children or to well young adults? We are not speaking here of the *research* value of the therapy—the findings are published elsewhere[8] and must be evaluated within their own frame of reference—but of the value of the therapy in itself. Was it worthwhile? Do patients have a right to this type of care as long as they live, just as they do to physical aid? Perhaps a comparison of the approaches of clinical medicine and psychotherapy may be helpful.

In some ways, clinical medicine and psychotherapy operate according to the same rules and goals, suiting the therapeutic approach to the needs and potentialities of the patient, and having as ther major goals the easing of pain and the restoration of function. However, a sharp dichotomy arises at one point. When the patient's life expectancy is clearly limited, clinical medicine does not abandon him. Although the physician may be aware that he cannot save the patient's life or restore his lost functions, he continues to attempt to soften the blow, to sustain and invigorate him, and to protect him from pain. Every medical resource is brought to bear on the situation. These efforts continue

8. Lawrence LeShan and Richard E. Worthington, "Some Recurrent Life History Patterns Observed in Patients with Malignant Disease," *Journal of Nervous and Mental Disease* 124 (1956): 460–65; LeShan, "A Psychosomatic Hypothesis Concerning the Etiology of Hodgkin's Disease," *Psychological Reports* 3 (1957): 565–75; LeShan and Marthe Gassman, "Some Observations on Psychotherapy with Patients with Neoplastic Disease," *American Journal of Psychotherapy* 12 (1958): 723–34; LeShan, Sidney Marvin, and Olga Lyerly, "Some Evidence of a Relationship between Hodgkin's Disease and Intelligence," *AMA Archives of General Psychiatry* 1 (1959): 477–79; LeShan, "Psychological States as Factors in the Development of Malignant Disease: A Critical Review," *Journal of the National Cancer Institute* 22 (1959): 1–18; LeShan, "Some Methodological Problems in the Study of the Psychosomatic Aspects of Cancer," *Journal of General Psychology* 63 (1960): 309–17; LeShan, "An Emotional Orientation Associated with Neoplastic Disease," *Psychiatric Quarterly* 35 (1961): 314–30.

as long as the patient lives—and sometimes extend even to massaging the heart after the patient is technically dead!

Psychotherapy operates quite differently in this area. As long as the patient's life expectancy is not clearly limited, it may be possible for him to get psychological help. Once the termination date is dimly seen, help becomes almost unobtainable. Even if he can afford private treatment and manages to secure it, the therapist's reluctance to become involved is likely to be manifested in a quality of remoteness and detachment which is quite different from his usual therapeutic approach. This is true not only of the patient with a known fatal disease, but also frequently of those in the later decades of life. Viewing this phenomenon on a superficial level, one might come to the altogether oversimplified conclusion that the therapist's preoccupation with the patient's continued ability to function and to relate to others is greater than his preoccupation with the patient himself.

A more careful consideration of this basic difference between clinical medicine and psychotherapy may make it possible to see some of the reasons why psychotherapists, by and large, avoid working with the dying patient, and it may, perhaps, suggest some implications about the basic values and goals of psychotherapy. There are many reasons why psychotherapists tend to feel that their task is to help the patient toward a long and healthy life. They feel that their function is not only to comfort and support—and in what denigrating terms do many psychotherapists contrast their cases in "supportive" therapy with those in "real" therapy!—but also to change him for the future. It may be worthwhile to look briefly at the reasons for this.

Each new science, as it develops, tends to exaggerate its potentialities, to see its future abilities in a somewhat magical light composed partly of hope and desire, to envision it serving as an elixir vitae answering mankind's greatest questions and needs. Psychotherapy is no exception—one recalls Freud's vision of

answering the question of the Sphinx.[9] Psychotherapists, in working very hard to help their patients for the future as well as in
the present, have often forgotten the unspoken assumption of
omnipotence which is part of this orientation. Psychotherapists
cannot mold the universe or control the future; they can help the
patient *now*, in the moment in which they are in contact with
him. They may perhaps need an attitude of more humility toward their own ability—one recalls someone's definition of psychotherapy as "the art of applying a science that does not yet
exist"—for at present the death of patients seems to threaten the
psychotherapists' basic assumption of their own omnipotence.
Psychotherapy, of course, has never had any right to expect
guarantees from the future. If the psychotherapist can justify
his work only by the results which he assumes will appear long
after he has lost contact with the patient, he had better think
through his basic assumptions.

This need to help the patient in the future may be strengthened
by the psychoanalytic view of the therapist as a father figure—
an image which may be held not only by the patient, but by the
therapist as well. As parents, therapists want their "children" to
grow up and to have long, happy, mature lives. The major flaw
in this orientation becomes immediately apparent if one looks at
actual parent-child relationships; if a parent receives all, or a
major part, of his satisfactions not from what his child is now,
but from what he will become when he grows up, the relationship
clearly leaves much to be desired.

Certainly it is vitally important for successful therapy that
the therapist wants the very best for his patient, that he has
dreams and visions for him. Only if this is true, in fact, can the
patient learn to accept and value himself. However, just as these
wishes must be reality-tempered by the potentialities of the pa-

9. Ernest Jones, *The Life and Work of Sigmund Freud*, vol. I (New York:
Basic Books, 1953).

tient and his environment, they must also be tempered by the therapist's knowledge of his own realistic limitations.

Another reason for the reluctance to treat patients with a limited life span has been suggested to us by a psychiatrist colleague. The medical man has, in his experience in medical school and in his internship, been constantly made to realize his own helplessness in the face of death. To be highly trained medically, to have at one's command all modern medical resources, and still to be unable to save a dying person can be a very heavy blow. Some of those who are most hurt by this go into psychiatry, where, theoretically, at least, death does not enter the picture. The prospect of then working with patients who will die can mobilize all of the doctor's earlier feeling of defeat and inadequacy, and arouse his resentment and resistance. In this context, remarks made by several psychiatrists about an earlier paper on the special problems and techniques involved in psychotherapeutic work with cancer patients[10] may be relevant. They did not criticize the technical concepts presented in the paper, but said that they felt the idea of intensive psychotherapy with dying patients to be "obscene" and "disgusting."

The fear of the therapist of his own hurt also seems to be a major factor in the reluctance to work with the dying patient. The feeling that a therapist develops for his patient consists of more than countertransference; there is also love and affection. When the patient dies during the process of therapy, it is a severe blow. Not only are the therapist's feelings of omnipotence damaged and his narcissism wounded, but also he has lost a person about whom he feels very deeply. It is entirely natural to wish to shield oneself from such an event, which becomes even more painful upon repetition. We believe, in fact, that a practice composed entirely or largely of patients with a limited life span is too painful to be dealt with successfully; treating a small

10. See LeShan and Gassman, "Some Observations on Psychotherapy." See footnote 8 above.

number of such patients seems to be a much more realistic approach.

The psychotherapist, too, cannot protect himself by the defense maneuver that necessity sometimes dictates to the purely medical specialist whose patients often die—the surgeon, for example, or the oncologist. This defense—the brusque, armored manner, the uninvolved relationship, the viewing of the patient's disease as of primary interest and the concentration on its technical details to the exclusion of as much else of the person as possible—may save the physician a great deal of heartache, but it is a defense which is impossible to assume for one who is in a psychotherapeutic role. The psychotherapist's answer to the heartache must come rather from a life philosophy which regards the time left for each person as an unknown variable, and holds that the expansion of the personality and the search for the self and its meaning are valid in themselves—valid as a process, valid when they are being done, and not just in terms of future results.

These are perhaps some of the reasons why psychotherapists have done so little with patients with a limited life span—why they have left this painful period of life to the minister, the rabbi, and the priest. To the question: What can one hope to accomplish with the dying patient? our answer is that the validity of the process of the search for the self is in no way dependent on objective time measurements, that the expansion of the psyche—in another age, one might have called it the growth of the soul—is not relevant to the fluttering of leaves on a calendar.

Some years after his psychotherapy, a patient wrote:

One of the primary contributions of the therapy was the certainty it has provided that I am truly alive. . . . I can recall the long years of my life and the full river of emotion that poured through me for thirty years. Surely I was alone, feeling and suffering intensely long before the analysis began. The whole record of my life until then showed intense fear and anxiety. But there is a difference now, and I believe it consists in this: I have become integrated with life; my body, mind and psyche are intimately bound to the real world around me; no longer do I project myself almost completely into the outer world to forget myself, to avoid the inner fears, panic and uncertainty. . . . I have the firm conviction now of being really made of one piece.[11]

A sister of a patient who had died said to the therapist:

She knew she was loved and lovable before she died. It was the first time in her life she had been able to accept this.

A patient's daughter wrote to the therapist:

. . . and I know that every day she grew in courage and understanding and was learning to fight the fears that surrounded her. With a woman like Mother—I suppose with any human being—an illness such as hers could have been the final fear to entirely hem her in and shut her off from human contact. But I do think that through her work with you, she somehow managed to win through her illness to greater understanding, not only of herself but of other people too. So please don't feel that your work was in vain. I don't believe that anything like that ever goes into a vacuum. Somehow it perpetuates itself. My father and I are changed because of the change in Mother, and I think it influenced her friends who visited her. Because of you, Mother's last months were filled with hope and thoughts of the future, to her very last hours. And the past few months were made far easier for those of us who loved her. . . . Because of you, we'll always have a wonderful memory of Mother's last days and of the courage that filled them.

Of these three patients, two died during the course of therapy, and one is still alive, years after completion. Who is to say which of the three therapies was most worthwhile?

11. John Knight, *The Story of My Psychoanalysis* (New York: Pocket Books, 1952), p. 201.

2 On Death and Dying

ELISABETH KUBLER-ROSS

Since I have been asked to talk about death and dying, I thought I would share with you today what we have learned from a kind of peculiar, special experience: from asking dying patients to be our teachers. I will be very brief in telling you about getting started in this peculiar specialty.

About five and a half years ago I was visited by some theological students from Chicago Theological Seminary who asked me for some help and advice in writing a paper on the Crisis in Human Life. Their class had decided dying was the biggest crisis man has to face. But they were stopped—because how can you write a paper on this? It's something you can't experience, and you can't ask one who has experienced it. I think they were sorry they had chosen this topic. So, they came to my office and we put our heads together and decided we wanted to put out a meaningful paper on this topic. We did not want to write a philosophical or theological paper, but rather a paper that could explain what it is really like to be dying, how we can recognize when a patient is dying, and what kind of things we can do (by "we" I mean the members of the healing profession) that are helpful to these patients.

I had a similar experience a few years earlier when I came to

Elisabeth Kubler-Ross has been one of the major influences in turning the attention of the medical profession to the dying patient as a person rather than to the exclusive problem of his disease. She has taught at the University of Chicago Center for Continuing Education and is the author of *On Death and Dying*.

this country. I was in a big ward in a state hospital with seventy schizophrenic patients. I didn't have the slightest idea what to do with those patients. I had no supervision, practically no teaching, no background, and here I was trying to be the therapist of persons who had been in a state hospital for up to twenty years. In my desperation I did something which proved to be a marvelously wonderful experience. I asked each of my schizophrenic patients to share with me what it is like to be schizophrenic, what kind of experiences he had, what kind of needs, fears, and fantasies he had, what kind of things we doctors can do. And after two years with these schizophrenic patients I found that they are marvelous teachers. Even the best textbooks cannot convey as well as they what it is like to be schizophrenic, how it all begins, and what kind of things are therapeutic.

I think it was because of that past experience that I recommended to my theology students to do the same thing with dying patients. I said, "Who knows what it is like to be dying other than someone who goes through the process of dying? Why don't we try to get the dying patients—I will ask them if they are willing—to talk and to share with us? I will do the interviews until you feel comfortable yourselves. You sit at the bedside and just listen, and eventually you will pitch in and I will wean myself off." That was five and a half years ago.

A week later there wasn't a single dying patient in the six-hundred-bed hospital. I went from ward to ward and asked, "Is there someone dying here?" and they said, "No." Nobody had anybody dying. But I knew better. I knew people were on the critical list, and we had a ward with cancer patients. So I started my rounds a second time. When I asked again, they looked at me and said, "What do you want to talk to them about?" I said, "About dying" (which was naïve), and they looked at me as though *I* needed a psychiatrist. It became very obvious, but it took me a long time to realize it, that there was a fantastic, massive denial in that big, very good, teaching hospital

—that the staff really did not want to admit that somebody is dying here. When I insisted on meeting the patient, instead of denial there was a tremendous amount of rationalization. "This patient is too weak" or "too sick" or "too depressed" or "would jump out of the window if you would do that." I didn't give up, and after the rationalization there came a tremendous amount of anger and uncooperativeness. I very soon had the nickname of "Vulture"—you know, the bird that waits.

Some formerly nice nurses asked me if I "got a kick out of telling a twenty-year-old boy he had only a week to live," or if I "enjoyed playing God." There was anger and hostility and uncooperativeness in this behavior, and I couldn't quite understand it. Finally, in my desperation I asked one of my colleagues in the elevator, "I wonder what it takes to get the patients for an interview." He said, half-jokingly, "There is a physician in the hospital who was a minister before. Maybe he would understand." So I went to this physician, and sure enough, he had a patient for me, an old man who was dying and apparently wanted very badly to talk about some unfinished business. I went to see him. He put his arms out, looked at me with pleading eyes, and said, "Please sit down now," with the emphasis on "now." Then I did something which I think we often do, but we are not really aware of it. I walked out of that man's room and said matter-of-factly, "No, not now—tomorrow. My students are coming tomorrow." I did hear and see him with my mind, but I did not hear or see him with my heart—that is a big, big difference. I answered my own needs, and I did not hear the patient's needs.

The next day when I went with the students, who were all ready for their first patient, the patient was elevated on pillows and in an oxygen tent, hardly able to breathe. The only thing he said was, "Thank you for trying anyway." He died about a half-hour later. I think it is fortunate that this happened to us. As painful as it was, I think it opened the door to something very important and very meaningful, because we had so many feelings of shame and guilt and frustration at that time that we would not otherwise have expressed.

We managed to gather in my office and we asked each other, "What did this patient do to us—not to our minds (the nice, fancy things we ought to say), but how do we really feel?" We call that now a "gut" reaction. How does it feel here? One of the theological students, the only one who was white like a bed-sheet, said, "It didn't bother me. I wasn't afraid. I am not afraid of dying patients." I looked at him and asked, "Why are you the only one who is so pale?" He looked up, and to prove he was not afraid said that a year ago he was in a state hospital and was called to one of those big wards where a woman was dying. He said, and I quote him now, "I walked in there and I yelled at the top of my voice, 'God is love. God is love,' until she dropped dead." That was his "proof" that he was not afraid. We had our own private "gut" reaction to him.

The question was: How do we teach the staff, theological students, medical students, nurses, that we are all afraid of death and dying—that this is normal and human? Perhaps we can teach them to overcome fear if we have the courage to admit that we are afraid? I looked at this young man and said, "You know, you looked at those people and yelled 'God is love.' That reminds me: When I was a little girl in Switzerland we had a big wine cellar. When we had guests our father would send us down there to get a bottle of wine. I remember vividly that the darker it was, the louder we yodeled." Can you understand what I tried to tell him? It conveys many things. It conveys that you are not alone. We are doing that all the time. This is a defense that children use more often than adults. We sing, we whistle, we yodel, I guess, depending on where we come from. It took this student a long time to learn that he, too, was petrified like everyone else. But he was able to overcome it, and he has become a marvelous counselor to dying patients.

What came out of these bedside interviews I can summarize very briefly. The hostility, resistance, disbelief that something like this can and should be done, was tremendous on the part of the staff. But we were impressed by the open arms and the great sense of relief of our dying patients. They welcomed us with open arms. Many times it was like opening floodgates when we came to them. It was okay to talk about anything, and anything included talking about cancer, death and dying—anything *they* wanted to talk about. We soon moved from the bedside interviews to a screened interview room because other students wanted to join the theological students. It has since become an accredited seminar on death and dying which is open to any member of the healing profession.

We have interviewed in the past five years about five hundred terminally ill patients. Each one of them knows that we are asking him to perform a service for us. We ask them explicitly to be our teachers. They know about the tape recording and the screened window. They know about the audience. And they also have the choice of being right in front of the audience or behind the screened window where we can interview with a bit more privacy. After a year and a half of doing this alone, I asked the chaplain's office for some help, because I was stopped with religious questions many times. Since then I always have a rabbi, a priest, or a minister available so that most of the interviews are done with one member of the clergy, the patient, and myself. I will summarize briefly what we have learned by asking our dying patents to be our teachers. But before I do that I would like to say a word about the society in which we live—a society in which it has become necessary to have seminars on death and dying, and to write books on death and dying. This is paradoxical. After all, man has experienced death as long as he has existed. It is very peculiar that we are not experts in this area, because nothing since man has existed has been so permanently with us as death and dying. And it seems that as

long as we live—and I now talk about mankind—the more difficult it becomes to die. We have to try to understand why this is
so. For this reason I have to talk like a psychiatrist for just a few
minutes.

When I ask you what you are afraid of when I talk about death
and dying, you will probably say you are afraid of pain, of
suffering, of nothingness, or of leaving loved ones behind. All
these fears of death are real, but they are not the real reasons
that make us so defensive and so anxious and uncomfortable in
the face of a dying patient. When you study drawings of children, when you study old pictures and cultures, and then you
study patients in psychiatric practice, you begin to understand
that the biggest part of the fear of death is unconscious. Fear of
death is like an iceberg: a tiny part is above the water (meaning conscious), and the biggest part is below the water (meaning unconscious).

I have a hard time conceiving of my own death. I can conceive
that one hundred years from now everyone in this room will be
dead; but somehow I am not among you. We believe like the
Psalmist who said, "A thousand shall fall at thy side, and ten
thousand at thy right hand, but it shall not come nigh thee." In
terms of our own ego, it is almost inconceivable to conceive of
our own death. You can conceive of someone else's death. If you
are forced to conceive of your own death you can conceive of it
as a malicious intervention from the outside. You can only be
killed. You cannot conceive of a natural death at the end of your
life and days. A person can only be killed. And it is because of
this catastrophic and destructive force that he can't do a thing
about it. If you understand that, you can understand a lot of
communications with the dying patient.

We asked an eight-year-old boy to draw a picture. He was
dying of a brain tumor. It is a beautiful picture of a child talking
about death and dying. If you do not know that, you will never
understand what this little boy was trying to convey. The fear

of death is a fear of a catastrophic, destructive force bearing upon you, and you cannot do a thing about it. This eight-year-old boy drew a tank with a cute little house behind the tank, with grass, sunshine, trees, doors, and windows. In front of the tank he drew a tiny person with a stop sign in his hand, trying to stop the tank. This is an expression of our unconscious fear of death. I will ask you afterwards how you would help this little boy to overcome his fear—which was done in this case. His last picture before he died was a beautiful flying bird with a little bit of yellow on the upper wing. When asked what this was he said, "This is the peace bird, flying up into the sky with a little bit of sunshine from my room." Do you see the difference between the two pictures? The second one is, I think, the picture of the stage of acceptance—no longer a fear of the catastrophic force. This is basically what this seminar is trying to do—to help people move from the picture of the tank to the picture of the bird. The question is why is death now so petrifying?

In the old days catastrophic death came through epidemic diseases. Man tried to postpone this event through vaccinations and injections. He has learned to conquer infectious diseases and all these catastrophic deaths. But he has also learned the mastery of killing. Man has now in this society—in this country —learned for the first time in the history of mankind the weapons of mass destruction. I am not thinking only of pollution. I am thinking of bacteriological warfare, chemical warfare, and atom bombs. They are man-made catastrophic forces; and I think if we would really face the monsters we have created, if we would really face the reality that it cannot only happen to "thee and to thee, but to me," we could not come here today, we could not enjoy a vacation, we could not make plans for our children, or our future. And because we cannot defend ourselves physically against this catastrophic destruction, we have to defend ourselves scientifically. This is perhaps why America, of all countries, is the most death-defying society that lives—because we have now made the monsters man has always been so afraid of.

In the old days and in the old country where I come from people were born at home and they died at home. There we still have no embalming. We do not put much makeup on our dead ones. We do not yet deep-freeze people and promise relatives to defrost them a hundred years from now. We do not yet have drive-in funeral homes where you can drive up in a sports car, sign a guest book, and drive off again—all of which are attempts to deny the reality of death. The nicest and briefest description of death in our society is perhaps written by Joseph Matthews, who describes the death of his own father:

My father, I say, was ninety-two. In his latter years he had wonderfully chiseled wrinkles. I had helped to put them there. His cheeks were deeply sunken; his lips pale. He was an old man. There is a kind of glory in the face of an old man. Not so with the stranger lying there. They had my Papa looking like he was fifty-two. Cotton stuffed in his cheeks had erased the best wrinkles. Makeup powder and rouge plastered his face way up into his hair and around the neck and ears. His lips were painted. He . . . looked ready to step before the footlights of the matinee performance.

I fiercely wanted to pluck out the cotton but was afraid. At least the makeup could come off. I called for alcohol and linens. A very reluctant mortician brought them to me. And I began the restoration. As the powder, the rouge, the lipstick disappeared, the stranger grew older. He never recovered the look of his ninety-two years, but in the end the man in the coffin became my Papa.

And then at the graveyard, he continues:

I say I smelled the fresh earth. There was none to be seen. What I did see is difficult to believe. I mean the green stuff. Someone had come before us and covered that good, wonderful raw dirt, every clod of it, with green stuff. Everything, every scar of the grave, was concealed under simulated grass: Just as if nothing had been disturbed here: Just as if nothing were going on here: Just as if nothing at all were happening. What an offense against nature, against history, against Papa, against us, against God.

I wanted to scream. I wanted to cry out to the whole world: "Something *is* going on here, something great, something significantly human. Look! Everybody, look! Here is my father's death. It is going on here!"

The banks of flowers upon the green façade only added to the deception. Was it all contrived to pretend at this last moment that my father was not really dead after all? Was it not insisting that death is not important, not a lively part of our lives, not thoroughly human, not bestowed by the Final One? Suddenly the great lie took on cosmic proportion. And suddenly I was physically sick!

Nowadays 80 percent of our population dies in the hospital. That means they are taken away from familiar environment— from their own beds, perhaps from the smell of good soup in the kitchen. They are rushed to the emergency room, where they are seen by an intern, extern, resident, lab technician, X-ray technician. Very few people personally introduce themselves there. Somebody takes blood, or sticks the patient's finger, and suddenly it becomes a very different kind of environment. We make decisions for the patient. We ask the family perhaps, but we rarely ask our patient, "How does it all feel? Do you want all this?" We rarely let them share in the decision making, and this is very scary for many of our patients.

Our dying patients have indicated that, more than anything else, they felt they were treated as if they had a contagious disease. Many of them shared with us their loneliness and their sense of great isolation. And in time, when they felt they went through their biggest crisis and needed people and human encounter more than they ever needed it before, we asked our patients what their biggest needs were. I would summarize briefly what we have learned from them.

The most impressive thing we learned is that all of our patients (and I must say all because I have not seen an exception yet) have known when they were close to death. If you can hear it, and if the patient knows that you are not using denial yourself, he will share with you not only the knowledge that he is dying but even the time of his death.

Our patients know that, and that includes children. I say good night to a patient, and she presses my hand in a special kind of way. I ask her, "Is this the last time?" and she nods her head. The next morning the bed is empty. This has also happened with children many times, and I think it is a question of picking their cues and having the courage and feeling free enough to talk about death.

We also asked our patients if they would have liked to have been informed that they had a serious illness at the time of its diagnosis. (About two hundred out of our five hundred had not been informed about their diagnosis or the seriousness of their illness.) They shared with us that they would like to have been told early when it was serious and not yet 100 percent sure to be fatal—under two conditions: that the physician allows for hope and does not present it to them black and white—that he does not tell them, "There is nothing else we can do"—and that the physician also conveys to them that he is not going to desert them. You may be surprised to know that they emphasize only the physician. It is significant that the physician at this moment of the patient's life is the most important person in the world, and the biggest request is always directed to him first. Only if the physician cannot give hope and cannot convey that he is not going to desert him will a patient look around for a substitute person. That, I think, is very important to know.

Many physicians say, "How can I give this patient any kind of hope when he comes to me in a hopeless condition already?" And that does not take into consideration that the hope of the relatively well is something totally different from the hope of the dying patient. Hope of the relatively well, and that includes patients who have been diagnosed as having cancer but are not yet in the process of dying, is always associated with treatment, cure, and prolongation of life. When this is no longer reasonable the patient's hope will change, and it is very important that you do not project your own hopes, but that you listen to the patient's hopes. I will give you a brief example of that:

I had the mother of small children as a patient. She was dying, and every day I visited her she would say, "Dr. Ross, I hope those research laboratories will develop those new miracle drugs and I will be the first one to get them, and I will respond and get out of here well." I shared these hopes with her, naturally. One day I visited her and she said, "You know, Dr. Ross, a miracle happened." I looked at her and said, "You got the new drug?" She said, "No, it's just that I know now that this miracle drug is not forthcoming, and I am no longer afraid." I asked, "What is your hope now, because nobody lives without hope?" She said, "I hope my children are going to make it."

Do you hear the difference? She has acknowledged that a miracle drug is probably not forthcoming, and her hope changes now to the hope that she will give her children enough strength and backbone, in a sense, so that they can stand on their own feet and "make it." It is important that we strengthen *her* hopes, that we do not tell her, "Come on now, last week you were so brave and hopeful about the new drugs. I am sure those new drugs are going to come." This is not going to help the patient. It is again protecting one's own needs and not listening to the patient's needs.

Most of our patients have gone through five stages. At the beginning of the illness they will react with shock and denial—"No, not me. It shall happen to thee and to thee." They will shop around from physician to physician. They will perhaps go back to work and pretend that it is not really true that it is so serious. But very quickly the patient will drop this denial if he has one human being—either in his family or on the medical staff—who is willing to talk about it. We have found that the majority of the patients who maintained denial maintained it only because they were afraid that they would be deserted. To be deserted does not mean that the physician has to make rounds with all his patients from beginning to end. I think one of my patients put it very nicely when I visited her in a nursing home just before she died. She looked at me nostalgically and said, "You know, it would have been tremendously helpful if Dr. P. would have called up just once to say, 'Hello, and how are you doing?'" That is what a patient means by not feeling deserted—not weekly or daily rounds, but just to know that he really counts as a person, that someone really cares, even though he is beyond medical help.

Of our patients only three out of five hundred maintained denial to the very end. I will give you a brief example of such a patient. There will always be exceptional patients who do need denial, and you would be very cruel if you would try to tear this denial down. (You can allow denial if you are sure not *your* needs, but the patient's needs are being met).

One of these patients who maintained denial was a twenty-eight-year-old mother of three small children. She had liver disease. She went in and out of hepatic coma, in and out of confusional stages and psychotic episodes. The family had depleted all their financial resources. Finally one day her young husband said, "You know, it would be better if you would live one day and be home and function as a housewife and mother and then die; but to go in and out, in and out, of hospitals like this—this is no life!" The woman was very desperate; she said her mother-in-law also wanted her dead—the sooner the better. So, in her desperate search for hope, she came back to the clinic, asking for some hope. A young physician who did not know her well and was not attuned to her needs told her, "There is nothing else we can do," and sent her home without another appointment. This was probably just an oversight, but to the patient it meant: My husband wants me dead, my mother-in-law can't wait, the hospital can't help me anymore—what next?

A neighbor who visited her and picked up her desperate search for hope told her about a faith healer who would help her. But she said she couldn't do that because the priest would never permit it. So, she was taken to the priest, in the hope that he would understand her needs and give her special permission to go there. But the priest said, "No." He, too, did not pick up how important it was for her to have some hope. Needless to say, this woman had only two possible paths to go. One was suicide, which was out of the question for her. The other was to go to the faith healer, which was the last resort for her. She did go this latter path. She walked out of the faith healer's office cured and healed. Then she wanted to tell the whole world about God's miracle—how He had cured her.

Since she felt that she was cured, she stopped taking her medication and following her diet. Two days later she slipped into a hepatic coma again. She was found in her house telling everyone about the miracle of God. But her own tiny children were in dirty diapers and not fed. Her family had had it. They brought her to the emergency room and did not want to see her anymore.

Something happened in the hospital that happens quite often, but we don't have the courage to talk about it. In the hospital nobody really wanted this woman—I think maybe because she didn't behave like one ought to behave. She floated up and down the hallways in a fancy nightgown, telling everyone about the glory of God—and very few people like to hear that all day long. She was a dying young mother of young children. The medical people thought she was psychotic, that she should go to the psychiatric ward. And the psychiatric ward realized she was dying and wanted her on a medical ward. Then we were asked for a consultation, and I think the thing that struck us most was that although this woman said she was cured and healed, she never left the hospital. Her night table was filled with the things that a woman would keep with her if she plans to stay in a place for a long time.

I realized that she was one of those few patients who can live only by denying the grim, sad, tragic realities of life. So I made a contract with her and told her that I would never, ever talk about her serious illness or about dying if she would continue to take her medication and stick to her diet, and I promised to visit her as often as I could. From then on, this woman stopped taking off for the cafeteria, where she stuffed herself once in a while, and she became a good patient.

But, tragically, she was not liked. She was put in the last room of the long hallway; not one but two doors were always closed. She was the loneliest patient I had ever seen in all my years as a physician. She sat one day on the edge of her bed, with quite disheveled hair. The telephone was off the hook. When I walked in I asked her what she was doing, and she said, "Just to hear a sound," meaning the click of the telephone. One day I visited her and she was lying in her bed, stiff and still with her arms folded across her body. There was a peculiar smile on her face (psychiatrists would call it a hebephrenic kind of smile). I asked her what she was doing, because there was nothing in her room that made me smile. She smilingly said, "Don't you smell and see the beautiful mimosas that my husband has surrounded me with?" Do you understand what she is doing? She is regarded as psychotic, which means poor reality testing, but this woman's reality testing was superb. She knew that she could not live without love and without care, which she hoped would be forthcoming from her husband. But she also knew this expression of love would not be forthcoming until she was in her casket. And so what she did in order to live was to develop the illusion of flowers and beauty, lying in the casket, surrounded by the flowers sent by her husband.

The question is then: If you enter a patient's room like this, how do you help the patient? Do you go in and open the windows and say, "Let's get some fresh air in here," which would be enforcing reality? Or are you phony and say, "Oh, I love mimosas. I think they are beautiful," when you know they are not there in reality? I think both extremes are cruel. I think what you have to learn is to read the meaning of the delusion and know that all this patient asks for is care and love. Since such concern is not forthcoming from her family, and you are not able to force them to give it, you must give her a little bit of care and love.

We spent every free moment with this patient, even if there were only perhaps five minutes a day, just holding her hand, sitting with her solemnly. On one of my last visits with her I was sitting, holding her hand. I couldn't talk much because I had promised not to talk about it. She smiled and said, "When my hands get colder and colder, I hope I have warm hands like yours holding mine." This was one of her last communications.

Does this patient know she is dying? It seems to me this expression also means to talk about dying. You can talk about dying without using the words "death" and "dying." I think when a patient like this says, "When my hands get colder and colder, I hope I have warm hands like yours holding mine," what she is really saying is, "I hope when I am dying someone sits with me and cares." If I include this kind of language, then I must say that there wasn't a single patient who did not talk about death and dying with us. Fortunately, most of our patients were not such tragic cases. Most of them dropped their denial very quickly.

When a patient stops saying, "No, not me," and he becomes nasty, mean, and angry, and begins to say, "Why me?" he is in the second stage, the stage of rage and anger. The tragedy is that very often we get angry back at them. They are nasty. Frequently they are obnoxious patients. They are ungrateful. We come in and try to start an infusion, and before we touch them they say, "Do you ever hit the vein the first time?" It is that kind of patient. The nurse wants to shake the pillow, and that moment they say, "Can't you leave me alone? I'm just trying to take a nap." We come either too early or too late; there are too many people or not enough people.

What is your "gut" reaction to people like this? How do you really feel in your heart—not in your mind? You stick the needle a bit harder; you wait perhaps twice as long before answering the light; you try to avoid them; or you get nasty back at them if you can; and if you are raised in a training center where you are taught "one ought always to be nice to patients" you take it out on the student nurse, or on the husband when you go home —or if you don't have a husband, then you take it out on the dog. But somebody's going to get it—and *that does not help!*

What helps, I think, is what we are trying to do throughout the seminar. That is not to judge but to try to understand why we are doing what we are doing. Why does the patient do what he is doing? What is the whole meaning behind it? The best example I can give is of a young man dying of lymphosarcoma who was in protective isolation for six weeks. He was lying in his bed, and every time someone walked in he turned his back. He wouldn't talk, he wouldn't communicate; he made everybody feel guilty. I went to him and really tried to get at his anger. He turned his back, and I was quite ready to take off again. Then for a glimpse of a moment I think what I tried to do was to identify with him.

I looked at this man who was dying, who had been six weeks in that room, isolated by the environment. People had to put a gown and mask on to go in (and thus very few people went in). Then I looked at the wall which he faced from his bed. The whole wall was filled with fancy, colorful get-well cards. Suddenly I got angry at those cards. I thought about all the nice people who went out shopping and bought those get-well cards, signed them, sent them, and thought they had done their duty. Most of these people knew that the young man was never going to get well, and it seemed like a big, big farce. I saw the gold-fish in the fishbowl, swimming around and around. I had the strong "gut" reaction to pick up that goldfish bowl and smash it at those get-well cards. Those "gut" reactions are only glimpses of moments that you feel if you are able to listen to your own feelings. I shared this with him, and he turned around and really poured out, like opening floodgates, his rage and his anger at the people outside—including his mother, who came there and spent the night and in the morning got up and said, "I have to go now because I have to go home and take a shower." He looked at me and said, "You, too—you're no different. You're going to walk out of here again."

Do you understand what he is saying? He is not angry with you as a person, but he is angry with you for what you represent —life, health, function, energy, all the things he is in the process of losing.

A mother whose child was dying of cancer was in the hallway of a hospital. I walked over to her and said, "You feel like screaming?" She said, "Do you have a screaming room in a hospital?" I said, "No, we have a chapel." Then she really gave it to me. She said, "The chapel! Who needs the chapel? In a chapel you have to be nice and quiet and grateful and grave, and I want to be angry and nasty and scream and curse and yell at God like I did last night in a cold car in a parking lot when I screamed and yelled at God, 'Why did you let this happen to me?' meaning 'Why did you let this happen to my child?'" That is the anger I am talking about. All our patients go through this stage of anger —the families go through this stage of anger, and to some extent also the staff. And we have to understand that—not judge it. You can pour fuel on the fire and let the patients express it without making them feel that they are not good Christians because they question God, or that they are ungrateful patients because you are working so hard, or because they are nasty and difficult. If you can help them to express it you see that sometimes after one five-minute session in which you let them pour it out, they never scream half as loud as you are afraid they will. Those patients and family members are greatly relieved and much more comfortable. From a hospital administration point of view, it is the most helpful thing you can ever do because you will see that the patient not only asks for less pain medication, but he rings for the nurses less often, and the staff is much more comfortable, too.

If the patient has stopped saying, "No, not me," and has stopped asking, "Why me?" he usually goes to the temporary stage of bargaining; this often demands the clergy because most of the bargaining is made with God: I will be a better Christian if you will give me one more year to live; I will donate my eyes or my kidneys. One woman asked for only one single day. She wanted to get dressed and attend her son's wedding. She was totally dependent on drugs for her pain. But we bent over backwards to give her this one day, partially because of our own needs, for we were hardly able to tolerate this angry woman. She looked like a million dollars when she left the hospital. We wondered what it was like when you ask for one single day. So I waited for her in the hallway the evening she came back, and she didn't like seeing me. Before I opened my mouth she called all the way down the hallway, "Dr. Ross, don't forget, I have another son." That's the briefest example of the bargaining. She wanted to attend her son's wedding, and the moment she was able to do that she reminded me that she had another son.

Mothers want to live until the children are out of school. The moment they are out of school, they want to live long enough to see them get married, and the day of the marriage they want to live long enough to become grandmothers. That is not important. It is not relevant what they promise, because the promise is hardly ever kept anyway. What is important is the significance of this bargaining. The bargaining is not peace yet, but it is a temporary truce. It serves a very important purpose, similar to recharging a battery or recollecting all your energy so that you have strength enough and courage enough and are relaxed enough for the final steps of the journey. This bargaining time is important for the patient, for the family, and for the staff.

When a patient stops saying, "No, not me," stops asking, "Why me?" and has said, "Yes, but . . . ," when he drops the "but" he enters a stage of depression, and the depression means, "Yes, me." The patient grieves first for what he has lost already—his job, his ability to be home. That kind of grief we can deal with relatively well. But then he goes through a preparatory grief, a silent kind of depression when he doesn't talk anymore —when he lies on his pillow and doesn't want to see anybody. That is hard for us to take. The nurses go in and want to be doing something; the minister goes in and wants to pray, and the patient doesn't want to pray; the family wants to be sociable and talk, and he doesn't want to talk. He doesn't even want to see his children anymore. And the staff and the family are very upset about this. What happens more often than not is that we go into such a patient's room and try to cheer him up by saying, "Come on, cheer up, it's not so bad." This is about the worst thing we can do for our patients in this stage.

If I were to lose one beloved person—if I were to become a widow—everybody in this room would allow me to grieve, to wear black clothes, to be in mourning—and that is for the loss of *one* beloved person. A man who is facing his death faces the loss of everybody and everything he has ever loved. This is a thousand times more sad, and he should be allowed to grieve. Only when we allow our patients to grieve, to separate, to decathect, as the psychiatrist calls it, will they ask once more to see all the relatives and acquaintances; then to see the children once more; and at the end to see only one beloved person. The tragedy is when the family does not reach the stages at the same time as the dying patient. Then you have to pay attention to the ones who limp behind in the stages.

I am thinking of a dentist who had a lot of unfinished business and who finally worked through and reached this final peace and acceptance after a lot of turmoil (and I think we were both pretty proud of it). His wife dashed into my office one day and said, "He doesn't talk anymore." I tried to explain that she should be very happy that he had finally reached this stage of acceptance and peace. But she said, "I know all that. You don't understand. I have called in all my relatives from far away." She obviously could not hear—just as I could not hear my first patient. So I thought: If she sees this man's peaceful face maybe she can understand. I went with her to her husband's room. He was surrounded with relatives who whispered and were uncomfortable. She walked straight over to him, pinched him on the cheeks, and said, "Be sociable."

Do you understand what she is doing? She cannot face her husband's imminent death, and she is still in the stage of partial denial. She still expects him to be the host and the sociable guy that he has always been. And that, too, you should not judge. But try to help her so that she, too, can reach this stage of acceptance.

The last stage, this peaceful stage of acceptance, is extremely hard to describe. The only way I can describe it is with actual examples. It is not resignation. Resignation is giving up—"What's the use?" "I'm tired of fighting." It's a kind of defeat. Acceptance is a victory, an inner kind of peace. Very few of our patients have need for pain medication at this time. They are not comatose. They are alert and conscious and can talk. There is very little need for verbal interaction. A patient lies rather comfortably in her bed and holds your hand and says, "My time comes very close now, and I am ready." Not happy, but ready. It is almost beyond feelings. It is not a happy stage, but it is also void of anguish, bitterness, and pain.

The best example I can give you, I think, is my favorite—a patient who is also a good example of hope. Before I mention her, I wanted to mention briefly that our patients use three basic languages to talk about dying.

Children usually use play, interaction, paintings, or drawings to talk about dying. I give you this example: If you hear a small child in an oxygen tent say, "Nurse, what happens when I'm here and a fire breaks out?" then I hope you remember what the fear of death is and don't tell the child, "But nobody smokes in here." A child who asks, "What happens if a fire breaks out and I am in an oxygen tent?" is fearing a catastrophic, destructive force and can't do a thing about it. That's the same question that this little eight-year-old boy raises with his drawing of the tank, when he stands in front of the barrel and tries to stop it, but he also knows he cannot stop it. It is symbolical language. Our patients either use plain English when they talk about death and dying or use symbolical language or drawings.

But plain English is not always plain English. Each time I visited one old man, he said, "Dr. Ross, the only thing you can do for me is to pray to the Lord that he will take me." And somehow I took it for granted that he really wanted the Lord to take him. He was eighty-three, he had had a full, meaningful life, and I assumed he was ready to die. I didn't question it.

In the fall before I went back to Switzerland I needed him—I guess to recharge my own battery because I was going to visit my own dying mother. I thought I had to see this wise old man, so I went to him. He was out in the hallway, very anxious and apprehensive—not at all the very wise old man that I wanted to see. He met me and said, "Dr. Ross, did you pray?" I said, "No—" I didn't finish my sentence before he said, "Thank the Lord. I was so afraid He might hear you." I asked him what happened, and he said, "You remember the seventy-three-year-old lady across the hall? We fell in love." He didn't want to die anymore. This is the best example of the inadvisability of taking things for granted. I took for granted that when you are an eighty-three-year-old wise man you have reached the stage of acceptance. He had not reached acceptance, only resignation—the resignation that you see in nursing homes so very often where people count the days and the weeks and the months until they die, not because they are ready or happy to die, but because they are not wanted much anymore; they are of no earthly use to anyone. That is resignation, not acceptance. And I always say, all it takes is a station wagon to change that. We tried that once.

We took a station wagon to an old-age home and asked for twelve grandmas. We got fifty volunteers. We took some to an orphanage and the others to a hospital where we have lots of children who need grandmas very badly—people to sit with them, paint with them, listen to them, read with them, or tell them stories. You have no idea what this station wagon did. It likely changed the chronological age of the nursing home by twenty years. Those old people waited from week to week, and I think this one and a half to two hours was the only time they felt like living. What I am trying to say is that you have to help people live until they die.

Sometimes we are fooled by thinking that old people are in the stage of acceptance when they really are in the stage of resignation, because they are not wanted and not loved and they have no feeling of purpose and meaning in their lives anymore. There are plenty and plenty of children who could benefit greatly from a grandma or a grandpa. The station wagon represents, I think, the catalyst, and that can be any one of you. To bring two needing people together takes just a little time and a little care; it doesn't take much money.

I am giving you my last example of my patient who I think represents this changing hope the best, and that is the most important lesson we learn. Last winter a thirty-five-year-old, black, single girl came to us with a big hope that if she came to this large hospital with all the specialists they would find out what was wrong with her, cure her, and then she would resume work and be all right. She had no idea how sick she was. She was soon told there was no cure for her ailment; then she was told there was very little treatment; and after a few more tests she was told the only way she could live any longer would be if she were accepted on a kidney dialysis program.

The problem was that we had two programs for indigent people on the kidney dialysis. The first place turned her down because she was not rich enough—and not poor enough (that's another problem we are facing now). And the second place was a hospital which would be very unlikely to accept her. Without our knowledge, this young woman, quite alone in a large hospital, tried to work and struggle through some sort of an acceptance. The staff, especially the nurse and the social worker, but also the resident and the priest, could not reach the stage of acceptance. They were rebelling against the possibility that this young, beautiful person had to die when the medical facilities for her continuing life existed. They could not accept it, and then the social worker acted. She kept calling the other hospital, nagging them, calling them, begging them, and asking them to consider the girl, until one evening I think they got tired of her pushing. They called up and said, "We have a free bed available. Why don't you send her over now?" A little while later the girl was sent back from the hospital rejected. Then the questions arose: What do we do now? Who is going to visit her? What do we tell her? And how do we face her when we ourselves cannot really accept it?

The minister and the social worker felt that they did not want to isolate her and keep her longer than necessary. But they also felt very uncomfortable seeing her, and finally asked if we would see this patient in our Death and Dying Seminar—to interview her in the seminar so that all the people who had anything to do with her could see how much she knew, how she was able to talk about it, and what kind of things we could do now when she was doomed to die in this society which could perhaps enable her to live. We went to visit her and told her that we needed her. In order for us to help her, she had to help us. We were frank and honest about it, and she was grateful that she was able to talk about it. Then she shared with us what happened in that hospital. The more she talked, the more upset I became about the silly, little trivial things that finally make the difference between a woman dying or living. At the very end, when I was very angry and really upset about it, she looked at me and said calmly, "Dr. Ross, don't worry. I know that I am

going to die soon, but when I die it is like going to be trans-
planted from this garden into God's garden." Just like that! I
said, "That simple?" which again is a reaction of mine—inability
to accept it. And she said, "No, not that simple; there is something that bothers me." During the seminar she was not able to
find out what her unfinished business was. So I said, "Well,
why don't I come back? Maybe when you are alone we can talk
about what bothers you."

I asked the priest and the social worker to go with me and
try to settle this unfinished business. None of them showed up.
We were alone together, and we were very strangely searching for something. We didn't know what we were searching for
—and I can't describe it to you any better. It's like two children
who look for something they have lost, but don't quite know
what it is they lost. The only thing she kept repeating was, "I'm
bad, I'm bad, I'm bad." It would have been simple for me to say,
"No, you are not bad. You are a beautiful person," but that would
not have helped her. It would have been a projection again of
my own image of her. And so we went down the line of all the
things people could regard as bad. Nothing. Finally I gave up
and said, "God only knows why you should be bad!" which is
an expression of my "gut" reaction, and she said, "That's it—God!
I asked God for help—'God help me. God help me.' And I hear
Him saying in the back of my mind, 'Why are you calling me
now? Why didn't you call me when things were all right?' What
do you say to that, Dr. Ross?"

What would you say? My "gut" reaction was to get up and
get the priest because that is a question that usually the priest or
minister answers. I am uncomfortable with questions like this
—and I am very frank with my patients. The minute I moved, she
looked at me and said, "What do *you* say to that?" I had learned
to listen to my patients, and so I was there, kind of stuck: I had
to give her my answer. I couldn't just give her a nice phrase, so
I told her, "You know, if you can think for a moment of the

children playing outside—the mother is in the house—and the little boy falls and hurts his knee. What happens?" She looked at me and said, "The mother goes out and helps him back on his feet and consoles him." And I said, "Well, what happens next?" She said, "Well, when he's okay, he goes back to play and mother goes back in the house." I said, "He has no use for her now." And she said, "No." I said, "The mother resents this terribly?" She looked at me almost angrily and said, "A mother? A mother would have resented that?" I said, "Strange—a mother wouldn't resent that and a Father should?"

Do you understand what I am trying to say? I am much more comfortable talking about mamas and children than I am talking about God. Did I not tell her in my own language what I think the answer would be? Then her face was very peaceful, comfortable—I can't describe how good it felt not only to her, but to me, too. But then this patient did something that no other patient of mine has ever done. Looking me straight in the face, she said, "Dr. Ross, what is your concept of death?" I almost fell off the chair. Do you know it shall happen to thee and to thee, but not to me? I ask those questions, and I mumbled something about liking the idea about the garden. She did not accept that because that was obviously not *my* concept of death before I met her. Then she said again, "What is your concept of death?" I looked at her face, and I said something that I really meant. I said, "Peace," because I looked at her marvelously beautiful, peaceful face. And she looked at me and said, "I am going very peacefully now from this garden into God's garden."

This is an example of what counseling the dying patient can be. We can do this with our "gut" reaction and our intuition, and just being with—very close and very intimately—the patient for a moment. You have to take off your white coat for a while. But then afterwards you have to think about it and try to understand what happened. Do you understand what this unfinished business was? Because if you don't understand it and think about it afterwards, you have not become receptive to the next patient's expression of unfinished business. Her hope was cure, then treatment, then prolongation of life; then, when she was not expected to live, her big unfinished business was the feat—"If I am not found acceptable in this garden, how do I know I am found acceptable in God's garden?" This was really a question of fear, but also of her last hope.

I think I am using this example also because many of you will say that you have to be a psychiatrist to do this sort of work. It is obvious you don't have to be a psychiatrist; sometimes it would be better if you were a priest (which I wished for at that moment), but I think what you have to be is a human being who cares. It does not take much time—it takes very little time. I knew this specific woman less than one hour in her whole lifetime. I think that shows you how little time it takes. It's how deeply and personally you dare to give your all to another human being, knowing that others will help you when you also have to face your own end one day. I want to be sure you get the feeling that the world of dying patients is not morbid, not depressing, not even terribly sad; it can be very, very beautiful, and you can learn a great deal from those facing death.

Someone once said: "People are like stained glass windows. They sparkle and shine when the light is out, but when the sun goes down their true beauty is revealed only if there is a light from within." I think counseling a dying patient is an attempt to find in each patient this light from within.

3 Anticipatory Grief, Death, and Bereavement:
A Continuum

AUSTIN H. KUTSCHER

It has been said that there are two things that man cannot face—the sun and his own death. Yet, from the very instant of birth, we are on a long, it is *hoped*, trajectory toward death. Notwithstanding, all too few of us realize that a life is filled with major and minor preparations for death. There are constant *superficial* losses whose value in the process of this preparation should not be underestimated. The loss of a job, even voluntary movement from one job to another, loss of job seniority, loss of social status, loss of financial security—all are certain, less evident, examples of factors in this preparatory process. How many children survive their first haircut without tears? How many long-haired youth today dread, with accompanying and often extreme emotional conflicts, the parturition from this possession? And speaking of parturition, all are aware of the postpartum "blues," which often are seen to follow childbirth, and the sometime devastating effects on many young mothers. All of these preparatory losses can be accompanied by and complicated by evidences of grief, both

Austin Kutscher teaches at the Columbia University College of Dentistry. He is the president of the Foundation of Thanatology, an institute concerned with the problem of death and dying from a variety of perspectives. He is also the author of *Death and Bereavement* and the editor of a volume on death, *But Not to Lose.*

anticipatory, prior to the loss, and consequent, following the loss.

Therefore, it has been concluded by some, Dr. Arthur Carr, for instance, that these losses prepare the human being for the *greater* losses in his life, the deaths of his loved ones and, finally, the loss of his own life. As caretakers in the economy of a human's being, we should theorize about his ability to *accept* these losses through certain adaptive processes which include anticipatory grief and the work of bereavement; and we should try to affect the psychosocial consequences and patterns of his recovery from them at the same time that we also assist our dying patients to the boundaries of mortality. Death must be accepted and faced—the death of the individual and the death of the loved ones who predecease him.

When a fatal illness is diagnosed, as death approaches, and after the patient's death, there are many who are involved in the care of the patient, as part of his trajectory: his family, the nurse who tends him, the physicians who treat his illness, and the minister and social worker, among others, who offer spiritual guidance and counsel. In addition to the dying patient, all of these important role players, some to a greater and others to a lesser extent, usually pass through stages of one or another form of grief and bereavement and/or deal with the emotional problems of terminal care by various defense mechanisms, such as denial. In trying to conceptualize this, the context of the title of this discourse is offered, to wit: the continuum of anticipatory grief, the dying of the patient, the death as experienced by survivors, and bereavement.

According to Dr. Elisabeth Kubler-Ross, in her book *On Death and Dying*, the dying patient proceeds along a path characterized by various stages until hopefully, but far from always, he reaches the point, or stage, of acceptance. These stages are (1) denial and isolation—failure to acknowledge the facts, disbelief in the face of overwhelming medical evidence, and a compulsion to be alone, to isolate himself, submerged in the depths of depressed and anxious thoughts; (2) anger—it can't be true, someone is lying, the doctors don't know what they are doing; (3) bargaining—if I do this, it won't be so; if I do that, perhaps something heroic, there will be a postponement of what seems to be inevitable; (4) depression—the sense of great loss; the reduction of the self-image; the realization of one's own shattered vulnerability and mortality; stress over the impact of medical expenses that go on and on; worry over the family at home; the realization that soon all will be lost, that the "me" will be gone from the scene; that death must be faced; and finally, if so, blessed; (5) acceptance—the inevitable will come no matter what is done; it must be faced by "me"; all *will* be lost; I do not know what will follow, but so be it: I have lived my life and tried to do my best.

Grief is the phenomenon of human behavior in survivors which accompanies loss; and its most striking effects are apparent when a beloved figure departs from life. The classic study of grief reactions was written by Dr. Erich Lindemann, who observed and treated both the victims and their survivors following the tragic Coconut Grove nightclub fire that took place in Boston in the 1940s. According to Lindemann, grief is a definite syndrome with somatic and psychological symptomatology, although medical definition may not recognize it as such. The most striking characteristics are weeping, a tendency to sighing respiration, complaints about lack of strength, feelings of physical exhaustion, digestive disturbances (such as inability to eat, repugnance toward food and/or abdominal discomfort), and so on. The bereaved may demonstrate a sense of unreality and detachment and may be intensely preoccupied with the image of the departed one. Guilt concerning acts done or not done may plague him; accompanying this guilt are extreme feelings of irritability and anger expressed toward others or toward the deceased. The bereaved person is frequently restless but unable to initiate meaningful activity. Even in the performance of his daily routine, he finds the smallest effort almost beyond his energies and capabilities. Depression, agitation, and insomnia aggravate his physical and mental status.

Frequently, however, grief may have found its fullest expression before the death of this loved person. Its effects strike the bereaved-to-be at the moment the hopeless prognosis is pronounced, as he becomes aware of the truth of the situation. Therefore, the process of mourning begins long before the significant loss. It is contended here that during this period of anticipatory grief, the bereaved-to-be passes through some parallel, if not identical or synchronous, stages in relation to the dying patient (stages which would be positively identifiable if accorded similar and adequate study): he denies and disbelieves the medical evidence; he isolates himself, fearing that a sharing of his thoughts and doubts will only aggravate his torment and that of the dying patient and other members of the family. He is angry—perhaps at the patient who "hadn't taken care of himself" and who is going to leave him to face the world alone, perhaps also to raise a family alone; or maybe at the doctors who refuse to do enough, or who are incapable of doing enough, or who may, he thinks, be lying to him or who are inordinately brutal in disclosing the facts; or perhaps he is angry at the nurse who brushes aside his agonizing questions because it is not in her province to answer them, or who is agonized herself by them and shields herself by denial, or who never seems to be around when she is needed, or who seems to be adding to the patient's discomfort when she fails to respond immediately to his ring—or perhaps his anger is directed at God; or various combinations of these and a host of others.

The family member, in this context almost always a spouse or a parent, begins to bargain: If I do this, maybe pain will disappear, maybe even my loved one will be healed; if only I pray hard enough; if I perform some other demanding effort, this misery will go away and life will continue as before. He becomes depressed by thoughts of the present, by facts and fantasies of what the future will bring in suffering for all concerned—both during and after the course of the illness; he finds that he cannot function, cannot summon up either his emotional or physical resources to face each day as it comes; and so he is anxious and depressed; he grieves—even mourns. Finally, hopefully, he accepts the facts: death will come; it must and will be faced; and I will be left to do as best I can in the future; there is no choice, and I must do what has to be done. And—eventually—I too will face my own mortality: will I and *how* will I be able to accept that?

There appears to be a timetable of grief, oriented to the date of the onset of a fatal illness as well as to the date of the loved one's death. And this timetable relates the period of grief to some undetermined finite period of time. The presence of grief in anticipation of the loss, both in subtle and in pronounced ways, alters the trauma of the aftermath. When death *has* been prepared for by those who will survive, these bereaved may more readily find their way back to normal functioning. The contention here, requiring intensive study, is that there is a kind of symmetry and replication of effects: the more the anticipatory grief reaction before the loss, the less the bereavement effects following it; the less the anticipatory grief reaction before the loss (as must be inevitable in cases of sudden accidental death or death from an acute myocardial infarction or heart attack), the more the bereavement effects after the loss. Anticipatory grief creates an atmosphere, however ineffable, of adjustment to the potential loss; and so, to continue our hypothesis, then, is not anticipatory grief in its most simplistic course and form a generally repressed projection backward of bereavement itself?

The physical symptomatology of grief is most apparent during the bereavement period. The bereaved person presents a multitude of symptoms, as Lindemann and more recently Dr. Paula Clayton have related. Further and more recent studies, by

Dr. Dewi Rees in Wales, Dr. C. Murray Parkes in England, and Dr. David Maddison in Australia, have also produced data which indicate a greatly and clinically significantly higher morbidity rate among the bereaved (particularly following the loss of a spouse and especially in the older age groups) and, more importantly even, a higher rate of mortality during the first six months of bereavement—tapering off thereafter. Neglect of the self, for instance, may play some part, but there are some disease processes that cannot truly be related in such a manner, among them perhaps even cancer. It is contended here that parallel studies of anticipatory grief would likely reveal findings comparable in one of many such aspects.

Emotionally, both the patient's attitudes and desires and those of the bereaved-to-be may change from day to day: now he may want to hear the truth and talk about it; tomorrow he may detach himself from it and/or deny it—depending on the stage achieved—and the changes of patient and family may be synchronous or may not. Not at all unrelated to the above, a new fact or sign or happening—and interactions involved—may occur, particularly within the cold walls of the institutional setting, with complicated emotional outcomes for all involved.

It is documented fact that most people today, in this country, die in hospitals and not at home (as was more often the case in the past). The hospital represents scientific achievement, the hope for cure with new and remarkable medications or machines, or, at the least, a dream of prolonging the life of a beloved one. But hospitalization in itself causes separation; separation results in anxiety; separation anxiety in turn further reduces the contact of both family and friends with the patient and, in so doing, increases everyone's anticipatory grief reaction; and the dying person, detached from his familiar surroundings and unable to be a vital member of society, goes through this period in a most extreme state of anxiety, suffering his own highly specific form of separation anxiety and anticipatory grief.

The patient may have complaints, but they frequently mask what his *real* complaints are—among many others, fear of death, distrust of those who, he often rightfully feels, may be concealing facts or at least something from him, and so forth. He truly has the right to grieve his own dying but is seldom given the opportunity to express his feelings and concerns. He usually finds himself being abandoned as his condition deteriorates; the living have already "written him off." He becomes the central figure in a great "conspiracy of silence"—forbidden to voice his fears and lied to concerning his condition and prognosis. The dying patient nearly always knows the truth but often doesn't know whether his kin have actually been told the worst. In the process, he may become antagonistic to them or, in many cases, may try to protect and shield his loved ones from the knowledge that he has. And this brings us to that widely debated question: Should the patient be told the truth, that death for him is imminent?

Although we have been debating this subject for decades, from the above it may be surmised that I think that this may actually be the wrong question. The question to be coped with should really be: How should we deal with what we must assuredly assume he "knows" or has discerned?—what Reverend Robert Reeves describes as the "moment of truth" between the patient and his bereaved-to-be.

First of all, let it be understood that the nurse often talks the most with the patient and is in the best position to "read his signals." Her counsel should always be considered as extremely relevant. The life style of the patient should be considered—how he handles trouble, reacts to bad news, responds in a crisis. And the life style of the person in attendance who does the "telling" —the doctor, family member, or pastor—is also a factor which will profoundly affect the patient's future relationships with all those about him. And let us not forget that these caretakers who themselves are often desperately anxious about death, including their own, whether consciously or unconsciously, may erroneously convince themselves through denial mechanisms that the patient does not know the truth—or want to.

Most patients actually seem to fear the process of dying more than the unknown quantity, death. Yet, if those who will mourn his death would share their feelings with him in the living *now*, if emotional *ex*pression rather than emotional *re*pression were to be allowed, many fears could be allayed; for many more, the terminal days could be a time for a kind of exquisite loving, sharing, and planning, and anticipatory grief for all would take on its most useful form and beneficent qualities. When there has been a free exchange of thoughts and emotions between two married people, or parents and a child—under these circumstances, the survivor is left with a substantial foundation on which to rebuild his life, a product of the positive effects of anticipatory grief, and with memories which become supportive during the days of sorrow and bereavement which follow the death. All such experiences represent a catharsis that ultimately allows the one to accept his own death with less fear (because he knows that he is loved and will not be abandoned) and his survivors to face the future with greater strength and a more suitably adjusted and positive life pattern. Hence, let us recapitulate the continuum of anticipatory grief, dying, and bereavement, well or badly enacted, as suggested in the title of this essay.

But too often the caretakers delude themselves into what I called above "the conspiracy of silence." The terminal patient *is* shielded from the truth. True, not all patients do want to know, and not all should necessarily be told; and if denial of the truth is the *only* way a patient can handle his dying, then he *should* be allowed his denial. But the greatest cruelty is inflicted when the patient *does* want to know and is *not* told. Observation has revealed that most patients crave an opportunity to ventilate their thoughts and feelings. Only in recent years, however, through the work of Dr. Herman Feifel, Dr. Elisabeth Kubler-Ross, and Dr. Avery Weisman, among others in the field of psychiatry and psychology, has the value of allowing the dying patient to ventilate his fears been appreciated. Perhaps above all, though, both for the patient and for his family, hope should never be utterly destroyed. The treatment plan should always be projected beyond the presumed life expectancy, recent conceivably hope-engendering developments in medical research can be discussed, and so on—so that at least a glimmer of hope never dies. And even when hope for survival is only a very dim and fading light indeed, a whole new series of realistic achievable goals *can* effectively be introduced for all involved so that life may be lived to the very end. Such realistic goals can be, for example, strong reinforcement of the already acknowledged and existent love of a spouse, the summoning of strength to live until a grandchild is born, the settling of unsettled and hence troubling personal affairs, the resolution of family difficulties and intensely personal differences between the dying patient and surviving members of the family, reconciliations, and perhaps most important of all, in some instances, the hope of achieving what Dr. Ross has called "acceptance"—in the wake of which death with dignity *can* then be achieved.

In Great Britain, Dr. Cicely Saunders has established a "resting place for the weary traveler," the dying person, called St. Christopher's Hospice, a unique—and I should not perhaps, since she does not, even call it this—hospital for the terminally ill, where heroic measures are not taken to sustain life or prolong dying, where pain is controlled even as it starts, where dying truly becomes a part of living as the very walls of the hospital are breached to allow the family to enter at will, where a staff of compassionate and believingly dedicated (in some instances highly religiously dedicated as well) people has been enlisted to support and tend the patient and permit him to die in dignity.

Such professionals, our caretakers, both on the scene and behind the scene, are involved not only in their professional capacities but also personally and emotionally with anticipatory grief and, thereafter, to some degree or other, with actual bereavement. How many—or perhaps we should ask how few—nurses and physicians don't reach a point of emotional overload during periods when it seems that one patient after another dies in spite of all their combined and/or individual efforts to save or extend a life? And so, by way of answer, we pose some further queries: Why do some professionals avoid service in wards where terminal patients are moved to die? Why do so many others tend to abandon the patient as his condition deteriorates; to visit him less frequently, to perform only those acts which treat his primary illness, to hustle and bustle in and out of the room as rapidly as possible, avoiding conversation which may prove to be embarrassing and avoiding answering questions, fearful that their own acknowledgment of the patient's psychological distress, *and their own,* will bring forth tears—maybe even their own? (Somehow or other, incidentally, we regard crying in ourselves and others as unworthy, unmanly, or an inappropriate reaction—when such is *not* the case at all.)

I would like at this point to offer some succinctly expressed words to serve, it is my hope, as a few effective tools for all who care for or surround the dying patient and his family.

1. The caretaker's chief obligation is to provide what Dr. Avery Weisman has so imaginatively called "safe conduct" for the dying patient.

2. The primary suffering of the patient is handled by those who can relieve the physical symptoms of his ailment, especially his pain or his disfigurement; but his secondary sufferings—the loss of self-esteem and body image, the fears of abandonment and separation, the anxieties and feelings of hopelessness—must also be treated—by *anyone* who can function well in this capacity.

3. The reactions of particularly close family members should be scrutinized in order to help them and to enable them, those who are losing the most, to also give the most in support of the patient's secondary suffering; and in so doing gain a measure of peace themselves.

4. High-risk family members, those adjudged to be most prone to suffer at some point from pathological and extended grief reactions following their loss, should be singled out for special counseling and treatment.

5. The patient should be allowed to make as many decisions regarding his own treatment, even his own manner of dying, as is consistent with *his* welfare, not heeding needlessly only the emotional welfare of his family or especially that of his *caretakers*.

6. Communication should always be maintained among all on the scene; self-esteem should be reinforced.

7. There are many, including especially family members, who can help the dying patient achieve his final goals—not only the physician and the nurse. Professional credentials are often less important than a person's ability to be present, to be readily available, to be alert, to be compassionate and willing to be on the team. *And,* touch the patient; let there be someone to hold his hand, literally, if possible, to the end.

8. The team should include, among others, the family, the clergy, social workers, psychologists, and psychiatrists *as well as* physicians and nurses.

9. The new ethics presented by the ability to transplant organs, or sustain failing ones mechanically, compels the physician to be the prime decision maker, the one in whose hands the "buck stops." But, nevertheless, these decisions and ethics involved pose profound and emotionally traumatic problems for the physician which he would be well advised to share with the family, clergy, or others.

10. The family should always be aware that to the physician,

regardless of his concerns about the patient, one death in particular is of even greater concern to him: his death.

11. The bereaved will have to deal retrospectively with the trauma of the deceased's illness and death, and he may be haunted by memories, even guilt, even anger. Caretakers must be available to contend with these also.

12. The passing of certain cultural and ethnic rituals, such as portions (at least) of the formal funeral, sitting *shibah,* and the wake, has probably been detrimental for the family as viewed sociologically and can hinder acceptance of the loss and the bereaved's ability to continue as a functioning human being. These rites and the attendant opportunities for loving companionship and self-expression often offer great emotional support to the bereaved (even if many do not choose to acknowledge such benefits because of often unfair financial burdens imposed by some funeral directors).

13. The grief experience can be transformed into a most meaningful and productive one through emphasis on the concepts and ideals of *creative* grief. The energies expended in grieving can be channeled with enormous productivity into good works or deeds, service to others in distress, devotion to tasks left undone by the deceased, etc., rather than dissipated in an unstructured and self-pitying melancholia.

But these are not, by any means, all the answers. We have scarcely scratched the surface. Even the few statistics drawn upon may be viewed dubiously because we are just beginning to gain insight into *what* to research, and such research has just barely begun. One more observation is in order: Our efforts in this field *may* need reappraisal, since it appears that for every fifteen investigators working with the care of the dying patient, there are probably only three dealing with bereavement, and only one with studies of anticipatory grief. This is discouraging to relate, in the opinion of many of our most informed workers, such as Mrs. Ruth Abrams, since the possibility for the most effective interventive medical action related to bereavement perhaps lies in the improved management of anticipatory grief.

We have turned around and around in our continuum: the classical picture of anticipatory grief, the dying experience *and* its management, and the final facet, bereavement. Nor have we neglected to mention our own psychological trauma at the thought of the dying "me." It should be apparent, then, that we have come full cycle and have, perhaps, even reached certain conclusions: (1) that our lives *are* spent in preparation for the bereavement which our great losses bring, including the death of "me"; (2) that there are doubtlessly stages of anticipatory grief which in one way or another parallel Dr. Ross's stages of dying—in a complementary fashion, sometimes and best of all in synchronization but sometimes out; (3) that, if we can achieve some degree of real synchronization, we can make the bereaved-to-be function more satisfactorily as members of the team that cares for the terminal patient; (4) that the mortality and morbidity of bereavement may well, with proper research and through the use of proper investigative expertise, be demonstrated in anticipatory grief, thereby reinforcing the decision to intervene at this point; (5) that it is logical to conceive of anticipatory grief as a repressed projection backward of bereavement; (6) that it would follow, then, that bereavement is the logical aftermath of repressed anticipatory grief; (7) that there is a symmetry and core of replication between anticipatory grief and bereavement from which it might well be hypothesized that the greater and better managed the one, the less of the other; and conversely, the less of the former, the greater the latter; (8) that these are challenging and critical areas for research.

Man cannot face the sun, but he must nevertheless face his own death, if he is to live. He must accept death as a part of his life—as a prerequisite for his enjoyment of and formal acceptance of the full beauty and tragedy of life. Just as it is possible for the dying person to achieve acceptance of his own death and die in dignity, so too the living who are bereaved can, with help, be brought to accept a life in which death is an integral part. The challenge to us all is at least twofold: Where is our place in the continuum at any time? How can we be effective as clinicians, as scientists, and as human beings?

4   The Moment of Grief

JACOB NEEDLEMAN

Surely, few of us believe that life is a preparation for death. As historical events and scientific progress nullify our trust in traditional religious forms, this idea is one of the first to fall: that there will come a final moment when we will be tested and weighed in the balance of some higher universal purpose, and that the central concern of our day-to-day lives should be to ready ourselves. All our knowledge seems to lead us to the certainty that death is our destruction, meaningless, which only madmen glorify and whose factuality only cowards avoid. We know that we are such cowards, but at least we value those rare moments when life seems so rich that death loses its terror. For the rest, we refuse to brood morosely.

And so, when a philosopher like Plato tells us that we should spend our life learning to die, we cannot really listen to him or even wish to. But in the time of grief we do turn to such thoughts and to many others which we avoid in the rest of our life. Is it simply that we are looking for comfort in the form of some intricate denial of the death we have encountered? For when we recover our customary balance, when we pass through this time, our attention is drawn far away from those thoughts.

Let us consider the possibility that in that moment of grief our consciousness comes into a new sort of relationship to the rest of us, and that it is precisely this relationship, and not the

Jacob Needleman teaches philosophy at San Francisco State College. He is the author of *The New Religions,* a book concerning newly emerging religious cults, and editor of *Being-in-the-World.*

outer event, for which we are unprepared. And that a better meaning of the idea of preparing for death has nothing at all to do with the gradual relinquishing of vital experience. What we wish to explore is the thought that the preparation for death is a preparation to be alive.

Obviously, this line of thought will yield no consolation in the ordinary sense. It cannot lead to proofs of life beyond the grave or to prescriptions about heroic acceptance of our destruction. On the contrary, it begins and ends with the thought that *we do not know* what death is. The agony of the search for proofs and prescriptions is not rooted in our ignorance about death, but in the fact that we are afraid to distrust our fears and imagination.

The point is this: It is a commonplace to say that man is afraid of the unknown. But is it really so? When I am afraid to enter a dark room isn't it because my imagination makes me *forget* that I don't know what is in there? And if someone then reminds me about my imagination, doesn't the fear lift for an instant? In other words, if somehow I were able to stand in front of my imagination, to see it, then at least that portion of myself would not be afraid. But somehow I cannot wish to do this. In some way I value my imagination and the fears that are in it; I trust it; I believe that it gets me through life, or that it brings me my satisfactions.

If we think of death as being like that dark room, then many of the proofs and prescriptions in the literature of philosophy and psychology read like reactions to the imagination, rather than attempts to awaken us to it. In the mainstream of modern thought this usually takes the form of proving that the mind cannot exist without the body, or that there is no soul. Of course we can also find proofs that go the other way: that there is a life after death, an immortal soul, and so on. Both sorts of effort are essentially the same, whatever the content of the particular proof. Each moves away from the fact of ignorance rather than toward it or into it.

The fact of ignorance is a fact about oneself, and to move away from it is to move away from oneself. This is to suggest that thought must be distinguished from self-awareness, since the thinking process is but one of the functions of that self or organism. Just as my fear lifts when I become conscious of my imagination, so it may be that if I can become conscious of my thought about death, I may begin to stand in a new relationship to that thought.

The ignorance about death is not an ignorance of some facts about the external world. Rather, it is possible to see this ignorance as the sensing of the inadequacy of thought, perhaps even the sensing of its surprisingly dependent place in the totality of our life.

It was also Plato who showed that our thought does not guide us, though we imagine it does, that thought always follows and serves some impulse, desire, or fear in us, creatures of the cave. The same Socrates who in *Phaedo* offers his pupils several external proofs of immortality also in the *Apology* reminds the whole Athenian community that no one but God knows what takes place after death.

Kierkegaard, a modern Christian pupil of Socrates, writes:

All honor to him who can handle learnedly the learned question of immortality! But the question of immortality is essentially not a learned question, rather it is a question of inwardness, which the subject by becoming subjective must put to himself. Objectively, the question cannot be answered, because objectively it cannot be put, since immortality precisely is the potentiation and highest development of the developed subjectivity. Only by really willing to become subjective can the question properly emerge, therefore how could it be answered objectively? . . . the consciousness of my immortality belongs to me alone, precisely at the moment when I am conscious of my immortality I am absolutely subjective. . . . Immortality is the most passionate interest of subjectivity; precisely in the interest lies the proof. . . . Quite simply therefore the existing subject asks, not about immortality in general, for such a phantom has no existence, but about his immortality, about what it means to become immortal, whether he is able to contribute anything to the accomplishment of this end, or whether he becomes immortal as a matter of course, or whether he is that and can become it.[1]

We thus come to the tentative conclusion that there is something valuable about this ignorance and that perhaps we should not be in too great a hurry to get rid of it. Whatever else they may be, are not the great sorrows of life also confusions? That is, don't they—and the death of loved ones more than any— bring us at least momentarily to the awareness that we do not understand? That we are ignorant? And are not our efforts to assuage our suffering often attempts to fly from that awareness back to our former "understanding"? When we suffer and we say, "I don't understand," are we not searching for some way to fit what has happened into our old categories?

So the question arises: What would it mean to want a new understanding rather than the retaining of our old understanding? Surely, the first thing it would mean would be the wish to remain cognizant of our ignorance and to see it as something which cannot be "corrected" by the selection (under the aegis of the old understanding) of external facts, proofs, or exhortations.

However, it is surely life and not we ourselves that brings us to moments of this awareness of ignorance. If we are to speak of any preparation it would have to be preparation for these moments.

We know we cannot change our emotions; we cannot, by thinking, change hate to love or erase our fears. In a minor sort of way, every emotional surprise in our lives is thus such a moment as we are speaking of. The material basis of any preparation lies right in front of us in the person of our everyday emotional life.

1. Søren Kierkegaard, *Concluding Unscientific Postscript*, ed., Walter Lowrie (Princeton, N.J.: Princeton University Press, 1941), pp. 154–156.

Our discussion having come to this, we can now connect it again with Socrates. In that same dialogue, *Phaedo,* which takes place on the day of Socrates' execution, he explains to his pupils that those who really apply themselves in the right way to the search for wisdom are directly and of their own accord preparing themselves for dying and death. At this

Simmias laughed and said: Indeed, Socrates, you make me laugh, though I am scarcely in a laughing humor now. If the multitude heard that, I fancy they would think that what you say of philosophers is quite true; and my countrymen would entirely agree with you that philosophers are indeed eager to die, and they would say that they know full well that philosophers deserve to be put to death.

Socrates answers

And they would be right, Simmias, except in saying that they know it. They do not know in what sense the true philosopher is eager to die, or what kind of death he deserves, or in what sense he deserves it.[2]

It is precisely in this context that Socrates explains this preparation as the turning of the attention toward the mind (or soul) and away from the pleasures and pains of everyday life. Most people are quick to see in this the thought that we should gradually relinquish the most vivid and valuable side of life. But, once again, does not this ready interpretation come also from the fact that we forget our ignorance about death? What could preparation mean if we are to continue, in our thought, to relate to our everyday emotions like undiscriminating beggars? If it is true that in our thought we are surprised by our emotions and confused by our powerful emotions, how else could we prepare ourselves than by searching for a new relationship to our thought? But we forget our ignorance, we forget that our emotions sur-

2. *Phaedo,* 64. Translated by F. J. Church (New York: Library of Liberal Arts, 1951).

prise us and lead us, we forget that they confuse us, we forget that we do not understand ourselves.

We think of the idea of preparing for death as preparing for something beyond the grave without our taking the initial steps of preparing for our fears and griefs. We reject the former idea as based on a presumption about life after death without realizing we live under the presumption that we stand in a right relationship to our fears and desires.

And so, when Socrates tells his pupils to despise everyday pleasures and pains, it is advice that follows from his (and the Oracle's) evaluation of ignorance. The Oracle said of him that he was the wisest in Athens because he alone was aware of his ignorance. We also recall the famous inscription "Know thyself" which was Socrates' watchword as well. Together, these two formulas about Socrates' wisdom and self-knowledge can lead to the practical goal of becoming aware of our ignorance about ourselves. And thus, to despise our everyday emotions is to despise the illusion that we are not confused by our emotions, an illusion that often takes the form of believing it is the world out there which confuses us, or perpetrates injustice, or destroys us, or (on the other hand) rewards us and makes us happy.

A man would have to be a fool to think lightly of the anguish of the moment of grief. But precisely because such an emotion is overwhelming and sweeps everything else in us aside, precisely because of this the question of preparation becomes important. If emotions are our source of life and yet not our responsibility it would seem that when we prepare for them we are preparing for being alive. It would follow that our search must be to struggle directly only with what is in our power to meet. Where, then, is our responsibility? What *is* in our power?

This question may perhaps reveal something about that weakening of trust in traditional religious forms which was mentioned at the beginning. For if the religions of our present culture take it as their task directly to legislate our emotions, the result may be for us only that we overlay the actual emotions which willy-nilly occur in us with imaginary feelings, i.e., thoughts about our emotions which are out of all congruity with the emotions themselves.

Nothing, of course, could be further from the awareness of ignorance, and nothing would more effectively block the growth of that awareness. For if I am told and if I believe that I ought to love my neighbor, how will I ever relate to my hatred of him? No wonder modern psychiatry seems more realistic in reminding us of our actual emotions. But unfortunately psychiatry, in passing judgment on our thought, just as effectively blocks our vision of confusion. Self-knowledge surely does not begin with the attempted refusal to judge my emotions, but with the search to see both my judgments and my emotions.

Yet what else but religion has the office of relating man with the question of death? In a sense this is its main, perhaps its only, task. It may be, however, just because we go to religion to escape our ignorance rather than to discover it that it can become undermined by such things as psychiatry, science, and political events. Thus, when a great fear or anguish overwhelms us we soon afterwards turn to religion either to have a counter-emotion evoked in us or to be commanded to feel something else, both of which serve the purpose of reinstating the illusion that we understand our emotions. And once it is reinstated, once we have "regained our balance," "passed through the difficult time," etc., we then avoid religion because it seeks to give us what we think we already have: a sense of moving in the right direction or—to put it in the language of this discussion—a turning away from our emotions in the form of a "contented relationship" toward them.

Thus religion, psychiatry, and science all leave us unprepared for death. And the moment of grief, a moment in which we may be genuinely face to face with the enormous forces that act in us in the form of our emotions, fails ultimately to make the rest of our inner life a question. On the contrary, our reactions to that moment pull us out of ourselves in the search for philosophical systems, proofs, exhortations, consolations, substitutes —in short, the search for a return to our former quality of life, a life which those very moments reveal to us, momentarily, as far less than our human right, as far closer to the death we confusedly fear than to the real life that lies hidden within us.

When the fact of death compels us outward to more recognizably metaphyical questions about man's place in the universe, perhaps it need not be wholly at the expense of an awareness of ignorance. Let us, therefore, assume that there is a difference between fantasy and speculation, taking fantasy as the absolutizing of partial or relative knowledge, and taking speculation as the effort to maintain a sense of the relativity of our thinking and our concepts of the universe. Thus, it is not only grandiose metaphysical systems that are fantasies. Equally fantastic is the absolutizing of those common standards of intellectual satisfaction associated with logical consistency, ordinary language, and pragmatic scientific theory.

How, then, are we to avoid fantastic thinking about death? And in what directions might metaphysical speculation about death take us?

One point is clear: For us, death is conceptually linked to a great many other things such as time, identity, consciousness, life, matter, change, birth. It would, therefore, be a great mistake to think about death without trying to see how these other ideas present themselves in our mind.

We may take as example what seems a truism: Death is the end of life. Yet this simple proposition contains many questions which, if totally avoided, leave us with nothing more than an empty verbal equation. *What* is that of which death is the end? How do we understand life? Biologically? Personally (my life)? If biologically, do we think of life as a complex trick of matter, an intricate organization of what is essentially dead? Does it seem more *natural* that things should die rather than that they should live? What concept of reality underlies this thought?

Or are we willing to settle for an unbridgeable dualism of the living and the nonliving in our universe? If so, what becomes of our *uni*verse? And in such a universe, how could anything die, that is, change from living to nonliving? What is lost or what is ended in such an event? How, in fact, do we understand an end? Disappearance? What is that? Vanishing into nothingness? Or disappearance from our view?

Furthermore, if we think of life as purposive activity, how do we recognize purpose? Is *our* activity the only sort of purpose that could exist? What is our standard of time against which we measure the accomplishment or effort toward purpose? Is there life that exists on totally different scales of time—incommensurably smaller or greater—than our own? If so, how would we ever perceive it?

For that matter, how can we perceive our own time scale? From what perspective, from what *place,* could we ever perceive our scale of time? Or are we condemned forever to stay within it, never directly perceiving how or if our beginnings are related to our endings? Is there in *us* the possibility of another order of time within which we can see the processes and changes which constitute the time of our everyday lives, both as individuals and as mankind? If not, is there no order of time other than our own? Or are we so cut off from the time of galaxies, planets, and molecules that it is foolish to think about them in this way? What sort of a universe would that be? And are we necessarily so cut off?

Or should we avoid these questions as unanswerable or meaningless? Unanswerable, meaningless, to whom? What sort of answers do we insist on? Why? What sort of meaning would we like to find? Why do we stop looking when we fail to find it? What sort of purposes is our thought supposed to serve? Are these purposes consonant with what exists in the universe?

What kind of certainty are we looking for? Why do we get weary of questions, and more questions? Why do we want to stop? What kind of resting place is the sense of certainty we prize? Is it that of fantasy?

Perhaps we take death as the end of *my* life. What kind of end can *I* have? What is it which ends? Can I believe in my own death? Can I imagine it? If not, why? Is it because I have no understanding of what I am? Can I even imagine my own life, not to mention my own death? Do I assume, only because of the rule of grammar and dictionary definition, that death is the end of experience? The end of consciousness? What are these? Is consciousness some weird, metaphyically unique phantom in a blind unconscious universe? Is there a consciousness that is different from thought? If so, how could I begin to *think* about it? Do I even have it? Or does it, can it, have me? Is it I?

And what do *I* ever experience? Is our past already dead? Is what dies, when I die, only the final member of a bundle of perceptions? Or is there a self that persists "through time"? If we would like to believe the latter, how do we experience it? Do we remember our life? What is there to do the remembering, one of the bundle? Or something above and beyond the bundle? And, again, if we believe the latter, who or what is believing? Another member of the bundle? That is, is this, too, fantastic thinking, a taking of the part for the whole?

There may be an interesting relationship between the notion that my self will be either destroyed or preserved in death and the degradation into fantasy of the impulse toward metaphysical speculation. The fantacist asks: What is the place in the universe of this being, man, who is destroyed by death? Or, alternatively: What is the place in the universe of this being, man, who is immortal? Fantasy would seem to be inevitable as long as we rely on part of our thought while questioning the other part. But in speculating about our place in the universe, is it not a fact that we have no real idea of what purpose our thought is to serve?

That our lives are dominated by fantastic thought may be because there is so little relationship between the *impulse* to speculate about our place in the universe and the *content* of our "speculative thought." If the emotion of the moment of grief represents one such impulse, surely another is what the ancients called *thaumazein,* and what we speak of as "wonder."

Most of us remember the rare moments when we have experienced this emotion: perhaps on a night away from the city, looking up toward countless worlds; perhaps as children directly observing some living thing—whatever; it would be futile to try to put this emotion in words. But what is it we forget when this moment passes and we are trying to think about the questions which we then associate with that moment: What am I? How can I respond to the fact that I exist? What is the meaning of my smallness? How can I know my part in this magnitude which I sense? Isn't this what we forget: that at that moment when we are presented with the emotion of wonder, that emotion and that state of mind *are themselves an element in the answer to our questions.* We know this at the moment—though perhaps not in so many words—and we forget it later.

Might it not be that such an emotion and state of mind is itself a kind of knowledge that truly takes us out of ourselves toward the universe? Might it not be that, just as in the moment of grief, this emotion is a brief individual connection with what to thought seems so far above us or outside of us? What do we trust when this emotion is no longer present? What do we then take to be knowledge? Is our fantastic thinking a mere expense of the knowledge or force with which we were temporarily connected? When we think of metaphysical systems which speak of man as a microcosm, embodying in himself in some way and to some degree all of the reality of the universe, do we value or even remember that our questions about the universe came to us originally in the form of an answering direction, and that this partial answer itself came in the form of a certain quality or force of questioning? Isn't it so, however, that our thinking flies away from that moment, forgets it by classifying it and distrusting it?

Thus, in this light, metaphysical speculation can be the study and the search for questions or, rather, for questioning, the study of what we desire and the possible attempt to be alert for help and direction when it appears. Do we want thoughts about death and immortality, or do we want immortality? Do we want answers or do we want to be?

MASS DEATH

*And the smoke of their torment
goes up forever and ever.*

Revelations 14:11

5 On Death and Death Symbolism:
The Hiroshima Disaster

ROBERT JAY LIFTON

The larger a human event, the more its significance eludes us. In the case of Hiroshima's encounter with the atomic bomb— surely a tragic turning point in man's psychological and historical experience—the meaning is perhaps only now, after nineteen years, beginning to reveal itself. Yet the event has much to teach us that is of considerable value in our struggles to cope with a world altered much more than we realize, and made infinitely more threatening, by the existence of nuclear weapons. In this article I shall describe a portion of a larger study of the psychological effects of the atomic bomb in Hiroshima.[1] I shall

Robert J. Lifton is Research Professor of Psychiatry at Yale Medical School. His books include *Boundaries: Psychological Man in Revolution* and *Death in Life: The Survivors of Hiroshima*. He was the winner of the National Book Award in 1969. This paper was presented at the Annual Meeting of the American Psychiatric Association, Los Angeles, California, May 7, 1964. From *Psychiatry*, Vol. 27, No. 3 (August 1964): 191–210. Copyright © 1964 by the William Alanson White Psychiatric Foundation. Reprinted by special permission of the Foundation.

1. The study was supported by research funds from the Department of Psychiatry, Yale University. Colleagues and friends from the various divisions of Hiroshima University (particularly the Research Institute for Nuclear Medicine and Biology), the Hiroshima City Office, and many other groups in the city lent indispensable help in making arrangements; and Miss Kyoko Komatsu and Mr. Kaoru Ogura provided skillful and dedicated

focus upon what I believe to be the central psychological issue in both the actual disaster and its wider symbolism—the problem of death and dying. The work represents a continuation of an effort, begun ten years ago, to develop a modified psychoanalytic research approach to broad historical problems.

There are many reasons why the study of death and death symbolism has been relatively neglected in psychiatry and psychoanalysis: not only does it arouse emotional resistances in the investigator—all too familiar, though extraordinarily persistent nonetheless—but it confronts him with an issue of a magnitude far beyond his empathic and intellectual capacities. Yet whatever the difficulties, the nuclear age provides both urgent cause and vivid stimulus for new efforts to enhance our understanding of what has always been man's most ineradicable problem. Certainly no study of an event like the Hiroshima disaster can be undertaken without some exploration of that problem.

I conducted the study over a six-month period, from April to September, 1962, mostly in Hiroshima itself. This was the last portion of a two-and-one-half-year stay in Japan, the greater part of which was spent investigating psychological and historical patterns of Japanese youth.[2] The Hiroshima study consisted primarily of individual interviews with two groups of atomic bomb survivors: one group of 33 chosen at random from the list of more than 90,000 survivors (or *hibakusha*) kept at the Hiroshima University Research Institute for Nuclear Medicine and Biology;

---

research assistance throughout. I have published one earlier, more general paper on the work ("Psychological Effects of the Atomic Bomb in Hiroshima: The Theme of Death," *Daedalus*, 92 [1963]: 462–97), and the present article draws upon a more comprehensive book-length report now in preparation. [The material appears in *Death in Life: The Survivors of Hiroshima* (New York: Random House, 1967). Editor.]

2. Robert J. Lifton, "Youth and History: Individual Change in Postwar Japan," *Daedalus* 91 (1962): 172–97; and "Individual Patterns in Historical Change: Imagery of Japanese Youth," in *Disorders in Communication*, Vol. 42, *Proceedings of the Association for Research in Nervous and Mental Disease*, ed. by David McK. Rioch (Baltimore: Waverly, 1964).

and an additional group of 42 survivors specially selected because of their prominence in dealing with atomic bomb problems or their capacity to articulate their experiences—including physicians, university professors, city officials, politicians, writers and poets, and leaders of survivor organizations and peace movements.

Hibakusha is a coined word which is by no means an exact equivalent of "survivor" (or "survivors"), but means, literally, "explosion-affected person" (or people), and conveys in feeling a little more than merely having encountered the bomb, and a little less than having experienced definite physical injury from it. According to official definition, the category of *hibakusha* includes four groups of people considered to have had possible exposure to significant amounts of radiation: those who at the time of the bomb were within the city limits then defined for Hiroshima, an area extending from the bomb's hypocenter to a distance of 4,000, and in some places up to 5,000, meters; those who were not in the city at the time, but within fourteen days entered a designated area extending to about 2,000 meters from the hypocenter; those who were engaged in some form of aid to, or disposal of, bomb victims at various stations which were set up; and those who were *in utero*, and whose mothers fit into any of the first three groups. In addition to these interviews with *hibakusha*, I tried to learn all I could, from a variety of sources and in a variety of informal ways, about the extraordinary constellation of influences felt by the city and its inhabitants in relationship to the bomb during the seventeen-year period that had elapsed between the disaster itself and the time of my research.[3]

Work in a foreign culture, or even in one's own, must depend heavily upon assistance from individuals and groups in the community. In Hiroshima the sensitivities inherent in the situa-

3. A listing of relevant Japanese and American writings on the various aspects of the atomic bomb problem can be found in Lifton, "Psychological Effects of the Atomic Bomb in Hiroshima." See footnote 1.

tion of an American psychiatrist undertaking a study of reactions to the atomic bomb made such assistance particularly imperative. Meetings and interviews were arranged, whenever possible, through personal introduction. And with the randomly selected group, my first contact with the survivor was made through a visit at the home, together with a Japanese social worker from Hiroshima University, during which I would briefly explain (either to the survivor himself or to a family member) my purpose in undertaking the work, and then arrange for a later meeting at the office I maintained in the city. In retrospect I feel that the consistently cooperative responses I encountered were significantly related to my conveying to both colleagues and research subjects my own sense of personal motivation in the study—the hope that it might shed light on these difficult problems and thereby in a small way contribute to the mastery of nuclear weapons and the avoidance of their use.[4]

Interviews generally lasted two hours, and I tried to see each research subject twice, though I saw some three or four times, and others just once. They were conducted in Japanese, with a research assistant always present to interpret; the great majority (particularly with subjects in the randomly selected group) were tape-recorded, always with the subject's consent. While I attempted to cover a number of basic questions with all research subjects, I encouraged them to associate freely to whatever ideas and emotions were brought up.

In an earlier publication I described the general psychosocial patterns of the atomic bomb experience, and related them to the predominant theme of death.[5] Now I wish to explore more spe-

4. Familiarity with various features of Japanese culture and the ability to speak some Japanese were also important; but always crucial in obtaining cooperation were introductions by trusted and respected individuals and groups in the Hiroshima community.

5. Lifton, "Psychological Effects of the Atomic Bomb in Hiroshima" (see footnote 1), describes the three basic emphases of the study: recollection and inner meaning of the experience seventeen years later; residual concerns and fears relating to delayed radiation effects; and survivors' sense of group identity. Many of the reactions mentioned in what follows were

cifically the psychological elements of what I have referred to as the *permanent encounter with death* which the atomic bomb created within those exposed to it. I shall discuss, in sequence, four different stages of experience with death—that is, four aspects of this encounter. Under examination, therefore, will be shared individual responses to an atmosphere permeated by death. Then I shall attempt to suggest a few general principles in the difficult area of the psychology of death and dying, essentially derived from this investigation but by no means limited to the Hiroshima experience.

The overwhelming immersion in death directly following the bomb's fall began with the terrible array of dead and near-dead in the midst of which each survivor found himself. Important here was the extreme sense of surprise and unpreparedness. Survivors were unprepared because, following an air-raid alarm, an all-clear signal had been sounded just a few minutes before the bomb fell; because of the psychological sense of invulnerability all people tend to possess, even in the face of danger; and because of the total inability of anyone to anticipate a weapon of such unprecedented dimensions. The number of deaths, both immediate and over a period of time, will probably never be fully known. Variously estimated from 63,000 to 240,000 or more, the official figure is usually given as 78,000, but the city of Hiroshima estimates 200,000; the enormous disparity is related to the extreme confusion at the time, to differing methods of calculation, and to underlying emotional influences, quite apart from mathematical considerations, which have at times affected the estimators. But the point here is that anyone exposed relatively near the center of the city could not escape the sense of ubiquitous death around him—resulting from the blast itself, from radiant heat, and from ionizing radiation. For instance, if

---

dealt with in somewhat greater descriptive detail in the earlier paper. The question of similarities to, and differences from, "ordinary disaster" was also taken up, and will not be discussed here.

the survivor had been within 1,000 meters (.6 miles) from the hypocenter, and out of doors (that is, without benefit of shielding from heat or radiation), more than nine-tenths of the people around him were fatalities; and if he had been unshielded at 2,000 meters (1.2 miles), more than eight of ten people around him were killed. For those indoors mortality was lower, but even then in order to have even a 50 percent chance of escaping both death and injury, one had to be about 2,200 meters (1.3 miles) from the hypocenter.[6] Therefore the most significant psychological feature at this point was the sense of a sudden and absolute shift from normal existence to an overwhelming encounter with death.

Recall of the experience was extremely vivid, despite the seventeen-year interval. For those closest to the hypocenter, first memories of the event were frequently only of a sudden flash, an intense sensation of heat, of being knocked down or thrown some distance and finding themselves pinned under debris, or of simply awakening from an indeterminate period of unconsciousness. Nonetheless, among the initial emotions experienced, many stressed (partly, undoubtedly, with retrospective reconstruction, but not without significance in any case)[7] feeling related to

6. See particularly Ashley W. Oughterson and Shields Warren, *Medical Effects of the Atomic Bomb in Japan* (New York: McGraw-Hill, 1956), for detailed studies of early mortality. Other sources for overall mortality estimates are listed in "Psychological Effects of the Atomic Bomb in Hiroshima" (see footnote 1), p. 492. Without here attempting to enter into the complexities of mortality estimates, one may say that it is significant that Japanese estimates are consistently higher than American ones.

7. Selectivity and distortion were inevitable in descriptions of an event that occurred seventeen years before. What the survivors' recollection revealed was not so much a literal rendition of what had occurred as the symbolic significance the event held for them at the time of the interviews. Nonetheless, a study of various accounts of the event recorded closer to the time that it occurred revealed surprisingly similar descriptions of behavior and psychological tendencies, suggesting perhaps that particularly impressive kinds of human experience (whether during childhood or adulthood) can create a lasting psychic imprint and, under conditions of reasonably good rapport, can be recalled with extraordinary vividness and considerable accuracy. See Lifton, "Psychological Effects of the Atomic Bomb in Hiroshima" (see footnote 1), pp. 491–92.

death and dying, such as: "My first feeling was, I think I will die"; "I was dying without seeing my parents"; and, "I felt I was going to suffocate and then die, without knowing exactly what had happened to me."

Beyond this sense of imminent individual death was the feeling of many that the whole world was dying. A science professor, covered by falling debris, found himself temporarily blinded: "My body seemed all black, everything seemed dark, dark all over. . . . Then I thought, 'The world is ending.'" A Protestant minister, himself uninjured, responded to the evidence of mutilation and destruction he saw everywhere around him when walking through the city: "The feeling I had was that everyone was dead. The whole city was destroyed. . . . I thought all of my family must be dead—it doesn't matter if I die. . . . I thought this was the end of Hiroshima—of Japan—of humankind." And a woman writer:

I just could not understand why our surroundings had changed so greatly in one instant. . . . I thought it might have been something which had nothing to do with the war, the collapse of the earth which it was said would take place at the end of the world, and which I had read about as a child. It was quiet around us. In fact, there was a fearful silence, which made one feel that all people and all trees and vegetation were dead.[8]

This "deathly silence" was consistently reported by survivors. Rather than wild panic, most described a ghastly stillness and a sense (whether or not literally true) of slow motion: low moans from those incapacitated, the rest fleeing, but usually not rapidly, from the destruction, toward the rivers (whose many branches run throughout the city), toward where they thought their family members might be, or toward where they hoped to find authorities of some sort or medical personnel, or simply toward accumulations of other people, in many cases merely

8. Yoko Ota, *Shikabane no Machi* [Town of Corpses] (Tokyo: Kaeade Shobo, 1955), p. 63.

moving along with a growing crowd and with no clear destination. This feeling of *death in life* was described by a store clerk as follows:

> The appearance of people was . . . well, they all had skin blackened by burns. . . . They had no hair because their hair was burned, and at a glance you couldn't tell whether you were looking at them from in front or in back. . . . They held their arms bent [forward] like this [and he proceeded to demonstrate their position] . . . and their skin—not only on their hands, but on their faces and bodies too —hung down. . . . If there had been only one or two such people . . . perhaps I would not have had such a strong impression. But wherever I walked I met these people. . . . Many of them died along the road—I can still picture them in my mind—like walking ghosts. . . . They didn't look like people of this world. . . . They had a special way of walking—very slowly. . . . I myself was one of them.

Characteristic here is the otherworldly grotesqueness of the scene, the image of neither-dead-nor-alive human figures with whom the survivor closely identifies himself. Similar emotions were frequently described in the imagery of a Buddhist hell, or expressed even more literally—as one man put it, "I was not really alive."

Examining the further psychological meaning of this early immersion in death, one is struck by the importance of feelings of helplessness and abandonment in the face of threatened annihilation. The fear and anticipation of annihilation dominate this phase, though it is not always easy to say exactly what it is that the *hibakusha* fears is about to be annihilated. Here I believe that his overall organism is included insofar as he is capable of symbolically perceiving it—in other words, he fears annihilation of his own self.[9] But one also must include his sense

9. This concept of self follows that of Robert E. Nixon, who states in "An Approach to the Dynamics of Growth in Adolescence," *Psychiatry*, 24 (1961): 18–31, that ". . . *self* is the person's symbol for his organism"

of relationship to the world of people and objects in which he exists: he anticipates the annihilation of both the field or context of his existence and his attachment to it—of his "being-in-the-world," as the existentialists would put it,[10] and his "non-human environment," as described in recent psychoanalytic writings.[11] And he fears the annihilation of that special set of feelings and beliefs which both relate him to others and allow for his sense of being a unique and particular person—in other words, his sense of inner identity.[12] This *anticipation of annihilation*—of self, of being, of identity—was related to overwhelming stimuli from without and within, an ultimate sense of threat that has been referred to by such names as "basic fear" and "the fear of the universe."[13]

And indeed so overwhelming was this experience that many

(p. 29). Also relevant is Susanne Langer's idea that "the conception of 'self' . . . may possibly depend on this process of symbolically epitomizing our feelings." *Philosophy in a New Key* (New York: Mentor Books, 1948), p. 111.

10. See, for instance, Rollo May's discussion on this concept in *Existence: A New Dimension in Psychiatry and Psychology*, ed. by Rollo May, Ernest Angel, and Henri F. Ellenberger (New York: Basic Books, 1958), pp. 55–61.

11. Harold F. Searles, *The Nonhuman Environment* (New York: International Universities Press, 1960).

12. See Erik H. Erikson, "The Problem of Ego Identity," *Journal of the American Psychoanalytical Association* 4 (1956): 56–121; and also Martin Grotjahn, "Ego Identity and the Fear of Death and Dying," *Journal Of Hillside Hospital* 9 (1960): 147–55.

13. See, respectively, Gert Heilbrunn, "The Basic Fear," *Journal of the American Psychoanalytical Association* 3 (1955): 447–66; and William James, *The Varieties of Religious Experience* (London: Longmans, Green, 1952). Erik H. Erikson, *Young Man Luther* (New York: Norton, 1958), p. 111, speaks of "a shudder which comes from the sudden awareness that our nonexistence . . . is entirely possible"; and I found similar responses in many exposed to Chinese thought reform; see Lifton, *Thought Reform and the Psychology of Totalism: A Study of "Brainwashing" in China* (New York: Norton, 1961), pp. 69–72. It seems particularly significant that this anticipation of annihilation can occur under a wide variety of circumstances in which one's sense of relationship to the world is profoundly impaired, whether or not actual death is threatened. It represents a symbolic expectation of death, which is the only kind of anticipation of death possible for humankind.

would have undoubtedly been unable to avoid psychosis were it not for an extremely widespread and effective defense mechanism which I shall refer to as "psychic closing off." In the face of grotesque evidence of death and near-death, people—sometimes within seconds or minutes—simply ceased to feel. They had a clear sense of what was happening around them, but their emotional reactions were unconsciously turned off.

A physicist, observing this process in himself, compared it to an overexposed photographic plate. A clerk who witnessed others dying around him at a temporary first-aid area reached a point where "I just couldn't have any reaction. . . . You might say I became insensitive to human death." And the woman writer quoted before described "a feeling of paralysis that came over my mind."

The unconscious process here is that of closing oneself off from death itself; the controlling inner idea, or fantasy, is: "If I feel nothing, then death is not taking place." Psychic closing off is thus related to the defense mechanisms of denial and isolation, as well as to the behavioral state of apathy. But it deserves to be distinguished from these in its sudden, global quality, in its throwing out a protective symbolic screen which enables the organism to resist the impact of death—that is, to survive psychologically in the midst of death and dying. It may well represent man's most characteristic response to catastrophe: one which is at times life-enhancing or even, psychologically speaking, life-saving; but at other times, particularly when prolonged and no longer appropriate to the threat, not without its own dangers. Certainly the investigator of nuclear disaster finds himself experiencing a measure of such closing off, as indeed does the reader of an account such as this one.[14]

14. In my paper "Psychological Effects of the Atomic Bomb in Hiroshima" (see footnote 1), I referred to this defensive maneuver as "psychological closure," and mentioned some of its wider implications for survivors, its necessity for me in carrying out the investigation, and its relationship to

Effective as it is, psychic closing off has its limitations even as a protective reaction. It cannot entirely succeed in neutralizing either the threatening stimuli from without nor those from within—the latter taking the form of self-condemnation, guilt, and shame. For at the very beginning of the atomic bomb experience a need is initiated for justifying one's own survival in the face of others' deaths, a form of guilt which plagues the survivor from then on, and to which I shall return. Here I shall only say *that the quick experience of self-condemnation intensifies the lasting imprint of death created by this early phase of atomic bomb exposure.* Contained within this imprint is something very close to witnessing in actuality that which ordinarily takes place only in psychotic fantasy—namely, an end-of-the-world experience. Normally a projection of inner psychological "death" onto the outside world, the process is here reversed so that an overwhelming external experience of near-absolute destruction becomes internalized and merged with related tendencies of the inner life.[15]

A type of memory which symbolizes this relationship of death to guilt appears in what I have called the *ultimate horror*—a specific image of the dead or dying with which the survivor strongly identifies himself, and which evokes in him particularly intense feelings of pity and self-condemnation. The scene may

---

attitudes concerning nuclear weapons in general. The term "psychic closing off," however, more directly conveys the threefold process involved: numbing of affect, symbolic walling off of the organism, and abrupt disconnection in communication between inner and outer worlds.

15. In other words, one may assume that everyone has some tendency toward this form of "psychological death"—toward withdrawal of psychic connection to the world—originating in earliest separation experiences, including that of birth itself; but that the tendency becomes most characteristically predominant in psychosis. Thus, when *hibakusha* underwent their end-of-the-world experience, they had, so to speak, a previous psychic model for it, upon which it could be grafted. For an interesting discussion of the significance of the end-of-the-world fantasy in the history of psychoanalysis, see Sheldon T. Selesnick, "C. G. Jung's Contributions to Psychoanalysis," *American Journal of Psychiatry* 120 (1963): 350–56.

include his own family members, or anonymous people in particularly grotesque physical array; or, as was frequent, pitiful images of women and children, universal symbols of purity and vulnerability, and especially so in Japanese culture.

One particular form of ultimate horror seemed, more than any other, to epitomize the association of death and guilt. It was the recollection of requests (whether overt or implicit) by the dying which could not be carried out, most specifically their pleas for a few sips of water. Water was withheld not only because of survivors' preoccupation with saving themselves and their own families, but because authorities spread the word that water would have harmful effects upon the severely injured. The request for water by the dying, however, in addition to reflecting their physical state, has special significance in Japanese tradition, as it is related to an ancient belief that water can restore life by bringing back the spirit that has just departed from the body.[16] These pleas were therefore as much psychological expressions of this belief as they were of physical need; indeed, one might say that they were pleas for life itself. The survivor's failure to acquiesce to them, whatever his reasons, could thus come to have the psychological significance for him of refusing the request of another for the privilege of life—while he himself clung so tenaciously to that same privilege.

The second encounter with death took the form of *invisible contamination.* After the bomb fell—sometimes within hours or even minutes, often during the first 24 hours, and sometimes during the following days and weeks—many *hibakusha* began to notice in themselves and others a strange form of illness. It consisted of nausea, vomiting, and loss of appetite; diarrhea with large amounts of blood in the stools; fever and weakness; purple spots on various parts of the body from bleeding into the skin

16. Shoji Inoguchi, "Funerals," in Vol. 4, *Nihon Minzoku Gakutaikei* [An Outline of the Ethnological Study of Japan], ed. by Oma Chitomi and others (Tokyo: Heibonsha, 1959).

(purpura); inflammation and ulceration of the mouth, throat, and gums (oropharyngeal lesions and gingivitis); bleeding from the mouth, gums, nose, throat, rectum, and urinary tract (hemorrhagic manifestations); loss of hair from the scalp and other parts of the body (epilation); extremely low white blood-cell counts when these were taken (leukopenia)—these symptoms in many cases taking a progressive course until death. Such manifestations of irradiation, and the fatalities associated with them, aroused a special terror in the people of Hiroshima, an image of a weapon which not only instantaneously kills and destroys on a colossal scale but also leaves behind in the bodies of those exposed to it deadly influences which may emerge at any time and strike down their victims. This image was made particularly vivid by the delayed appearance of these radiation effects—often two to four weeks after the bomb fell—in people who had previously seemed to be in perfect health, externally untouched by atomic bomb effects.[17]

No one at first had any understanding of the cause of the symptoms, and in the few medical facilities that were still functioning, isolation procedures were instituted in the belief that they were part of some kind of infectious gastrointestinal condition.[18] Ordinary people also suspected some form of epidemic, possibly in the nature of cholora. But very quickly, partly by word-of-mouth information and misinformation about the atomic bomb, people began to relate the condition to a mysterious "poison" emanating from the weapon itself. Whatever their idea

17. See particularly Ashley W. Oughterson and Shields Warren in footnote 6. They and other authors demonstrate statistically that the great majority of cases of radiation effects occurred within the 2,000-meter radius (depending partly upon degree of shielding); but this correlation with distance was not understood at the time, nor has it eliminated subsequent years of aftereffects in survivors exposed at greater distances.

18. For a vivid description of these reactions in one of the hospitals that remained functional, see Michihiko Hachiya, *Hiroshima Diary*, admirably edited and translated by Warner Wells (Chapel Hill: University of North Carolina Press, 1955).

of cause, survivors were profoundly impressed not only by the fact that others were dying around them but by the way in which they died—a gruesome form of rapid bodily deterioration which seemed unrelated to more usual and "decent" forms of death. They were struck particularly by the loss of scalp hair, the purple spots on the skin, and (whether or not always true) the way in which victims appeared to remain conscious and alert almost to the moment of their death. As a middle-aged electrician relates,

> There was one man who asked me for help and everything he said was clear and normal. . . . But in another three hours or so when I looked at him he was already dead. . . . And even those who looked as though they would be spared were not spared. . . . People seemed to inhale something from the air which we could not see. . . . The way they died was different . . . and strange.

Some were intrigued, and even attracted, by the weirdness of the symptoms—as in the case of a doctor quoted in a later written account: "I know it is terrible to say this, but those spots were beautiful. They were just like stars—red, green, yellow, and black . . . all over the body, and I was fascinated by them."[19] But the predominant feeling among survivors was that they themselves were imminently threatened by this same "poison"— as conveyed in such statements as: "Soon we were all worried about our health, about our bodies—whether we would live or die"; "I thought, sooner or later I too will die. . . . I never knew when some sign of the disease would show itself"; and, "We waited for our own deaths."

The nature of the death symbolism of this second stage was revealed in three rumors which swept Hiroshima during the period immediately following the bomb. The first rumor simply held that all those who had been exposed to the bomb in the city would be dead within three years. The psychological mes-

19. Ota, *Shikabane no Machi.* See footnote 8.

sage here was: None can escape the poison; the epidemic is total; all shall die.

But a second rumor, even more frequently related to me, and, I believe, with greater emotion, was that trees, grass, and flowers would never again grow in Hiroshima; from that day on, the city would be unable to sustain vegetation of any kind. The message here was: Nature was drying up altogether; life was being extinguished at its source—suggesting an ultimate form of desolation which not only encompassed human death but went beyond it.

The third rumor, closely related to the other two, held that for a period of seventy or seventy-five years Hiroshima would be uninhabitable; no one would be able to live there. Here was the sense that Hiroshima was to become totally deurbanized—literally, devitalized—that the bomb's invisible contamination had more or less permanently deprived the area of its life-sustaining capacity.

Other rumors, particularly during the first few days after the bomb fell, expressed further ramifications of these emotions: there were rumors that there would be new attacks with "poison gases" or "burning oil"; that America, having dropped such a terrible "hot bomb," would next drop a "cold bomb" or "ice bomb" which would freeze everything so that everyone would die; and there was even a rumor that America would drop rotten pigs so that, as one man put it, "Everything on the earth would decay and go bad." These additional rumors conveyed the sense that the environment had been so fundamentally disturbed, and the individual sense of security and invulnerability in relationship to life and death so threatened, that further life-annihilating assaults must be anticipated.

The psychological aspects of the second encounter with death may thus be summarized as follows: There was a fear of epidemic contamination to the point of bodily deterioration; a sense of individual powerlessness in the face of an invisible, all-enveloping, and highly mysterious poison (and in regard to this mysteriousness, there has been some evidence of psychological resistance toward finding out the exact nature of radiation effects); the sense, often largely unconscious and indirectly communicated, that this *total contamination*—seemingly limitless in time and space—must have a supernatural, or at least more than natural, origin, must be something in the nature of a curse upon one's group for some form of wrongdoing that had offended the forces which control life and death. This latter formulation was occasionally made explicit in, for instance, survivors' Buddhistic references to misbehavior in previous incarnations; it was implicit in their repeated expressions of awe, in the elaborate mythology (only a portion of which I have mentioned) they created around the event, and in their various forms of self-condemnation relating to guilt and punishment as well as to shame and humiliation.

The third encounter with death occurred with later radiation effects, not months but years after the atomic bomb itself, and may be summed up in the scientifically inaccurate but emotionally charged term "A-bomb disease." The medical condition which has become the model for "A-bomb disease" is leukemia, based upon the increased incidence of this always fatal malignancy of the blood-forming organs, first noted in 1948 and reaching a peak between 1950 and 1952.[20] The symptoms

20. For extensive studies of delayed physical aftereffects of radiation, see the series of Technical Reports of the Atomic Bomb Casualty Commission (an affiliate of the United States National Academy of Sciences, National Research Council, functioning with the cooperation of the Japanese National Institute of Health of the Ministry of Health and Welfare), as recently summarized in "Medical Findings and Methodology of Studies by the Atomic Bomb Casualty Commission on Atomic Bomb Survivors in Hiroshima and Nagasaki," in *The Use of Vital and Health Statistics for Genetic and Radiation Studies, Proceedings of the Seminar Sponsored by the United Nations and the World Health Organization,* held in Geneva, 5–9 September 1960, A/AC.82/Seminar, United Nations, New York, 1962; pp. 77–100. Additional Japanese and American studies are cited in Lifton, "Psychological Effects of the Atomic Bomb in Hiroshima" (see footnote 1); references 2, 13, and 14, pp. 489–93.

of leukemia, moreover, rather closely resemble those of acute radiation effects, both conditions sharing various manifestations of blood abnormalities, as well as the more visible and dreaded "purple spots" and other forms of hemorrhage, progressive weakness, and fever; leukemia, however, unlike acute irradiation, inevitably results in death.

Psychologically speaking, leukemia—or the threat of leukemia—became an indefinite extension of the earlier "invisible contamination." And individual cases of leukemia in children have become the later counterpart of the "ultimate horror" of the first moments of the experience, symbolizing once more the bomb's desecration of that which is held to be most pure and vulnerable—the desecration of childhood itself. Indeed, Hiroshima's equivalent of an Anne Frank legend has developed from one such case of leukemia in a twelve-year-old girl, Sadako Sasaki, which occurred in 1954; her death resulted in a national campaign for the construction of a monument (which now stands prominently in the center of Hiroshima's Peace Park) to this child and to all other children who have died as a result of the atomic bomb.[21]

And just at the time that the incidence of leukemia was recognized as diminishing and approaching the normal, evidence began accumulating that the incidence of various other forms of cancer was increasing among survivors—including carcinoma of the stomach, lung, thyroid, ovary, and uterine cervix. Leukemia is a rare disease (even with its increased incidence, only 122 cases were reported in Hiroshima between 1945 and 1959), but cancer is not; and should the trend continue, as appears likely, the increase in cancer will undoubtedly give further stimulus to various elaborations of death symbolism, just as some of these were beginning to decline. Thus, on a chronic level of

21. Betty Jean Lifton, "A Thousand Cranes," *The Horn Book Magazine* (April 1963); and Robert Jungk, *Children of the Ashes* (New York: Harcourt, Brace & World, 1961), pp. 289–90.

bodily concern, there is again evoked the feeling that the bomb can do anything, and that anything it does is likely to be fatal.

I shall not dwell on the other medical conditions which, with varying amounts of evidence, have been thought to be produced by delayed radiation effects. These include impairment in the growth and development of children; a variety of anemias and of liver and blood diseases; endocrine and skin disorders; impairment of central nervous system (particularly midbrain) function; premature aging; and a vague but persistently reported borderline condition of general weakness and debilitation. The exact consequences of radiation effects remain in many areas controversial, and are still under active investigation by both American and Japanese groups. My concern here, however, is the association in the minds of survivors of any kind of ailment with atomic bomb effects—whether it be fatigue, mild anemia, fulminating leukemia, or ordinary cardiovascular disease; and whether a scientific relationship to radiation effects seems probable, or possible but inconclusive, or apparently nonexistent. Bodily concerns of survivors are also intensified by the continuous publicizing of "A-bomb disease" by the mass media and by survivor and peace organizations, often in the form of lurid reports of patients dying in the "A-bomb hospital" (a special facility set up for the exposed population) of "A-bomb disease." Even though in many cases the relationship between the actual condition and the atomic bomb effects may be questionable, the ordinary survivor tends to identify himself directly with the victim and with the process of dying. As one man stated, "When I hear about people who die from A-bomb disease . . . then I feel that I am the same kind of person as they."

The survivor thus becomes involved in a vicious circle on the psychosomatic plane of existence: he is likely to associate even the mildest everyday injury or sickness with possible radiation effects; and anything he relates to radiation effects becomes in turn associated with death. The process is accentuated, though not created, by the strong Japanese cultural focus upon bodily symptoms as expressions of anxiety and conflict. The psychosomatic dilemma can also take on complicated ramifications. For instance, some survivors develop vague borderline symptoms, inwardly fear that these might be evidence of fatal "A-bomb disease," but resist seeking medical care because they do not wish to be confronted by this diagnosis. When such a pattern occurs in relationship to physical disease, it is usually referred to as "denial of illness"; but here the "illness" being denied is itself likely to be a symbolic product of psychological currents; and the "denial" is a specific response to the death symbolism associated with these currents. Others become involved in a lifelong preoccupation with "A-bomb disease," referred to by Hiroshima physicians as "A-bomb neurosis"; they become weak and sometimes bedridden, are constantly preoccupied with their blood counts and bodily symptoms, and precariously maintain an intricate inner balance between the need for their symptoms as an expression of various psychological conflicts and the anxious association of these symptoms with death and dying. At best, survivors find themselves constantly plagued with what may be called a nagging doubt about their freedom from radiation effects, and look upon themselves as people who are particularly vulnerable, who cannot afford to take chances.

Beyond their own sense of impaired body image, survivors carry the fear that this impairment will manifest itself in subsequent generations. The issue of genetic effects from the A-bomb is also controversial and unresolved. Fortunately, studies on comparative populations have revealed no increase in abnormalities among children of survivors. But it is widely known that such abnormalities can be caused by radiation, and there are again the problems of variation in medical opinion (some Japanese pathologists think that some evidence of increase in genetic abnormalities exists), and of lurid, sometimes irresponsible, journalistic reports. There is, moreover, one uncomfortably positive genetic finding among significantly exposed survivors, that of a disturbance of sex ratio of offspring, the significance of which is difficult to evaluate.[22] Still another factor in the survivors' psychological associations has been the definite damage from radiation to children exposed *in utero*, including the occurrence of microcephaly with and without mental retardation; this phenomenon is, scientifically speaking, quite unrelated to genetic effects, but ordinary people often fail to make the distinction.

Thus, at this third level of encounter with death, the sudden "curse" mentioned before becomes an *enduring taint*—a taint of death which attaches itself not only to one's entire psychobiological organism, but to one's posterity as well. Although in most cases survivors have been able to live, work, marry, and beget children in more or less normal fashion, they have the sense of being involved in an *endless chain of potentially lethal impairment* which, if it does not manifest itself in one year—or in one generation—may well make itself felt in the next. Once more elements of guilt and shame become closely involved with this taint. But the whole constellation of which they are part is perceived not as an epidemiclike experience, but as a permanent and infinitely transmissible form of impaired body substance.

The fourth level of encounter is a lifelong identification with death, with dying, and with an anonymous group of "the dead." Indeed, the continuous encounter with death, in the sequence described, has much to do with creating a sense of group identity as *hibakusha*, or survivors. But it is an unwanted, or at best ambivalent, identity, built around the inner taint I have discussed and symbolized externally by disfigurement—that is, by

22. See particularly the extensive work on genetic problems by James V. Neel and W. J. Schull, as well as additional studies listed in reference 14 in Lifton, "Psychological Effects of the Atomic Bomb in Hiroshima." See footnote 1.

keloid scars which, although possessed only by a small minority of survivors, have come to represent the stigmata of atomic bomb exposure.

A central conflict of this *hibakusha* identity is the problem of what I have come to speak of as *survival priority*—the inner question of why one has survived while so many have died, the inevitable self-condemnation in the face of others' deaths. *For the survivor can never, inwardly, simply conclude that it was logical and right for him, and not others, to survive. Rather, I would hold, he is bound by an unconscious perception of organic social balance which makes him feel that his survival was made possible by others' deaths: if they had not died, he would have had to; and if he had not survived, someone else would have.* This kind of guilt, as it relates to survival priority, may well be that most fundamental to human existence. Also contributing greatly to the survivor's sense of guilt are feelings (however dimly recalled) of relief, even joy, that it was the other and not he who died. And his guilt may be accentuated by previous death wishes toward parents who had denied him nurturance he craved, or toward siblings who competed for this nurturance, whether this guilt is directly experienced in relationship to the actual death of these family members, or indirectly through unconsciously relating such wishes to the death of any "other," however anonymous.

In ordinary mourning experiences, and in most ordinary disaster, there is considerable opportunity to resolve this guilt through the classical psychological steps of the mourning process. But with the atomic bomb disaster, my impression was that such resolution has been either minimal or at best incomplete. As in other mourning experiences, survivors have identified themselves with the dead (in this case, with the latter both as specific people and as an anonymous concept), and have incorporated the dead into their own beings; indeed, one might say that survivors have imbibed and incorporated the entire destruction of their city, and in fact the full atomic bomb experience. But they have found no adequate ideological interpretation—no spiritual explanation, no "reason" for the disaster—that might release them from this identification, and have instead felt permanently bound by it. They have felt compelled virtually to merge with the dead and to behave, in a great variety of ways, *as if* they too were dead. Not only do they judge all behavior by the degree of respect it demonstrates toward the dead, but they tend to condemn almost any effort which suggests strong self-assertion or vitality—that is, which suggests life.

The *hibakusha* identity, then, in a significant symbolic sense, becomes an identity of the dead—taking the following inner sequence: I almost died; I should have died; I did die, or at least am not really alive; or if I am alive it is impure for me to be so; and anything I do which affirms life is also impure and an insult to the dead, who alone are pure. Of great importance here, of course, is the Japanese cultural stress upon continuity between the living and the dead; but the identity sequence also has specific relationship to the nature of the disaster itself.[23]

Yet one must not conclude that all survivors are therefore suicidal. This is by no means the case, and I was in fact struck by the tenacity with which *hibakusha*, at all of the stages mentioned, have held on to life. Indeed, I have come to the conclusion that this identification with death—this whole constellation of inwardly experienced death symbolism—is, paradoxically

23. The various elements of *hibakusha* identity are developed in somewhat greater detail in Lifton, "Psychological Effects of the Atomic Bomb in Hiroshīma." See footnote 1. The point of view I wish to suggest about cultural factors in this response—and in other responses to the disaster—is that they are particular emphases of universal tendencies. Here, for instance, survivors' identification with the dead reflects a strong Japanese cultural tendency related in turn to a long tradition of ancestor worship; but this cultural emphasis should be seen as giving a special kind of intensity to a universal psychological pattern. Thus, "extreme situations" such as the Hiroshima disaster, through further intensifying culturally stressed behavior patterns, throw particularly vivid light upon universal psychological function.

enough, the survivor's means of maintaining life. In the face of the burden of guilt he carries with him, and particularly the guilt of survival priority, his obeisance before the dead is his best means of justifying and maintaining his own existence. But it remains an existence with a large shadow cast across it, a life which, in a powerful symbolic sense, the survivor does not feel to be his own.[24]

Through the experiences of Hiroshima survivors we have been thrust into the more general realm of the interrelationship between the anticipation of death and the conduct of life. It is an interrelationship that has been recognized and commented

24. This "identity of the dead" strikingly resembles findings that have been reported in survivors of Nazi concentration camps. William G. Niederland ("The Problems of the Survivor: Part I, Some Remarks on the Psychiatric Evaluation of Emotional Disorders in Survivors of Nazi Persecution," *Journal of Hillside Hospital* 10 [1961]: 233–47) describes a "psychological imprint" in concentration camp survivors which includes elements of depressive mood, withdrawal, apathy, outbursts of anger, and self-deprecatory attitudes which, in extreme cases, lead to a "living corpse" appearance; this is in turn attributed to their owing their survival to maintaining an existence of a "walking corpse" while their fellow inmates succumbed. Without attempting a full comparison here, one may say that in Nazi concentration camps, in addition to the more prolonged physical and psychological assault upon identity and character structure, the problem of survival priority was more directly experienced: each inmate became aware that either he or someone else would be chosen for death, and went to great lengths to maintain his own life at the expense of the known or anonymous "other." See Bruno Bettelheim, *The Informed Heart: Autonomy in a Mass Age* (Glencoe, Ill.: Free Press, 1960). In the atomic bomb experience, the problem of survival priority was more symbolically evoked, as I have described, though the end result may be psychologically quite similar. Moreover, two additional factors—the fear of aftereffects (of "A-bomb disease") and the survivors' tendency to relate their experience to the present world threat of nuclear weapons—have the effect of perpetuating their death symbolism and their sense of permanent encounter with death in a manner not true for concentration camp survivors (although the latter have had their anxieties and concerns over survival priority revived and intensified by such reminders of their experience as outbreaks of anti-Semitism anywhere in the world and, more importantly, the Eichmann trial). Despite their importance, these psychological problems of death symbolism have too often been overlooked or minimized by psychiatric examiners and other investigators concerned with later behavior of concentration camp victims, and by those studying other forms of persecution and disaster as well.

upon by generations of philosophers, though mentioned with surprising infrequency in psychiatric work. There are many signs that this psychiatric neglect is in the process of being remedied,[25] and indeed the significance of problems in this area so impresses itself upon us in our present age that matters of death and dying could well serve as a nucleus for an entire psychology of life. But I will do no more than state a few principles which I have found to be a useful beginning for comprehending the Hiroshima experience, for relating it to universal human concerns, and for examining some of the impact upon our lives of the existence of nuclear weapons. Attempting even this much is audacious enough to warrant pause and examination of some rather restraining words of Freud, which are made no less profound by the frequency with which they have been quoted in the past:

It is indeed impossible to imagine our own death; and whenever we attempt to do so we can perceive that we are in fact still present as spectators. Hence the psychoanalytic school could venture on the assertion that at bottom no one believes in his own death, or, to put the same thing in another way, that in the unconscious every one of us is convinced of his own immortality.

These words, which were written in 1915, about six months after the outbreak of World War I,[26] have found many recent

---

25. Among recent psychiatric and psychological studies of death and death symbolism, see K. R. Eissler, *The Psychiatrist and the Dying Patient* (New York: International Universities Press, 1955); Herman Feifel, ed., *The Meaning of Death* (New York: McGraw-Hill, 1959); and Norman O. Brown, *Life against Death: The Psychoanalytical Meaning of History* (Middletown, Conn.: Wesleyan University Press, 1959). In addition, a good deal of research is now in progress. See, for instance, Avery Weisman and Thomas P. Hackett, "Predilection to Death: Death and Dying as a Psychiatric Problem," *Psychosomatic Medicine* 23 (1961): 232–56; and Edwin S. Shneidman, "Orientations toward Death: A Vital Aspect of the Study of Lives," in Robert W. White, ed., *The Study of Lives* (New York: Atherton, 1963).

26. Sigmund Freud, "Thoughts for the Times on War and Death," *Standard Edition of the Complete Psychological Works* (London: Hogarth,

echoes. (Merleau-Ponty, the distinguished French philosopher, has said, "Neither my birth nor my death can appear to me as *my* experiences . . . I can only grasp myself as 'already born' and 'still living'—grasping my birth and death only as pre-personal horizons.")[27]

Profound as Freud's words are, it is possible that psychological investigations of death have been unduly retarded by them. For they represent the kind of insight which, precisely because of its importance and validity, must be questioned further and even transcended. I believe it is more correct to say that our own death—or at least our own dying—is not entirely unimaginable but can be imagined only with a considerable degree of distance, blurring, and denial; that we are not absolutely convinced of our own immortality, but rather have a need to main-

---

1957), 14: 289. The editor of this edition, James Strachey, states (p. 274) that the two essays contained in the paper were written "round about March and April, 1915." Eissler (see footnote 25; pp. 24–25) dates them "at the end of 1914 or at the beginning of 1915," emphasizing that they were not written after exhausting years of despair and horror but were "a rather quick response to the very evident fact . . . that there is more aggression in man than one would have thought from his behavior in peacetime and that man's attitude toward death is usually the outcome of the mechanism of denial, so long as he does not face death as a reality which may befall him or his loved ones at any moment." Ernest Jones, *The Life and Work of Sigmund Freud* (New York: Basic Books, 1955), 2: 367–68, points out that the essays were written in response to a request from the publisher (Hugo Heller) of the psychological periodical *Imago*, though he adds that Heller probably did not suggest the theme and that Freud, in writing them, must have been "like all highly civilized people . . . not only greatly distressed, but also bewildered, by the frightful happenings at the onset of the first World War, when so many things took place of which no living person had any experience or any expectation." Jones adds that these two essays "may be regarded as an effort to clear his mind about the most useful attitude to adopt to the current events." In any case it seems clear that with this paper, more than with most of his writings, Freud was responding to the stimulus of a great and highly threatening historical event; it is also significant that while his private reactions to the war were at times impulsive and quite variable, his public statement contained only a controlled series of ideas growing directly out of his previous concepts.

27. *Phenomenologie de la Perception;* pp. 249–50, as quoted and translated by Arleen Beberman in "Death and My Life," *Review of Metaphysics,* 17 (1963): 31.

tain a *sense of immortality* in the face of inevitable biological death; and that this need represents not only the inability of the individual unconscious to recognize the possibility of its own demise but also a compelling universal urge to maintain an inner sense of continuous symbolic relationship, over time and space, to the various elements of life. Nor is this need to transcend individual biological life *mere* denial (though denial becomes importantly associated with it): rather it is part of the organism's psychobiological quest for mastery, part of an innate imagery that has apparently been present in man's mind since the earliest periods of his history and prehistory. This point of view is consistent with the approach of Joseph Campbell, the distinguished student of comparative mythology, who has likened such innate imagery or "elementary ideas" to the "innate releasing mechanisms" described by contemporary ethologists. It also bears some resemblance to Otto Rank's stress upon man's longstanding need of "an assurance of eternal survival for his self," and to Rank's further assertion that "man creates culture by changing natural conditions in order to maintain his spiritual self."[28]

The sense of immortality of which I speak may be expressed through any of several modes. First, it may be expressed biologically—or, more correctly, biosocially—by means of family continuity, living on through (but in an emotional sense, *with*) one's sons and daughters and their sons and daughters, by

28. In developing his ideas on the "inherited image," Joseph Campbell (*The Masks of God: Primitive Mythology* [New York: Viking, 1959], pp. 30–49, 461–72) follows Adolf Bastian and C. G. Jung. Otto Rank (*Beyond Psychology* [New York: Dover, 1958], pp. 62–101) develops his concepts of man's quest for immortality through the literary and psychological concept of "The Double as Immortal Self." While I do not agree with all that Rank and Campbell say on these issues (I would, in fact, take issue with certain Jungian concepts Campbell puts forward), their points of view at least serve to open up an important psychological perspective which sees the quest for immortality as inherent in human psychology and human life.

imagining (however vaguely and at whatever level of consciousness) an endless chain of biological attachment. This has been the classical expression of the sense of individual immortality in East Asian culture, as particularly emphasized by the traditional Chinese family system, and to a somewhat lesser extent by the Japanese family system as well. But it is of enormous universal importance, perhaps the most universally significant of all modes. This mode of immortality never remains purely biological; rather it is experienced psychically and symbolically, and in varying degree extends itself into social dimensions, into the sense of surviving through one's tribe, organization, people, nation, or even species. On the whole, this movement from the biological to the social has been erratic and in various ways precarious; but some, like Julian Huxley and Pierre Teilhard de Chardin,[29] see it as taking on increasing significance during the course of human evolution. If this is so, individual man's sense of immortality may increasingly derive from his inner conviction: I live on through mankind.

Second, a sense of immortality may be achieved through a theologically based idea of a life after death, not only as a form of "survival" but even as a "release" from profane life burdens into a "higher" form of existence. Some such concept has been present in all of the world's great religions and throughout human mythology. The details of life after death have been vague and logically contradictory in most theologies, since the symbolic psychological theme of transcending death takes precedence over consistency of concrete elaboration. Christianity has perhaps been most explicit in its doctrine of life after death, and most

29. Huxley and Père Teilhard, of course, go further, and visualize the development of a unifying, more or less transcendent idea-system around this tendency. Huxley refers to this as "evolutionary humanism" (*The Humanist Frame,* ed. by Julian Huxley [New York: Harper & Row, 1961], pp. 11–48), and Père Teilhard speaks of the "Omega point," at which a "hyperpersonal" level of advanced human consciousness may be attained (*The Phenomenon of Man* [New York: Harper & Row, 1959], pp. 257–63).

demanding of commitment to this doctrine; but intra-Christian debate over interpretation of doctrine has never ceased, with present thought tending toward a stress upon transcendent symbolism rather than literal belief.

Third, and this is partly an extension of the first two modes, a sense of immortality may be achieved through one's creative works or human influences—one's writings, art, thought, inventions, or lasting products of any kind that have an effect upon other human beings. (In this sense, lasting therapeutic influences upon patients, who in turn transmit them to their posterity, can be a mode of immortality for physicians and psychotherapists.) Certainly this form of immortality has particular importance for intellectuals conscious of participating in the general flow of human creativity, but applies in some measure to all human beings in their unconscious perceptions of the legacy they leave for others.

Fourth, a sense of immortality may be achieved through being survived by nature itself: the perception that natural elements—limitless in space and time—remain. I found this mode of immortality to be particularly vivid among the Japanese, steeped as their culture is in nature symbolism; but various expressions of Western tradition (the romantic movement, for instance) have also placed great emphasis upon it. It is probably safe to say—and comparative mythology again supports this—that there is a universal psychic imagery in which nature represents an "ultimate" aspect of existence.

These psychological modes of immortality are not merely problems one ponders when dying; they are, in fact, constantly (though often indirectly or unconsciously) perceived standards by which people evaluate their lives. They thus make possible an examination of the part played by death and death symbolism during ordinary existence, which is what I mean by the beginnings of a death-oriented psychology of life. I shall for this purpose put forth three propositions, all of them dealing with death as a standard for, or test of, some aspect of life.

1. Death is anticipated as a *severance of the sense of connection*—or the inner sense of organic relationship to the various elements, and particularly to the people and groups of people, most necessary to our feelings of continuity and relatedness. Death is therefore a test of this sense of connection in that it threatens us with that which is most intolerable: *total severance.* Indeed, all of the modes of immortality mentioned are symbolic reflections of that part of the human psychic equipment which protects us from such severance and isolation.

Another expression of the threat to the sense of connection represented by death is the profound ambivalence of every culture toward the dead. One embraces the dead, supplicates oneself before them, and creates continuous rituals to perpetuate one's relationship to them, and (as is so vividly apparent in the case of the Hiroshima survivors) to attenuate one's guilt over survival priority. But one also pushes away the dead, considers them tainted and unclean, dangerous and threatening, precisely because they symbolize a break in the sense of connection and threaten to undermine it within the living. These patterns too were strongly present in Hiroshima survivors (and can be found in general Japanese cultural practice), although less consciously acceptable and therefore more indirectly expressed. Indeed, in virtually every culture the failure of the living to enact the rituals necessary to appease the dead is thought to so anger the latter (or their sacred representatives) as to bring about dangerous retribution for this failure to atone for the guilt of survival priority.

2. Death is a test of the meaning of life, of the symbolic integrity—the cohesion and significance—of the life one has been living. This is a more familiar concept, closely related to ideas that have long been put forth in literature and philosophy, as well as in certain psychoanalytic writings of Freud, Rank, and Jung; and it has a variety of manifestations. One is the utilization of a *way or style of dying* (or of anticipated dying) as an epitome of life's significance. An excellent example of this is

the Japanese samurai code, in which a heroic form of death in battle on behalf of one's lord (that is, a death embodying courage and loyalty) was the ultimate expression of the meaning of life.[30] Various cultures and subcultures have similarly set up an ideal style of dying, rarely perfectly realized, but nonetheless a powerful standard for the living. The anticipation of dying nobly, or at least appropriately—of dying for a meaningful purpose—is an expression of those modes of immortality related both to man's works (his lasting influences) and to his biosocial continuity. And I believe that much of the passionate attraction man has felt toward death can be understood as reflecting the unspoken sense that only in meaningful death can one simultaneously achieve a sense of immortality and articulate the meaning of life.

Apart from dramatically perfect deaths on the samurai model, timing and readiness play an important part. Can one visualize, in association with death, sufficient accomplishment to justify one's life? Or has life become so burdensome and devoid of meaning that death itself (whatever the style of dying) seems more appropriate? The latter was the case with a remarkable group of people undergoing surgery recently described by Avery Weisman and Thomas P. Hackett. These "predilection patients" were neither excessively anxious nor depressed, and yet correctly predicted their own deaths. For them, "death held more appeal . . . than did life because it promised either reunion with lost love, resolution of long conflict, or respite from anguish,"[31] and one is led to conclude that this psychological

30. The *Hagakure*, the classical eighteenth-century compilation of principles of *Bushido* (The Way of the Samurai), contains the famous phrase: "The essence of *Bushido* lies in the act of dying." And another passage, originally from the *Manyoshu*, a poetic anthology of the eighth century: " 'He who dies for the sake of his Lord does not die in vain, whether he goes to the sea and his corpse is left in a watery grave, or whether he goes to the mountain and the only shroud for his lifeless body is the mountain grass.' This is the way of loyalty." Robert N. Bellah, *Tokugawa Religion* (Glencoe, Ill.: Free Press, 1957), pp. 90–98.

31. Avery Weisman and Thomas P. Hackett, "Predilection to Death," p. 254. See footnote 25.

state interacted with their organic pathology and their reactions to surgical procedures to influence significantly the timing of their deaths. Their surrender to death was apparently related to their sense that they could no longer justify their continuing survival.

A classical literary expression of anticipated death as a test of the integrity of one's entire life (and one which has inspired many commentaries) occurs in Tolstoy's "The Death of Ivan Ilych."[32] Here the protagonist, in becoming aware of the incurable nature of his illness, reviews his past and is tormented by the thought that "the whole arrangement of his life and of his family, and all his social and official interests, might all have been false," and that the only authentic expressions of his life have been "those scarcely noticeable impulses which he had immediately suppressed." His lament in the face of approaching death is that of wasted opportunity ("I have lost all that was given me and it is impossible to rectify it") and existential guilt: the awareness of the enormous gap between what he has been and what he feels he might have been. But his torment disappears through a sudden spiritual revelation, his own capacity to feel love and pity for his wife and son. And at this point, for Ivan Ilych, "death" disappears: "Death is finished . . . it is no more!" "Death" has meant emptiness, the termination of a life without significance; death is transcended through a revelation which revivifies Ivan Ilych's sense of immortality by transporting him, even momentarily, into a realm of what he can perceive as authentic experience, and one in which he can feel in contact with eternal human values of pity and love, whether these are derived from a theologically defined supernatural source or from man's own creative works and influences.

Highly significant in Ivan Ilych's search for integrity is his disgust for the lying and evasiveness of those around him con-

---

32. Leo Tolstoy, *The Death of Ivan Ilych and Other Stories* (New York: Signet Classics, 1960). The quotations which follow are from pp. 97, 138, 152, and 156.

cerning the true nature of his illness (and concerning everything else), his yearning for an end to "this falsity around and within him [which] did more than anything else to poison his last days." But his family members are incapable of acting otherwise, because their deception is also self-deception, their own need to deny death; and because they are immersed in their own guilt over survival priority in relationship to Ivan Ilych—guilt made particularly intense by their hypocrisy, lack of love for him, and relief that death is claiming him and not them. Similar emotions are present in his colleagues and friends immediately after his death: "Each one thought or felt, 'Well, he's dead but I'm alive!'" The one voice of integrity around Ivan Ilych is that of a simple peasant servant who makes no effort to hide from him the fact that he is dying but instead helps him understand that death is, after all, the fate of everyone, that "We shall all of us die. . . ." Here the "survivor" lessens the emotional gap between himself and the dying man by stressing their shared destiny; this in turn enables the dying man to see his experience in relationship to the larger rhythms of life and death, and thereby awakens his biologically linked mode of immortality.[33]

33. Psychiatrists attending dying patients serve functions similar to that of the peasant servant in "The Death of Ivan Ilych." K. R. Eissler (see footnote 25) speaks of helping the patient during the "terminal pathway" to "accomplish the maximum individualization of which he is capable." And Weisman and Hackett similarly stress psychiatric intervention "to help the dying patient preserve his identity and dignity as a unique individual, despite the disease, or, in some cases, because of it." I would hold that achieving these goals depends also upon restoring the patient's sense of immortality through the various modes which have been discussed. Weisman and Hackett describe a "middle knowledge," or partial awareness, which patients have of their impending death, and find that attending physicians, because of their own conflicts over death, often have a greater need to deny this outcome than the patient himself. A situation is thus created in which the patient is reluctant to admit his "middle knowledge" to those around him for fear (and it is by no means an inappropriate fear) that they will turn away from him—so that he feels threatened with total severance. (Avery Weisman and Thomas P. Hackett, "Human Reactions to the Imminence of Death," Symposium on Human Reactions to the Threat of Impending Disaster, presented at the 1962 Annual Meeting of the American Association for the Advancement of Science.)

Very similar in theme to the death of Ivan Ilych, and probably influenced by it, is *Ikiru* (To Live), a film made by the accomplished Japanese director Akira Kurosawa. The film is also about a dying man who critically reviews his life—a petty official whose past actions have been characterized by bureaucratic evasion, and who overcomes his self-condemnation by an almost superhuman dedication to a final task, the building of a park for children. He thus achieves his sense of immortality mainly by his "works," by the final monument he leaves behind for others (even though surviving fellow bureaucrats, who had actually tried to block the enterprise, claim complete credit for it). This form of immortality is more consistent with East Asian stress upon the contribution to the social order—and with the Japanese *deification of the human matrix*[34]—than is the Western mode of spiritual revelation or faith expressed in the Tolstoy story. Moreover, the sequence of the bureaucrat's behavior on discovering he is dying—first his withdrawal into petulant inactivity and then his extraordinary rush of productive energy—provides evidence of the East Asian tendency to deal with problems of despair over life and death by means of a polarity of purposeless withdrawal or active involvement, rather than by the more characteristically Western pattern of self-lacerating inner struggle against the forces creating despair.[35] But con-

34. Lifton, "Youth and History," in footnote 2, p. 229. There are, of course, East Asian forms of spiritual revelation, particularly in Buddhism, but these are of a somewhat different nature; moreover, as Buddhism has moved eastward from its Indian origins—and particularly in its expressions in Japan—it has lost much of its original concern with spiritual revelation, and with doctrine in general, and these have become in various ways subordinated to the sectarian tendencies of the various human groups involved. See Hajime Nakamura, *The Ways of Thinking of Eastern Peoples* (Tokyo: Japanese National Commission for UNESCO, 1960), pp. 311–15.

35. Again the distinction should be understood as reflecting patterns emerging from varying degrees of psychological emphasis rather than absolute difference. Nonetheless, this East Asian, and perhaps particularly Japanese, pattern of despair has considerable importance for such problems as the emotional context of suicide in Japanese life, and the differences in Japanese and Western attitudes toward psychological constellations which the Westerner speaks of as tragedy. In all of these, I believe, Japanese

cerning the problems of death and the sense of immortality, the essential message of *Ikiru* is not different from that of "The Death of Ivan Ilych."

The foregoing may suggest some of the wider meaning of the concept of the survivor. All of us who continue to live while people anywhere die are survivors, and both the word and the condition suggest a relationship which we all have to the dead. Therefore, the Hiroshima survivors' focus upon the dead as arbiters of good and evil, and invisible assigners of guilt and shame, is by no means as unique as it at first glance appears to be. For we all enter into similar commitments to the dead, whether consciously or unconsciously, whether to specific people who lived in the past or to the anonymous dead; or whether these commitments relate to theological or quasi-theological ideas about ties to the dead in another form of existence, or to more or less scientific ideas about a heritage we wish to affirm or a model we wish to follow. In fact, in any quest for perfection there is probably a significant identification with the imagined perfection of the dead hero or heroes who lived in the golden age of the past. Most of our history has been made by those now dead, and we cannot avoid calling upon them, at least in various symbolic ways, for standards that give meaning to our lives.

3. And a last proposition: Death, in the very abruptness of its capacity to terminate life, becomes a test of life's sense of movement, of development and change—of sequence—in the continuous dialectic between fixed identity on the one hand and

---

show less of an inner struggle against the forces of nature or man creating the despair, potential suicide, or tragedy, and instead a greater tendency either to acquiesce to these forces or else to cease life-involving activity altogether. The degree of relevance of Western writings on despair for the Japanese situation can best be appreciated by keeping these distinctions in mind. See Leslie H. Farber, "Despair and the Life of Suicide," *Review of Existential Psychology* 2 (1962): 125–39; and "The Therapeutic Despair," *Psychiatry* 21 (1958): 7–20.

individuation on the other. To the extent that death is anticipated as absolute termination of life's movement, it calls into question the degree to which one's life contains, or has contained, any such development. Further, I would hold that a sense of movement in the various involvements of life is as fundamental a human need, as basic to the innate psychic imagery, as is the countervailing urge toward stillness, constancy, and reduction of tension which Freud (after Barbara Low) called the "Nirvana principle."[36] Freud referred to the Nirvana principle as "the dominating tendency of mental life" and related it to the "death instinct"; but I would prefer to speak instead of polarizing psychic tendencies toward continuous movement and ultimate stillness, both equally central to psychic function. Given the preoccupation with and ambivalence toward death since mankind's beginnings, Freud's concept of the death instinct may be a much more powerful one than his critics will allow. At the same time, it may yield greater understanding through being related to contemporary thought on symbolic process and innate imagery, rather than to older, more mechanistic views on the nature of instinct.[37]

36. Sigmund Freud, "Beyond the Pleasure Principle," *Standard Edition of the Complete Psychological Works* (London: Hogarth, 1955), 18: 55–56. Maryse Choisy (*Sigmund Freud: A New Appraisal* [New York: Philosophical Library, 1963]) has pointed out that Freud (and presumably Barbara Low), in employing this terminology, misunderstood the actual significance of Nirvana—to which I would add that Nirvana (whether the ideal state or the quest for that state) probably involves various kinds of indirect activity and sense of movement, and not simply ultimate stillness.

37. See, for instance, Susanne Langer (footnote 9); Joseph Campbell (footnote 28); Kenneth Boulding, *The Image: Knowledge in Life and Society* (Ann Arbor: University of Michigan Press, 1956); S. A. Barnett, "'Instinct,'" *Daedalus* 92 (1963): 564–80; and Adolf Portmann, *New Paths in Biology* (New York: Harper & Row, 1964). What Freud refers to as the death instinct may well be an innate imagery of death which the organism contains from birth, which becomes in the course of life further elaborated into various forms of conscious knowledge, fear, and denial; and which interacts with other forms of innate imagery relating to life-enhancement (sexual function, self-preservation, and development) as well as to mastery. From this perspective, the need to transcend death involves

To express this human necessity for a sense of movement, I find it often useful to speak of "self-process" rather than simply of "self." And I believe that the perpetual quest for a sense of movement has much to do with the appeal of comprehensive ideologies, particularly political and social ones, since these ideologies contain organized imagery of wider historical movement, and of individual participation in constant social flux. Yet ideologies, especially when totalist in character, also hold out an ultimate vision of utopian perfection in which all movement ceases, because one is, so to speak, *there*. This strong embodiment of both ends of the psychic polarity—of continuous movement as well as perfect stillness—may well be a fundamental source of ideological appeal. For in this polarity, ideologies represent a significant means of transcending linear time, and, at least symbolically, of transcending death itself. In the promise of an interminable relationship to the "Movement," one can enter into both a biosocial mode of immortality and a very special version of immortality through man's works, in this case relating to man's symbolic conquest of time. Nor is it accidental that ideologies appear and gather momentum during periods of cultural breakdown and historical dislocation, when there tends to be a sense of cessation of movement and of prominent death symbolism. For central to the revitalizing mission of ideologies is their acting out, in historical (and psychological) context, the classical mythological theme of death and rebirth.[38]

The psychic response to a threat of death, actual or symbolic, is likely to be either that of stillness and cessation of movement or else that of frenetic, compensatory activity. The former was by far the most prominent in the Hiroshima situation, though

the interrelationship of all three of these forms of imagery, with that of mastery of great importance.

38. For a discussion of psychological and historical aspects of ideology, and particularly of ideological extremism, see Lifton, *Thought Reform and the Psychology of Totalism: A Study of "Brainwashing" in China* (New York: Norton, 1961), Chap. 22.

the latter was not entirely absent. The psychic closing off which took place right after the bomb fell was, in an important sense, a cessation of psychic motion—a temporary form of symbolically "dying"—in order to defend against the threat of more lasting psychological "death" (psychosis) posed by the overwhelming evidence of actual physical death. And the same may be said of the later self-imposed restraint in living which characterizes the "identity of the dead," an identity whose very stillness becomes a means of carrying on with life in the face of one's commitment to death and the dead. But there were occasional cases of heightened activity, usually of an unfocused and confused variety, even at the time of the bomb. And later energies in rebuilding the city—the "frontier atmosphere" that predominated during much of the postwar period—may also be seen as a somewhat delayed intensification of movement, though it must be added that much of this energy and movement came from the outside.

Can something more be said about these propositions concerning death, and about the various modes of immortality, as they specifically apply to the nuclear age? I believe that from these perspectives we can see new psychological threats posed by nuclear weapons—right now, to all of us among the living.

Concerning the first proposition, that death is a test of our sense of connection, if we anticipate the possibility of nuclear weapons being used (as I believe we all do in some measure), we are faced with a prospect of being severed from virtually all of our symbolic paths to immortality. In the postnuclear world, we can imagine no biological or biosocial posterity; there is little or nothing surviving of our works or influences; and theological symbolism of an afterlife may well be insufficiently strong in its hold on the imagination to still inner fears of total severance. Certainly in my Hiroshima work I was struck by the inability of people to find adequate transcendent religious explanation—Buddhist, Shinto, or Christian—for what they and others had experienced. This was partly due to the relatively weak state of such theological symbolism in contemporary Japan, but perhaps most fundamentally due to the magnitude of the disaster itself. And whatever the mixed state of religious symbolism in the rest of the world, there is grave doubt as to whether the promise of some form of life after death can maintain symbolic power in an imagined world in which there are none (or virtually none) among the biologically living. This leaves only the mode of immortality symbolized by nature, which I found to be perhaps the most viable of all among Hiroshima survivors—as expressed in the Japanese (originally Chinese) proverb quoted to me by several of them: "The state may collapse, but the mountains and rivers remain." And with all the other modes of immortality so threatened, we may raise the speculative possibility that, independent of any further use of nuclear weapons, one outcome of the nuclear age might be the development of some form of natural theology (or at least of a theology in which nature is prominent) as a means of meeting man's innate need for a sense of immortality.

Concerning the second proposition, relating to the meaning and integrity of life, we find ourselves even more directly threatened by nuclear weapons. As many have already pointed out, nuclear weapons confront us with a kind of death that can have no meaning.[39] There is no such thing as dying heroically, for a great cause, in the service of a belief or a nation—in other words, for a palpable purpose—but rather only the prospect of dying anonymously, emptily, without gain to others. Such feel-

---

39. See, for instance, Hans J. Morgenthau, "Death in the Nuclear Age," *Commentary* (September 1961). Among psychological studies, see Jerome D. Frank, "Breaking the Thought Barrier: Psychological Challenges of the Nuclear Age," *Psychiatry*, 23 (1960): 245–66; *Some Socio-psychiatric Aspects of the Prevention of Nuclear War*, report of the Committee on Social Issues of the Group for the Advancement of Psychiatry; and Lester Grinspoon, "The Unacceptability of Disquieting Facts," presented at the 1962 American Association for the Advancement of Science Symposium.

ings were prominent among Hiroshima survivors both at the time of their initial immersion in death and during the months and years following it. They could not view their experience as purposeful, in the sense of teaching the world the necessity for abandoning nuclear weapons, but rather saw themselves as scapegoats for the world's evil, as "guinea pigs" in a historical "experiment," or else as victims of a war made infinitely more inhuman by the new weapon. Part of their problem was the difficulty they had in knowing whom or what to hate, since, as one of my colleagues put it, "You can't hate magic." They did find in postwar Japanese pacifism an opportunity for organized rechanneling of resentment into a hatred of war itself; this was of considerable importance, but has by no means resolved the issue. The only consistent "meaning" survivors could find in all of the death and destruction around them was in the application of an everyday expression of East Asian fatalism—*shikata-ganai* ("It can't be helped")—which is a surface reflection of a profoundly important psychological tendency toward accepting whatever destiny one is given. But however great the psychological usefulness of this attitude, one can hardly say that it enabled survivors to achieve full mastery of their experience. And concerning the question of the "appropriateness" of anticipated death, Hiroshima survivors were the very antithesis of the "predilection patients" mentioned before: rather than being ready for death, they found its intrusion upon life to be unacceptable, even absurd; and when seeming to embrace death, they were really clinging to life.

But considering the destructive power of present nuclear weapons (which is more than a thousandfold that of the Hiroshima bomb), and considering the impossibility of a meaningful nuclear death, is not life itself deprived of much of its meaning? Does not nuclear death threaten the deep significance of all of our lives? Indeed, the attraction some feel toward the use of nuclear weapons might be partly a function of this meaninglessness, so that in a paradoxical way they want to "end it all" (and perhaps realize their own end-of-the-world fantasies) as a means of denying the very emptiness of the nuclear death toward which they press. Here the principle of individual suicide as an attempt to deny the reality of death[40] is carried further to encompass nuclear suicide-murder as an attempt to deny the threat to meaningful human existence posed by these weapons.

And finally, in relationship to the proposition of death as a test of life's sense of movement, I think the matter is more ambiguous, though hardly encouraging. There is a sense in all of us, in greater or lesser degree, that nuclear weapons might terminate all of life's movement. Yet there is also, at least in some, a strange intensity and excitement in relationship to the confrontation with danger which nuclear weapons provide; and this, it might be claimed, contributes to a sense of movement in present-day life. But this exhilaration—or perhaps pseudoexhilaration—is less a direct function of the nuclear weapons themselves than of the universal historical dislocation accompanying a wider technological revolution. In other words, there is in our world an extraordinary combination of potential for continuously enriching movement and development of self-process, side by side with the potential for sudden and absolute termination. This latter possibility, which I have called the *potentially terminal revolution,*[41] has not yet been seriously evaluated in its full psychological consequences; and whatever its apparent stimulus to a sense of movement, one may well suspect that it also contributes to a profound listlessness and inertia that lurk beneath.

I am aware that I have painted something less than an opti-

40. K. R. Eissler (footnote 25; pp. 65–67) notes the frequently observed psychological relationship between suicide and murder, and goes on to speak of suicide as "the result of a rebellion against death," since "for most suicides the act does not mean really dying" but is rather a means of active defiance of, rather than passive submission to, death.

41. Lifton, *Thought Reform and the Psychology of Totalism* (New York: Norton Library [paperback] Edition, 1963), Preface, pp. vii–ix.

mistic picture, both concerning the Hiroshima disaster and our present relationship to the nuclear world. Indeed it would seem that we are caught in a vicious psychological and historical circle, in which the existence of nuclear weapons impairs our relationship to death and immortality, and this impairment to our symbolic processes in turn interferes with our ability to deal with these same nuclear weapons. But one way of breaking out of such a pattern is by gaining at least a dim understanding of our own involvement in it. And in studying the Hiroshima experience and other extreme situations, I have found that man's capacity for elaborating and enclosing himself in this kind of ring of destructiveness is matched only by his equal capacity for renewal. Surely the mythological theme of death and rebirth takes on particular pertinence for us now, and every constructive effort we can make to grasp something more of our relationship to death becomes, in its own way, a small stimulus to rebirth.

THE DEATH THROES
OF CULTURE

6 The Games of Life and the Dances of Death

BENJAMIN NELSON

A premier Poet of our time once sang:

> *This is the way the world ends*
> *This is the way the world ends*
> *This is the way the world ends*
> *Not with a bang but a whimper.*[1]

The Poet would almost certainly have been mistaken had he meant his remarks to apply to civilizations. Civilizations do not end with a *bang* or a *whimper*. Civilizations generally die laughing!

The more closely great societies approach the point of checkmate, the deeper the indulgence of great numbers in their favorite games. In fact, the worse the situation, the more hectic the abandonment. It is when all is fun and joy, on the go-go,

Benjamin Nelson is Professor of Sociology and History at the Graduate Faculty of the New School for Social Research. His books include *The Idea of Usury: From Tribal Brotherhood to Universal Otherhood.*

1. T. S. Eliot, "The Hollow Men" (1925). In *The Collected Poems: 1909–1962.* Reprinted by permission of Harcourt Brace Jovanovich.

Clues to the wider perspectives adopted in this essay will be found in the writings of Durkheim, Jane Harrison, Johan Huizinga, and others who place strong stress on the structures of experience in the shaping of men's expressions. See esp., Durkheim ([1912] 1915); Harrison (1912); Huizinga (1924); also see some earlier essays listed under the author's name in the References below (1963, 1964, 1965, 1969, 1972).

when the dancers in the charades are at the edge of ecstasy and frenzy, that the hoped-for oblivion prevails. At this juncture, treasured elements of the legacy of civilizations slip unnoticed out of focus.[2]

Abundant evidence for these statements is available to those students of history and sociology who attend strongly to the ways in which the classes and the masses alike have related to certain of the very critical transitions in their histories. The more closely we study the episodes, the more we discover that relatively few can sense or understand the changes which occur in peak structures of value or in all of those sensibilities which might have had to be maintained if civilizations are somehow to be preserved.

The depictions by Samuel Dill and others of Roman society of the late fourth and fifth centuries A.D.[3] tell the story eloquently. The available evidence on political and economic developments makes it clear that the Imperial Establishment was sagging. In losing to the Visigoths at Adrianople (A.D. 378), the Romans had suffered a crucial break in their frontiers. Very decisive structures at every level appeared to be crumbling. Yet, when we read their letters and other literary efforts, we discover that only a handful of men cared to relate to the circumstances of their undoing.

Christian thinkers were, in the main, more prone to respond to the crisis than were the pagans. The reasons are easy enough to see. For St. Augustine, the sack of Rome in 410 offered the needed proof that the only true grounds for hope lay in the promise of a city uncontaminated by Rome's persisting corruptions, a city of God (*civitas Dei*).

But if we read the pagan letters of the time, we get a much

2. The evanescence of civilizations has rarely been rendered as poignantly as in Paul Valéry's "Crisis of the Mind." See his *History and Politics* (1962). A striking contrast to Valéry's view of civilization will be found in R. Nisbet (1969), p. 3, but cf. B. Nelson (1969a).

3. S. Dill (1898, ed. 1957).

more serene picture. We discover that long before the time of the worst onslaughts, the well-to-do had left the cities for country villas where they would regularly meet and engage one another in sports, charades of sociability, and polite banter about their literary traditions. How effete their favorite rhetoric was may be judged from stilted missives they wrote to one another from time to time. The situation continued to get worse, but the classes and for that matter the masses, neither truly understood nor cared to analyze their predicaments.[4]

Masses do not usually have the alternatives that the classes do. They cannot, for the most part, put things out of mind by devising genteel distractions. Masses are likely to be stirred into states of effervescence, to coalesce into collectivities and to move toward ways—whether political, prepolitical, or post-political—of achieving some new sense of vitality and existence. Masses often get to be completely involved in efforts to discover a collective oneness.

Patterns of this sort have occurred again and again. Sometimes a religion is formed in the midst of the effervescence; always there are powerful components goading men into mindlessness and into "trances of action." The reasons are not hard to find: the older ways have become tedious, everything that comes to mind in these times proves frightening. Rather than "minding," great numbers resort to drink, drugs, Dionysiac abandonment, disaster politics. No prejudice is intended in these words. A great deal of dying and being reborn is in process. This is one form of the equation of our essay.

There is another form of our equation which links the games of life men play in their hours of despair to their dances of death.[5] I begin with some paragraphs from Somerset Maugham's

---

4. *Ibid.*, bk. V, ch. 1, *passim*, esp. 415, 428–439; on the Christian side, see the earlier exceptional work, *On the Government of God*, by Salvianus, a presbyter of Marseilles; cf. Dill (1957), 137–141.

5. See, e.g., Huizinga (1924).

Of Human Bondage. Maugham is describing a Paris dance hall around 1900:

The hall was lit by great white lights low down which emphasized the shadows on the faces, although the light seemed to harden under it and the colors were most curious. Philip leaned over the rails staring down. He ceased to hear the music. They danced furiously. They danced around the room, slowly talking, but very little, with all their attention given to the dance. It seemed to Philip that they had thrown off the guard which people wear on their expression, and he saw them now as they really were. In that moment of abandon they were strangely animals. Some were foxy; some were wolf-like. Others had the long foolish faces of sheep. Their skins were sallow from the unhealthy life they led. Their features were blunted by mean interests and their little eyes were shifty and cunning. They were seeking escape from a world of horror.

Fate seemed to tower above them, and they danced as though everlasting darkness were about their feet. It was as if life terrified them, and the shriek that was in their hearts died within their throats. Notwithstanding the beastly lust which disfigured them and the meanness of their faces, and the cruelty. Notwithstanding the stupidity which was the worst of all, the anguish of these fixed eyes made all that crowd terrible and pathetic.[6]

Maugham's grim description locates the main elements of our scenario: the haste to stave off horror; the growing fascination with and the anguished flight from a sense of impending death; the experience of vertigo. It is against this background that men come to play their games of life.

A not so surprising effect occurs as the games grow more abandoned; the takeoff into oblivion accelerates. Played with enough frenzy, the games promise escape from the horrors of existence; precisely, then, the masks of the actors fall: *the games of life turn out to be dances of death.*

6. Maugham (1930), 263–4. Reprinted by permission of Random House (Vintage Books).

The equation I have just stated is one which has been very well understood by all those attuned to divining the signs of the times. Depictions of the agonies of interims recur throughout literature and art. My subsequent examples will be drawn mainly but not exclusively from the nineteenth and twentieth centuries.

In the arts, there are those who run ahead and who are especially sensitive to the quakes and tremors of their times. One such a spiritual seismographer was Rimbaud, whose *Season in Hell* is a supreme illustration of the sorts of games that life suggests to those in the extremities of despair. Anyone wishing to have a more than superficial understanding of the twentieth century must come to know that Rimbaud's logbook offers us more insights into the profiles of our future sense of reality than myriad "futurological" publications which are now concerned with the Year 2000. Rimbaud was truly a visionary, one who saw far ahead in respect to the spiritual itineraries we would all encounter in our efforts to find our ways out of the maze.[7]

None of us ever really learns to live life. The living of death comes to us more or less naturally. We do not need to receive special lessons on how to live death. We move toward death with faultless ease and skill. Is this not exactly what many of our foremost playwrights, poets, and painters have been telling us? Among the playwrights I would mention only a few whose works make no sense unless they are read and experienced in the spirit of the equations I have been suggesting here.

Samuel Beckett's whole work is devoted to the notion that the boring charades which comprise our games of life are in their own little way *dances* on the way to a death—if, indeed, there is any reality to either life or death. Beckett never settles the question; we read him or listen to him in *Waiting for Godot*, in *Malone Dies*, and other plays and novels; we sense that he

7. Rimbaud (1873, tr. 1961).

doesn't ever decide whether he is alive or dead or has yet been born. The whole of life has the quality of being a silly turn on the way to death, itself an illusory end to meaninglessness.[8]

The resistances men exhibit to facing the realities of their lives and deaths have provoked one playwright after another in our time. Audiences have worked wonders in fending off these messages. I recall the perplexities of more than one elegant and cultivated group when *The Iceman Cometh* of Eugene O'Neill first appeared on Broadway. In my naïveté, I originally supposed that everyone who saw or read the play would instantly recognize that *The Iceman Cometh* was a passion play. I found it the single most searing *contemporary* statement of this theme I had until then seen, relentlessly depicting the ways by which people seek to assure themselves that life eternal is theirs for the asking, exposing the "moonshine" and "pipe-dreams," everything—including the arts and sciences—which was fashioned in the attempt to make reality more bearable.

Those who remember the play cannot forget how stark were the alternatives with which O'Neill confronts us. As I was to learn only recently, O'Neill's stage directions directly recall the eve of the sacrifice of the paschal lamb. On Hickey's return to the saloon for the purpose of having a reunion with his old cronies, they throw themselves into having a wonderful time, living just as they always wanted to live and avoiding all the mess of the actual world. O'Neill's stage directions call upon Hickey and his cronies to be grouped in a manner which recalls Leonardo's painting of the Last Supper.[9] It turns out the "Last Supper" is not only with Christ but also with Freud. What O'Neill wants to argue is the proposition that neither Christ nor Freud will get us out of the "bum rap" of this living death.[10]

8. This scheme is given insistent stress in the script written for—and acted by—Beckett's friend, Jack McGowran.

9. C. Day in J. H. Raleigh (ed.) (1968), 83.

10. Karl Schiftgriesser concludes an interview with O'Neill saying, "But as it [the play] proceeds, the 'Iceman' who started as a ribald joke, takes

We must not be astonished that the disciples turn on Hickey-Christ-Freud. They wish to destroy him. In fact, they put him out of the way as hopelessly mad; what else could they do? Was he not telling them that the illusions they insisted upon living and reliving in this womb, that they had recreated for themselves, could not in the end suffice?

It is startling that I have not yet found the author or critic who has noticed that Hickey's old cronies set upon him exactly when he comes to deliver a message meant to bring them into close touch with reality. Are not those who come to deliver some message too hard for our ears, too strong for our hearts and minds, regularly set aside as being beside themselves? Who among us can look straight into the eyes of life and death?

Countless illustrations of the relationship between the games of life and the dances of death are found in major living playwrights, Sartre, Genet, Ionesco, Peter Weiss, and others less removed.

Most recently, the works of art which have spelled out our equation most profoundly are films, but for some reason, not easy to state in a formula, many critics of films seem to miss critical dimensions of what is happening. Too often in our day, we get psychoanalytic pathographies of the directors rather than interpretations of the film. A case in point is an essay which offers proof that Fellini's *Satyricon* illustrated Fellini's inability to shake his way free of the perversions and psychopathologies which consumed him. Was it not obvious that he had voyeuristic tendencies, that he was dedicated to sadistic perversion, that he had addictions to necrophilia, and so forth?

Are we prepared to overlook the fact that Fellini's most interesting and most recent pictures are located in Rome, the historic city of Rome? *La Dolce Vita*, which is certainly about Rome, has the nobility wandering through catacombs and old

on a different, deeper and even terrifying meaning and before the end becomes Death itself." J. H. Raleigh (ed.) (1968), p. 28.

villas engaging in orgiastic, frenetic efforts to shake themselves
free of agonizing obsessions of one kind or another. As many
will recall, *La Dolce Vita* begins with a helicopter carrying
aloft the image of Jesus.

When I first saw *La Dolce Vita*, I felt certain that Fellini's
future work would have to include *The Satyricon*. Fellini had
to film *Satyricon* because *Satyricon* was *our* story, spoke to *our*
condition. Fellini's reputed perversions—his sadism, his scatol-
ogy, and his necrophilia—proved to be in the service of other
purposes. What did Fellini really want to say? All the evidence,
in my view, points to the fact that Fellini wanted to re-present
us to ourselves by helping us, compelling us to re-live critical
phases in the experiences of Western men during the anguished
hours of Rome's age-old history.

La Dolce Vita is the prelude to *The Satyricon*. Both are the
working out of deeply committed experiments in Fellini's
spiritual efforts to read our times. Knowing that Rome had been
—and continues to be—one of the navels of the world, an ir-
radiating nucleus of civilizational development, Fellini sought
to depict a dilemma revealed by Rome's history. Fellini was
sensitive to the fact that when Rome sought to be starkly pagan,
it had a way of going berserk, out of its mind; when it sought to
be altogether—totally and totalistically—Christian, it became
absurd. How does one get beyond this impasse? Fellini under-
took an experiment: he tried to establish whether those who
escaped being thrown off course by the distortions of the Christian sense of guilt, who hoped to be able to enjoy "pagan" innocence in their indulgences, are in fact able to manage to have
joy without shame or whether the games they play destroy them.

I am now able to cite Fellini himself as a witness that my
conjectures tally with the key facts. A recently published guide
to Fellini's *Satyricon* permits us to read his own words. Interest-
ingly, the setting of the interviews might almost be one from a
Fellini film. A party is going on, starlets and international re-

porters are everywhere, and the renowned Moravia is one among them; he is the chief interviewer. Everyone explains Fellini to himself, but Fellini tells his own story clearly in his Preface. He explains he first read *The Satyricon* "many years ago at school," and that the reading remained a "vivid memory" and exerted "a constant and mysterious challenge." He continues:

After the lapse of many years I reread the *Satyricon* recently. . . . This time [there was] more than just a temptation to make a film out of it, there was a need, an enthusiastic certainty.

The encounter with that world and that society turned out to be a joyful affair, a stimulation of fantasy, an encounter rich in themes of remarkable relevance to modern society.[11]

Clearly, Fellini expects us to know that *La Dolce Vita* was for him a first step along this way. His remarks go forward to describe the "disconcerting analogies" between . . . society today and Roman society "before the final arrival of Christianity."[12]

Fellini is quick to explain that his intentions went far beyond transcribing Petronius on film. His work was to be as much an experiment as a satire.

. . . If the work of Petronius is the realistic, bloody and amusing description of the customs, characters and general feel of those times, the film we want to freely adapt from it could be a fresco in fantasy key, a powerful and evocative allegory—a satire of the world we live in today. Man never changes, and today we can recognise all the principal characters of the drama: Encolpius and Ascyltos, two hippy students, like any of those hanging around today in Piazza di Spagna, or in Paris, Amsterdam or London, moving on from adventure to adventure, even the most gruesome, without the least remorse, with all the natural innocence and splendid vitality of two young animals. Their revolt, though having nothing in common with traditional revolts— neither the faith, nor the desperation, nor the drive to change or

11. Fellini (1970), 43. Reprinted by permission of Ballantine Books.
12. *Ibid.* (As this essay goes to press, word comes from Italy that Fellini has now completed a new film entitled *Roma: The Decline of the Roman Empire: 1931–1972.*)

destroy—is nevertheless a revolt and is expressed in terms of utter ignorance of and estrangement from the society surrounding them. They live from day to day, taking problems as they come, their life interests alarmingly confined to the elementaries: they eat, make love, stick together, bed down anywhere. They make a living by the most haphazard expedients, often downright illegal ones. They are dropouts from every system, and recognize no obligations, duties or restrictions. . . .

They are totally insensible to conventional ties like the family (usually built less on affection than on blackmail): they don't even practice the cult of friendship, which they consider a precarious and contradictory sentiment, and so are willing to betray or disown each other any time. They have no illusions precisely because they believe in nothing but, in a completely new and original way, their cynicism stays this side of a peaceful self-fulfillment, of a solid, healthy and unique good sense.[13]

That last remark offers Fellini's most compelling statement of the new credo. The new faith is expressed in the conviction that if previous structures of commitment, including commitment to one's dearest friends, are held in total abeyance, if there is a total rejection of any image of reciprocity, this may well be the very remedy which this dementing society apparently requires. Self-fulfillment then seems to be "solid, healthy and unique good sense."

Is this situation conceivable or possible? Has the new credo the makings of some new faith which will recover us from our alienation? The story fills out as we follow the details of the interview. On more than one occasion evidence develops that Moravia was not able to understand what Fellini was saying. Despite Moravia's vaunted moralism, he seems to enjoy the spectacle of ongoing decays. Fellini runs very much deeper. He reminds us here of Nietzsche! He explains:

When I think that at the time of Hadrian the cultivated, sensitive, cosmopolitan emperor who traveled constantly throughout the em-

13. *Ibid.,* 44.

pire, in the Coliseums at Rome, one could witness the massacre of seventy-five pairs of gladiators in a single afternoon. . . . What escapes us is the mentality of the world in which you went to the box office or the theater and bought a ticket which entitled you to entertain yourself with the agony of a fellow human being killed by the sword or devoured by a wild beast. Death probably constituted the most entertaining part of these spectacles. People watched men die as today Spaniards watch bulls die: joking, laughing, having a drink.[14]

Moravia, ever the cultured critic, remarks, "Agony as a spectacle comes to an end in history with the coming of Christianity."

This seems to be as questionable an assertion as has been uttered in our century. Agony as a spectacle *does not come to an end in history with the coming of Christianity;* it takes myriad new forms. We, in our own time, are witnessing many of those forms. We, you and I, are able to look at our TV and see agonies far beyond the imagination of Roman proletarians and emperors alike, the agonies now occurring across the world which regularly appear on our TV screens—Vietnam, Biafra, East Pakistan, the agonies displayed in gladiatorial sport spectacles, football, and so on. Our films more than match the fantasies of de Sade.

It was the era of the late Middle Ages—in many ways a prototype of our own times—which best understood that the games of life are the sources of the dances of death. The men of those days were fascinated by the image of the confrontation of the living and dead. Introducing a medieval dance of death, Florence Warren reminds us that the theme of the encounter of the three living and the three dead occurs again and again. Actual dancing was frequently held at the times and places of death, and during the plague it was even encouraged as a means of raising people's spirits. There was a dance in which the dancers circled others who played dead. Death has an ironic and humorous tone,

14. *Ibid.*, 26.

though there is the usual grim message underneath, for death takes liberties in addressing his subjects. He tells the abbot, for example, to dance "even though you're nothing light." The dance was jolly, and when it came time for each of the dancers to kiss their "dead" fellow goodbye, each would do an exaggerated parody of the act, which caused mirth. In the poem, "the grim confrontation of death with the living becomes a game of the living," Florence Warren explains.[15] (This last metaphor, introducing a moving variation of the image I had already selected for my own title, surprised me on running across it in Florence Warren's pages.)

Perhaps the most powerful explicit rendering of a medieval dance of death by a modern master will be found in Ingmar Bergman's *The Seventh Seal*. Indeed, the entire action of that great work occurs in an interlude or a reprieve between the sittings of a great game of chess, whose outcome the Knight-Crusader knows in advance: he will be checkmated by his opponent, Death. At the end, he learns that Death has "no secrets," "nothing to tell him." The central project under consideration among the people of the everyday world in interaction in the play is the planning of a re-presentation of the dance of death. Here again we have the links between the games of life and the dances of death.

As in the case of Fellini, we have Bergman's own word that the grim equations I have touched upon on these pages depict pangs and blights of modern existence. We dare not close our comparison of these two men, however, without remarking that a chasm seems to separate their images of world and future. Bergman sums up his own creed in the following stark lines:

. . . In former days the artist remained unknown and his work was to the glory of God. He lived and died without being more or

15. Warren (1931), in introduction.

less important than other artisans; 'eternal values,' 'immortality' and 'masterpiece' were terms not applicable in his case. The ability to create was a gift. In such a world flourished invulnerable assurance and natural humility.

Today the individual has become the highest form and the greatest bane of artistic creation. The smallest wound or pain of the ego is examined under a microscope as if it were of eternal importance. The artist considers his isolation, his subjectivity, his individualism almost holy. . . . The individualists stare into each other's eyes and yet deny the existence of each other. We walk in circles, so limited by our own anxieties that we can no longer distinguish between true and false, between the gangster's whim and the purest ideal.

Thus if I am asked what I would like the general purpose of my films to be, I would reply that I want to be one of the artists in the cathedral on the great plain. I want to make a dragon's head, an angel, a devil—or perhaps a saint—out of stone. It does not matter which; it is the sense of satisfaction that counts. Regardless of whether I believe or not, whether I am a Christian or not, I would play my part in the collective building of the cathedral.[16]

I allow myself some summary theses on the *dramas* of life and death which constitute the fabrics of our several and joint histories. I do this by way of conclusion and reprise.

The present essay argues that societies do undergo changes in their images of their states of being; their senses of their past, present, and future; their experience of the balances of hoped-for fruitions and dreaded failures.[17] At times in the histories of societies, the tensions verge upon the unendurable. Deep confusion and perplexities begin to manifest themselves at every turn—in some as agony, in some as apathy, in some as effervescence, in some as immense urgency to engage in mindless acts of ecstasy, terror, fusion with others.

The most compelling instances or signs of the crisis state of

16. Bergman (1960). Reprinted by permission of Simon & Schuster.
17. Cf. Nelson (1973).

civilization may be described as *anomie* and *vertigo*.[18] When this occurs, societies séem to be caught up in maelstrom. In the omnipresence of the grotesque,[19] all of the rules have been suspended and no longer appear to apply. A precedent seems to be absurd. Among the critical developments are new religious statements and truths allegedly derived from the sciences and the pseudosciences, that death has no power over man, that it is possible to eliminate it by the expansion of consciousness or by some particular device of a new science or an old science, whether it be reincarnation or cryonic suspension.[20] Whenever societies are close to the state of vertigo, we discover the increase of frenzied efforts to fight off the sense of impending doom. Vast numbers of people are propelled into violent motions, whether in dance, marathon,[21] nomadism, or in brutal sports of an agonistic character.

The most interesting of all of the responses of individuals and groups to the sense of impending doom is the increase in pressure to create games and dances which distract one's mind from brooding over one's fate. I have called these games "the games

18. Durkheim (1912), R. K. Merton (1938, ed. 1968), B. Nelson (1964).
19. B. Nelson (1972).
20. Evidence indicates that the key source of this movement is the 1964 book by Robert Ettinger. An exceptionally interesting recent case is described in Bill Barry, "Playing It Cold," Long Island, New York, *Newsday* (Nov. 12, 1971), pp. 7W–15W.
21. Robert Coates offers the following "Afterword" to Horace McCoy's novel:

> The dance marathon was truly a *danse macabre,* and the violent contrasts inherent in the scene: the band (always, as the author notes, playing overly loud), the gaudy festoons and ribbons of bunting strung all over the hall, the bars and hot dog counters along the walls, the intermittently booming loud speakers, all centering on the weaving array of close-to-collapsing contestants, almost literally walking in their sleep—these contrasts only served to heighten the resemblance to a kind of Surrealist, latter-day Inferno. (All this, too was punctuated—and this the author brings out skillfully indeed—by the fiendish jocularity of the promoter, who was always at his most expansive when he was ordering an extra sprint to thin out some of the contestants.)

See Coates (1966). Cf. Jonathan Eisen's review of R. Neville's study of the "international underground" of "play power." Eisen (1971).

of life," and when they are looked at very carefully, it is observed that these games of life, whose purpose one would suppose would be to stave off the dances of death are after their own fashion, dances of death; for, in the playing of the games of life, we actually lose our lives or cast them away in one or another fashion.

The connections between the games of life and the dances of death were very well understood by men of another time, especially the men of the Middle Ages. It is, therefore, no wonder whatever that they gave so much stress to the idea of the dances of death. Indeed, these were always projected as the games of life which were being played by hectic and frenzied dancers.[22]

The stuff which we produce as "plays" in our theaters is the dramas of our lives and deaths. Who does not relive these histories will not be able to reappropriate these re-presentations. We are the authors, the audience, the actors, and the acts. The stories we are telling and are being told are about ourselves.[23]

De nobis fabulae narrantur.

---

22. Backman (1952), 146–54.
23. Cf. B. Nelson (1963, 1964, 1972, 1972a); Foucault (1965).

References

Backmann, E. Louis
1952
    Religious Dances in the Christian Church and Popular Medicine. Tr. E. Classen. London: Allen & Unwin.

Beckett, Samuel
1938   *Murphy.* N.Y.: Grove Press.
1953   *Watt.* Paris: Olympia Press.
1954   *Waiting for Godot.* N.Y.: Grove Press.
1955   *Molloy.* N.Y.: Grove Press.
1956   *Malone Dies.* N.Y.: Grove Press.
1957   *All That Fall.* London: Faber & Faber.

Bergman, I.
1960   *The Seventh Seal: A Film.* N.Y.: Simon & Schuster. Intro. by I. Bergman.

1966   *Four Screen Plays.* Tr. by Lars Malstrom and David Kushner. 3rd pb. printing. N.Y.: Simon & Schuster. Orig. ed., 1960.

Coates, Robert
1966   "Afterword: Life and Death." See below under McCoy.

Day, Cyrus
1968   "The Iceman and the Bridegroom: Some Observations on the Death of O'Neill's Salesman." In J. H. Raleigh (ed.), 79–86.

Dill, S.
(1898) 1957   *Roman Society: The Last Century of the Western Empire.* N.Y.: Meridian. (Original ed., 1898).

Durkheim, Emile
(1897) 1951   *Suicide.* Tr. J. Spaulding. Glencoe, Ill.: Free Press.
(1912) 1915   *The Elementary Forms of the Religious Life.* Tr. J. W. Swain. London: Allen & Unwin; N.Y.: Macmillan.

Eisen, Jonathan
1971   "Selling the Underground." *Book World,* Jan. 10, 1971. (Review of R. Neville below).

Eliot, T. S.
1925   "The Hollow Men." In *The Collected Poems: 1909–1962.* N.Y.: Harcourt Brace Jovanovich, 1962.

Ettinger, Robert, C. W.
1964   *The Prospect of Immortality.* Garden City, N.Y.: Doubleday & Co.

Fellini, F.
1970   *Satyricon.* Dario Zanelli (ed.); E. Walter and J. Matthews (trans.). N.Y.: Ballantine.

Foucault, Michel
1965   *Madness in Civilization: A History of Insanity in the Age of Reason.* N.Y.: Pantheon.

Harrison, Jane
1912   *Themis.* Cambridge: Cambridge University Press. Reprinted in *Epilogomena to the Study of Greek Religion and Themis:* A Study of the Social Origins of Greek Religion. New Hyde Park, N.Y.: University Books, 1962.

Huizinga, J.
1924   *The Waning of the Middle Ages.* N.Y.: Longmans, Green (also published in 1937, London: Arnold & Co.).

Jacobsen, J. &
  W. R. Mueller
1964   *The Testament of Samuel Beckett.* N.Y.: Hill and Wang.

Lydgate, William
  (c1370–1450)
    See below under Warren.

Marin, Peter
1972   "Children of Learning." *Saturday Review,* May 6, 58–63.

Maugham, Somerset
1930   *Of Human Bondage.* N.Y.: Modern Library (also N.Y.: Vintage, 1956).

McCoy, Horace
1966   *They Shoot Horses, Don't They?* N.Y.: Avon. With "An Afterword" by Robert M. Coates.

Merton, R. K.
(1938) 1968   "Social Structure and Anomie." (Originally printed in *ASR,* 3, 1938, pp. 672–682.) Revised and enlarged version in R. Merton, *Social Theory & Social Structure,* N.Y.: Free Press, 1968, pp. 131–161.

Nelson, B.
1963   "[Genet's] *The Balcony & Parisian Existentialism." Tulane Drama Review,* 7:3, 60–79.

1964   "Actor's Directors, Roles, Cues, Meanings, Identities: Further Thoughts on 'Anomie'." *Psa. Rev.,* 51:1, 135–160.

1969   Preface to G. Rosen (1969).

1969a   "Metaphor in Sociology." Review of Robert Nisbet's *Social Change and History: Aspects of the*

Western Theory of Development. Science Magazine, 166 (Dec. 19), 1498–1500.

1971   "Afterword: A Medium with a Message: R. D. Laing." In *R. D. Laing & Anti-Psychiatry*, R. Boyers & R. Orrill (eds.). N.Y.: Harper & Row. Pp. 297–301. (Originally appeared in *Salmagundi Review, 16* (Spring), 1971, 199–201.

1972   "The Omnipresence of the Grotesque." Reprinted in *The Discontinuous Universe*, S. Sears & G. Lord (eds.). N.Y.: Basic Books. Pp. 172–185. (Originally published in *Psa. Rev., 57*:3, 505–518.)

1972a   "Myths, Mysteries, and Milieux." Presented to the Annual Congress of Fellows, Society for the Arts, Religion and Contemporary Culture, Feb. 26, New York, N.Y.

1972–73   "Civilizational Complexes and Intercivilizational Encounters." In *New Visions of the Sacred*, Lorin Loverde (ed.). N.Y.: Grossman Publishers (Viking). Forthcoming. (Originally delivered to the American Sociological Association Meetings, Denver, Colorado, August 30, 1971.)

1973   "*Eros, Logos, Nomos, Polis:* Their Shifting Balances in the Vicissitudes of Communities and Civilizations." In *New Bottles for New Wine? Possible Bases for the Scientific Study of Religion.* A. Eister (ed.). Forthcoming.

Neville, Richard
1970   *Play Power: Exploring the International Underground.* N.Y.: Random House. See review by Jonathan Eisen in *Book World,* Jan. 10, 1971.

Nisbet, Robert
1969   *Social Change and History.* N.Y.: Oxford Press. *Cf.* B. Nelson (1969).

O'Neill, Eugene
(1946) 1949 *The Iceman Cometh.* N.Y.: Vintage, n.d. Copyright 1946. First performance, 1949.

Petronius Arbiter
n.d.   *The Satyricon.* Tr. J. M. Mitchell. 2nd ed. N.Y.: E. P. Dutton.

Raleigh, J. H. (ed.)
1968   *Twentieth-Century Interpretations of* The Iceman Cometh. Englewood Cliffs, N.J.: Prentice-Hall.

Rosen, G.
1968   *Madness in Society. Chapters in the Historical*
(1969)   *Sociology of Mental Illness.* Preface by B. Nelson. Chicago: U. of Chicago Press. (Paperbound ed., N.Y.: Harper Torchbooks, 1969).

Rosenfeld, Hellmut
1954   *Der mittelalterliche Totentanz.* Münster-Köln: Bohlau Verlag.

Rimbaud, Arthur
   (1873) 1961

A Season in Hell. Tr. L. Varèse. Norfolk, Conn.: Laughlin.

Salvianus of Marseilles
   (439–50 A.D.)1930

On the Government of God. Tr. from the Latin by E. M. Sanford. N.Y.: Columbia University Press. (Records of Civilization).

Turner, V. W.
   1968

The Ritual Process: Structure & Anti-Structure. Chicago: Aldine.

Valéry, Paul
   (1919) 1962

"The Crisis of Mind." In P. Valéry, *History and Politics.* Tr. D. Folliot and J. Matthews. N.Y.: Pantheon (Bollinger Series, XLV).

Warren, Florence (ed.)
   1931

The Dance of Death. Collected from Mss. by F. Warren. With Intro. and Notes by Beatrice White. (Early English Text Society, orig. series, no. 181). (William Lydgate's free trans. of French original).

7 The Resurrection of the Body

RALPH W. SLEEPER

The claim that I shall make is that the notion of the resurrection of the body is uniquely relevant to an understanding not only of the "phenomenon of death" but of the "phenomenon of life." The manner in which this claim will be pressed forward will be philosophical rather than theological; rather than an essay in the tradition which theologians have come to call "demythologization," the defense here will be conducted quite independently of any theological presuppositions. While it may be evident that theological "demythologization" could come to a similar, if not identical, view of the meaning of the "doctrine" in question, it is precisely because the present essay approaches bodily resurrection as a philosophical idea or "notion" *rather* than as "doctrine" that distinguishes it from the "demythologization" that might be offered by a theologian.

The problem of the meaning of death is especially baffling to philosophers who are persuaded that we ought to ground our cognitive claims, as good philosophers have always done, in the firm soil of experience. For though we can experience the death of others we do not—at least in any useful philosophical way—experience our own deaths. There is good evidence, of course, that some philosophers have *expected* to experience their own deaths—Socrates and William James, for example. But evidence

Ralph Sleeper is Professor of Philosophy at Queens College of the City University of New York. He has published widely in such journals as *Religious Studies, The Journal of Philosophy,* and *Cross Currents.*

that they *did* experience what they expected is notoriously lacking, even though there have been those among us who, like the late Bishop Pike, have believed that it would not always be so. And even if it were the case that Socrates and William James— or Bishop Pike—were to somehow be able to convey to us *their* experiences of death this would not do much for the notion of bodily resurrection. For involved in this notion is the condition that death is not only experienceable, but is experienceable as something which the body survives. The testimony of spiritualists, even if acceptable, would confirm only the "spiritual" survival of the persons in question and not their *bodily* resurrection.

Nor will the good empirical philosopher be relieved of his bafflement by those who would, on surviving some particularly striking threat to bodily life, talk of their "postmortem" life and the experience that they have undergone.[1] Interesting as these experiences may be, they can at best be only evidences of what the experience of bodily death *may* be like; they are but *analogies* of the experience of bodily resurrection and not the experience itself. And yet, if we dismiss both the "spiritualist" account and the "analogical" account, what remains as ground for an empirical understanding of death and bodily resurrection?

My own view is that a possible answer lies rather nearer at hand than is supposed by those who would turn to either the "spiritualist" or the "analogical" positions. I want to call into question the basic presupposition which underlies both

1. An interesting example of this kind of talk is the testimony of the distinguished psychologist Abraham Maslow, who reported on his survival of a massive heart attack in the following words: "My attitude toward life changed. The word I used for it now is the post-mortem life. I could just as easily have died so that my living constitutes a kind of an extra, a bonus. It's all gravy. Therefore I might just as well live as if I had already died. One very important aspect of the post-mortem life is that everything gets doubly precious, gets piercingly important. . . . I guess you could say that post-mortem life permits a kind of spontaneity that's greater than anything else could make possible. . . ." *Psychology Today* (August 1970), p. 16.

positions: i.e., the notion that we have, at present, no useful evidence about our own death, no philosophically important experience of what our own deaths mean. It will, in other words, be a most significant part of my defense that we *do* have empirical evidence about our *own* deaths and not merely about the deaths of others. Unlike the "spiritualist," I do not believe that we must wait for death to happen to us in order to have philosophically meaningful experience of it. Unlike the "analogists," I do not believe that we lack *direct* empirical evidence as to the nature of death or its relation to life. Finally, I believe that the concept of the resurrection of the body is both empirically defensible and philosophically useful.

My case for all of this begins with a factual claim. It is the claim that death is a general fact and that *consciousness* of death as a general fact is pervasive of human history. By this I mean only that the concrete actuality of temporal death as inevitable is part and parcel of human experience. Historians and prehistorians, anthropologists and social psychologists, tell us that there never have existed men who were not aware of the inevitability of their own deaths. So, as it were, from the beginning it has been the consciousness of his own mortality, the experience of himself as finite, that has separated the human from the rest of the animals. And it is no small part of the consequences of this fact that it helps to account for the rise of human culture per se, as well as the different implications of death for different peoples, determining the different characteristics of different cultures, distinguishing them from one another in terms of what we come to know as customs, mores, folkways, and social institutions.

One does not have to wait for Bergson or Freud to demonstrate the fact that human civilization is in very large measure simply a defense against death. Or that societies are, by and large, more or less elaborately organized systems for dealing with the threats to life arising on every side. But the point deserves stress all the same, for the fact with which we begin is not always as simple as it may seem. That is, it is not the bare and unvarnished fact of death that causes men to bind themselves into groups in defense against it, but rather the more complex fact that men are *aware* of death as an imminent threat to life. It is the fact that they are in some way *conscious*—or even *self-conscious*—of death as an inevitable fact in their own case, inescapable and threatening, a constant companion. So it is not the mere fact of death itself, but consciousness of it, that drives the human animal to transcend the herding instincts of his fellow creatures and to create those very *unnatural* conditions of life and death that we call human cultures.[2]

Now, here I have inserted a term which is sure to alert the philosophical critic—the term "unnatural." Why, it will be asked, do you assume socialization to be an unnatural process? My response is as follows: Let us grant, at least for the sake of argument, that the "herding" instinct is natural, that the formation of animal societies by ants, bees, apes, elks, and such is an instinctive reaction when survival is threatened. Let us grant further that every such animal society exhibits rules of behavior which govern the actions of individuals within the group, rules

2. Although I am suspicious of the ancient philosophical distinction between art and nature, I do want to distinguish between the behavior of animals who do not seem to be aware of the inevitability of their own deaths and those who *are* aware. It may be that one of the chief functions of art in culture is to remind us of our own mortality. In speaking of his recent play *All Over*, Edward Albee said: "One of the points of the play is to make us aware of our mortality. And that bothered the critics. In *Virginia Woolf*, they saw people they knew, not themselves. But this play is not about others. It's about us, because it's about death, and you can't fob off death." Albee then goes on to make a confession which stands in sharp contrast with the point which Maslow makes; consciousness does for Albee what a heart attack does for Maslow. Thus: "I had an awareness of death when I was 15, but when I turned 36 or 37 I became aware that *I*, Edward Albee, was going to die. . . . I'm so much more aware of things around me now. I find that I make love more often, and much better than before. I'm more aware of colors, of seasons, of textures." *New York Times*, April 18, 1971, Sec. D, p. 10.

without which neither the society nor its members could survive. Let us even go so far as to grant that these animal societies practice minimal *moral* constraints on behavior. But let us *not* commit the contradiction of also saying that those moral constraints are "repressive" of instincts, "repressive" of the very impulses of nature from which those societies spring and of which they are the more or less perfect expression. And let us not assume, for we lack both evidence and reason for it, that the restriction on behavior in animal societies is any different from the minimal "rules" governing the behavior of falling leaves and roaring winds—not to mention swirling electrons and the halflives of radioactive elements.

To the extent that human societies also exhibit such minimal rules and restrictions, to that extent they are in no significant sense different from animal societies. There is a difference, though, in other respects. And it is in reference to those other respects that I have introduced the term "unnatural" and applied it to human societies alone and exclusively. The term itself—and I am quite aware of this—is more than a little controversial. For some it is a pejorative term. Think of Rousseau, to whom all unnatural elements are anathema, to whom the highest commendation of a human society would be to say that it is perfectly natural. Or think of St. Thomas Aquinas, to whom it was a divine task and a saintly achievement to reconcile the natural law with the supernatural will of God. Or think of the ecological faddists in our midst, to whom natural foods, natural hair styles, natural sex, and natural childbirth are among those qualities of life that are, in this fake and synthetic world, alone worth pursuing, are alone among the true, the good, and the beautiful. Think of Charles Reich and "Consciousness III," the naturalistic optimism of *The Greening of America.*

For all these—as, of course, for many others—nature is not only that which is given, that which is, but also that which is good, that which ought to be. In terms of the history of philosophical thought, this view of nature is most closely associated with the classical Greeks, although it does not seem to be either exclusive or original with them. For there is a tradition from the ancient Egyptians onward that nature is ultimately orderly, disciplined, and rational, a tradition which flowered among the Greeks and has been, ever since, a distinctive element within our Western ways of thinking about the world and all that's in it.

But against this view, and also of ancient vintage, has been the conception of nature as fruitfully chaotic, an undisciplined and disorderly resource, fertile but fickle, an untamed well of infinite energy and limitless variety—a nature at once both terrifying and beautiful. In such a view of nature it is, of course, impossible to read off "natural law" as normative of human society. Nature is incapable of supplying the standards of virtue, the rules of good government, the duties and obligations of citizens. Nor can man himself be regarded as a "social animal," an animal possessed of reason in accordance with his essential nature, a nature from which can spring the understanding of—and conformity to—the natural laws of the true, the good, and the beautiful. Think of Mani and Zarathustra, the witches and diabolists of every age, the Nietzsches and the Freuds, the Dostoevskys and the Genets. Think of all those to whom it has been amply clear that "nature" is a "house divided against itself," that "there is a beast which lurks within the jungle of the human heart."

In speaking of these two quite contrasting views of nature let me, from here on, use a rather traditional shorthand terminology. For the conception of nature as orderly, inherently rational, and serene, let me use the term "Apollonian." And for the conception of nature as wild and chaotic, a mixture of futility and fertility, let me use the term "Dionysian." The two terms used in this way are probably already familiar ones, but let me risk a word or two of explanation.[3] The Greek god Apollo represents,

3. See also the explanation advanced by the theologian Sam Keen in his "Manifesto for a Dionysian Theology" in *Transcendence*, ed. by H. W. Richardson and D. R. Cutler (Boston, 1969). I have profited from Keen's insights but, as will become obvious, disagree rather sharply with his proposals.

in mythology, the most complete embodiment of the rational ideals of truth, goodness, and beauty that we associate with classical culture; the god of reason, illumination, purity, moderation, and self-discipline. Dionysus, on the other hand, was a god foreign to the Greek mainstream; he appears to have invaded the Greek pantheon from Thrace, where he served as the primitive god of fertility, of *dynamis*, the blind, striving energy of creation and destruction alike. In Athens Dionysus took to wine, women, and song; he was worshiped in wild revelry and orgiastic enthusiasm. He became the symbol of unfettered will and desire, the explosive source of energy as prone to destruction as creation. Dionysus meets us in the ecstatic beauty of the dance of life—and in the horrible beauty of the dance of death.

But let me now try to focus in on the phenomenon of death as viewed, first from the Apollonian perspective, then from the Dionysian. It is a basic feature of the Apollonian angle of vision on death that the essence of nature lies beyond, behind, or above the finite limits of all that is material, all that is mortal, all that is temporal and changing. True nature is form without matter, pure spirit without body, pure ego without id. So the death of the body is of no great consequence to the soul, which is, in principle, immortal. Think of Socrates' words of consolation to his disciples as he was about to die: ". . . no anxiety ought to be felt about his own soul by a man who all his lifetime has renounced the pleasures of the body and its adornments as alien to him and likely to do him more harm than good . . . but with even temperament and justice and courage and freedom and truth . . . awaits that journey to [the other world] which he is ready to make whensoever destiny calls him" (*Phaedo*, 115a). From such a perspective the body, as indeed Socrates says, is viewed as the "prison house of the soul"—the trap from which the soul is mercifully released upon the death of the body.

To the Appollonian, then, immortality has nothing at all to

do with the resurrection of the body. The body has no place whatsoever in the economy of salvation, as, indeed, matter has no status in the innermost reality of nature, no standing with the true, the good, and the beautiful, no part in the One, no share in the unity of all that is ultimately real. Matter—the human body—is that which individuates, that which circumscribes and limits, that which restricts the self from participating in the ultimate reality of being itself. Put another way, it is the material body which stands in the way of human perfection in wisdom and virtue, the source not only of human fallibility but the very ground of evil and destruction. Individuality, personal uniqueness, the self as private and particular: these are equated with the surface world of imperfection and hubris, of folly and pride. In a striking way the body is *repressive* of the soul.

There is in all this, of course, a very fundamental ambiguity about nature. The Apollonian must take it that nature itself is perfect, finished, complete, and unchanging. All that changes, all that grows and develops, all that declines and decays: these must be somehow less than ultimately real, must belong to a second-rate order of reality which falls short of being perfectly *natural*. So the death of the body, its material change and decay, does not and cannot belong to ultimate reality at all. What is *natural* is the *immortality* of the soul. It is death that is unreal. But, by so idealizing nature, the Apollonian society becomes "Puritanical" and repressive of all that is instinctive. It becomes, from another point of view, profoundly *un*natural. For what is natural to the Apollonian is exactly what is *un*natural to the Dionysian. As Nietzsche so clearly shows in his comparison of the Apollonian and Dionysian ways of life and death, it is the god Prometheus who is the true incarnation of the Dionysian way. For it is Prometheus who renounces the life of moderation and balance, who dares to defy the Apollonian rules and restrictions, who commits the crime of stealing fire from the gods and who presents it as a gift to mortal men. The symbol *is* fire, warmth and desire. The body is no longer alien. It becomes "polymorphously perverse": what Norman O. Brown calls "Love's Body." But the stolen gift of fire is also the symbol of power; power both for incredible creation and for terrible destruction. The power of modern science and technology, nuclear fission and fusion, "the bomb."

As Nietzsche saw it in *The Birth of Tragedy*, man's highest good must be bought with a crime and paid for by the flood of grief and suffering. The penalty exacted by the offended divinities is visited upon the whole of the human race. Man's noble ambition is flawed from birth. The Promethean crime, the Dionysian crime, is the same as that of Adam in Genesis: man becomes man, becomes "naturalized" as a citizen of the world, only through breaking the laws which would keep him ignorant, which would deprive him of personal knowledge of good and evil, which would bind him forever in a pristine state of impotent innocence, forever unfree, forever repressed and enslaved.

Yet, for the Dionysian, the price that man pays in grief and suffering is not unjust. It buys the infinite possibilities of freedom. Nietzsche again:

> The earth offers its gifts voluntarily, and the savage beasts of the mountain and desert approach in peace. Now the slave emerges as a freeman; all the rigid hostile walls which either necessity or despotism has erected between men are shattered . . . each individual becomes not only reconciled to his fellow but actually at one with him . . . he feels himself to be godlike and strides with the same elation and ecstasy as the gods he has seen in his dreams. No longer the *artist*, he has himself become a *work of art*; the productive power of the whole universe is now manifest in his transport, to the glorious satisfaction of the Primordial One.[4]

So there is, in this Dionysian view also, a fundamental ambiguity as to what is and what is not *natural*. As Nietzsche indi-

4. Friedrich Nietzsche, *The Birth of Tragedy* (Garden City, N.Y.: Doubleday, 1956), p. 24.

cates, there is a profound tension between the Dionysian cele-
bration of the body *as* body, flesh *as* flesh, and the ultimate
coalescence of individuals, their final renunciation of autonomy
as private "freemen," their union in the eyes of the "primordial
One." So the Dionysian as well as the Apollonian must view
nature as divided into "levels" of reality, as having about it a
superficial and false dimension as well as an ultimate and real
dimension. *But the Dionysian reverses the Apollonian order.*
Where the Apollonian finds truth in the order of reason, the
Dionysian finds it in the order of instinct. What the Apollonian
praises, the Dionysian disparages.

And yet the odd result is, in both cases, that we end up as
having to lose our individuality if we are to fulfill our natural
telos. The difference is, perhaps, that the Apollonian dreams of
losing his individuality through a certain bodiless immortality, a
life of the mind after the death of the body, a life wherein the
mind sees the Good and becomes one with it, mastering all
truth and beauty in an act transcending the body, fully and
finally. The Dionysian, on the other hand, envisages the final
union as a sort of mindless merger with being itself, a merger
so complete that the self is no longer *a* self, but a body being
lived by being itself, the "One."

In Heidegger, for example, this Apollonian concern with the
ultimate union of individuals is manifested by the fact that he
is able to make a complete analysis of the "human condition"
without ever once referring to *man.* For man is simply *dasein,*
"being-there," an instance of *sein,* but without autonomy, without a "nature" of his own. It is not *we* who live out our lives, but
being (*sein*) that lives in and through us. We are, as it were,
inhabited by powers outside of ourselves. It is a theme that
Norman O. Brown puts this way:

> The *id* is instinct; the Dionysian "cauldron of seething excitement,"
> a sea of energy out of which the ego emerges like an island. The term
> "*id*"–"it"–taken from Nietzsche (via Groddeck), is based on the
> intuition that the conduct through life of what we call our ego is

essentially passive; it is not so much we who live as that we are lived, by unknown forces. The reality is instinct, and instinct is impersonal energy, an "it" who lives in us. I live, yet not I, but it lives in me, as in creation, *fiat*. Let it be; no "I," but an it. The "I-Thou" relationship is still a relation to Satan; the old Adversary; the Accuser; to whom we are responsible or old Nobodadddy in the garden, calling, Adam, where art thou? Let there be no one to answer to.[5]

The Dionysian way of life, then, is egoless; an exercise in allowing the primordial id to live through the self until the self-lessness of Nirvana is reached. Thus Alan Watts, that prophet of Zen trips and psychedelic satoris: "Nirvana is a radical transformation of how it feels to be alive; it feels as if everything were myself, or as if everything—including 'my' thoughts and actions—were happening of itself. There are still efforts, choices, and decisions, but not in the sense that 'I make them'; they arise of themselves in relation to circumstances.[6]

In the Christian scheme of things this Dionysian-Nietzschean emphasis on the importance of "losing oneself" in the divine Other has, of course, long been represented by the spiritual enthusiasts. The Shakers and Quakers, those who "speak with tongues," the followers of the "inner voice," the inspired generally cry, "Not my will but thine, O Lord!" For the paths of Dionysus and Christ have often been joined. Norman O. Brown is most explicit:

Dionysus, the mad god, breaks down boundaries; releases the prisoners; abolishes repression; and abolishes the *principium individuationis*, substituting for it the unity of man and the unity of man with nature. In this age of schizophrenia, with the atom, the individual self, the boundaries disintegrating, there is, for those who would save our souls, the ego-psychologists, "the Problem of Identity."

5. Norman O. Brown, *Love's Body* (N.Y.: Random House, 1966), p. 88.
6. *Psychotherapy East and West* (N.Y.: Pantheon Books, 1961), p. 60.

But the breakdown is to be made into a breakthrough; as Conrad said, in the destructive element immerse. The soul that we call our own is not the real one. The solution to the problem of identity is, get lost. Or as it says in the New Testament: "He that findeth his own psyche shall lose it, and he that loseth his psyche for my sake shall find it."[7]

And it is, I think, possible to observe without cynicism at all that it is characteristic of our age that more and more of us are doing just what Brown recommends; we meet our "identity crises" by getting lost. In the words of Timothy Leary, we "tune in, turn on, and drop out." Thus: communes, unisex, transcendental meditation, encounter groups, sensitivity training, the Woodstock Nation, and, perhaps, the Charles Manson "family."

But here we reach the heart of the Dionysian way of death. Body mysticism. It means that the resurrection of the body must be understood as the abolition of repression, the return to the polymorphous perversity of childhood, riddance of the taboo on all but genital sex—all equated with the elimination of morbid concern with death. "O death, where is thy sting?" Death accepted as a part of life; death not as the enemy of life, but as friend; the body reconciled with death. Brown puts the challenge to Christianity—among the major religions the most confused and troubled about its own doctrine of the human body—in terms that make it clear that there has been all along a strong Dionysian element in the Christian experience. But also in words that suggest the extent to which that Dionysian element has been continually repressed and distorted by the Apollonian-Pauline attitude imported into Christianity from the Greeks, an attitude which still controls the Christian "establishment."

But Christianity, if it has often been hostile to the material world, hostile to the body in its attitude toward death, has never completely succumbed to the Apollonian vision. As Brown

7. Brown, *Love's Body,* p. 161.

acknowledges, the "empty tomb" symbolizes something of the utmost importance about the Christian conception and experience of life—as well as of death. "The specialty of Christian eschatology lies precisely in its rejection of Platonic hostility to the human body and to 'matter,' its refusal to identify the Platonic path of sublimation with ultimate salvation, and its affirmation that eternal life can only be life in a body."[8] There is reason for this refusal and this affirmation. And the reason is this: On neither Apollonian nor Dionysian grounds is it possible to work out a really satisfactory philosophy of the individual self, of the human person *as* a person. And it is because of this that neither the Apollonian nor the Dionysian attitude toward death can be fully satisfactory.

The claim that this essay is designed to support is that the notion of the resurrection of the body is uniquely relevant to the understanding of death. But to show this it has been necessary to show also, using the specific examples of the Apollonian and Dionysian, how views of life relate to views of death. For nothing seems quite like a philosophical conception of death in its power to illuminate the philosophical conception of life. Both the Apollonian and the Dionysian conceptions of death, stressing as they do the ultimate immersion of the self in the One, loss of individuality, absorption of individuality, the cancellation—in effect—of the person as a person, both reflect the philosophical denial of the meaning and value of individual life, of the life of the person *as* a person. Such a life can have no ultimate meaning, no ultimate value, on either Apollonian or Dionysian grounds. To this the Christian view of the individual stands in stark contrast.

It is not, admittedly, the easiest thing in the world to see how the Christian conception of the self, of the individual person, is

8. *Life Against Death* (Middletown, Conn.: Wesleyan, 1959), p. 309.

implicit in the notion of bodily resurrection. But that, despite its difficulties and obscurities, is what the notion of the resurrection of the body is all about. Forgetting the theological setting of this doctrine, at least for a moment, it seems amply clear that the purely philosophical question that is answered by the notion of personal bodily resurrection is the question of the value of the self, the meaning of individual life in terms of the worth of the person *as* a person. Only, it seems, if we approach the idea of bodily resurrection from this angle can we make philosophical sense of it at all. But when we *do* view it from this perspective the whole human context in which the notion arises in the Christian experience becomes important and relevant: the idea of "natural" man symbolized by Adam, man's "second nature" as symbolized in the person of Jesus *as* "the Christ." The death to the world of Adam, the birth to the new world in the "new being" of the Incarnation: thus contextualized there emerges an outline of a philosohpical thesis in which death is "conquered" by being accepted, and it is this thesis which the accounts of the bodily resurrection of Jesus as the Christ mythologize.

What this means in philosophical terms can, perhaps, be best seen in terms of the experience of a new awareness, a new consciousness of death. No longer is death a punishment for sin (Genesis), but it becomes a necessary and inevitable part of life. Neither enemy nor friend of life, death is simply one of life's conditions, a condition which is, in itself, neither good nor bad, neither meaningful nor meaningless, except as it is *given* meaning or value by life. And all in such a way that death must be understood as *completely* personal, an event *in* the life of the individual which must be made into an integral element *of* that life. In an affirmative sense, then, the idea of death which bodily resurrection represents means acceptance of the body, acceptance of the flesh. It means acceptance of the body *as* dying—for death is not, as is sometimes supposed, all-at-once; the meaning of death is not *apart* from the meaning of life when death is accepted as the dying that is an inevitable condition of living. And at the same time, acceptance of the condition of death means that the body is no longer the "prison" of the soul, no longer a drag on the spirit, but rather the vehicle of spirit—its means of self-expression.

Perhaps the most important philosophical implication of this new notion of bodily resurrection is the acceptance of the body as having an appropriate role in the "kingdom of God." For it is here that the ethical and political implications of the Christian consciousness of death as wholly "natural" comprise a radical departure from the implications of both the Apollonians and the Dionysians. Against the Apollonians it implies that the body is no barrier to the "kingdom"—quite the contrary. Life in the "kingdom" is inconceivable *without* the body. For what is now at issue is not the merger of the soul of the individual into some sort of "world soul," some sort of union with the One in which the private self ceases its existence as a particular, and in which the identity of the self is forever lost. But, rather what is at stake is, the "redeemed" life of the self *as* a self, the individual *as* an individual. And likewise, in contrast to the Dionysian thesis, the soul is no longer "repressive" of the body. No longer is there an assumed antagonism between the functions of reason and the purposes of instinct; no longer is the price of freedom the grief and suffering of the private self.

Moreover, if the resurrection body is taken as the prime element—or even as *one* prime element—in the constitution of the "kingdom of God" it becomes possible to clear away much of the confusion as to "when" and "where" the "kingdom" is to come. For it is evident that *now* is the time and *here* is the place. This, despite the later theological speculations of Apollonian Christianity about bodily "assumption" into an otherworldly "heaven," is the clear and logical consequence of the resurrection body when analyzed from a purely philosophical perspective. For one of the obvious and most important characteristics of a "resurrected body" is that it must be a *historical* body, existing in time and space, having a particular duration and location and, as a consequence, a particular *identity*. So, if the "kingdom of God" is to be made up of resurrected bodies it must then be a realm in this and not another world, beginning *here* and *now* and not in some vague eschatological future "place" and "time."

Perhaps the clearest example of what all this means, at least in the philosophical sources of Christianity, is the conception of the City of God which is due to St. Augustine, the Bishop of Hippo in Northern Africa. For in Augustine both the Dionysian and the Apollonian visions of how a redeemed society should look are rejected in favor of historical pragmatism.[9] Here the task of the Christian is nothing more or less than the historical one of founding the "City of God" in the midst of the "City of Man"—the practical and everyday work of building a community of persons, a society in which individuals can achieve self-realization *as* individuals.

In this Augustinian conception of society there will be no repression either of soul or body. There is no place for the Dionysian impulse toward the submergence of the self in the primordial sea of being, nor a need to lose the ego in the all-embracing id. For in the City of God the ego does not "repress" and the id is not enslaved. Nor is there room for the Apollonian dream of eternal peace in which the soul is lost in the transcendent One, the final sublimation in which all individuality is gone, all particularity of matter transcended in timeless, spaceless transcendence. Rather, the self *as* self, a self in relation to and in interaction with other selves, is charged with the responsibility of working out his own salvation, charged with the freedom both to succeed and to fail.

9. I have developed this theme of Augustine as a "social pragmatist" in "John Dewey's Empiricism and the Christian Experience," *Cross Currents* IX, 4 (1959): 367–78.

But now let me return to the theme which I introduced earlier, the notion that human culture is essentially *un*natural, by which I meant that the conditions which human culture supplies for living and dying are not the same conditions as nature itself supplies. For now I think it ought to be clear that the Apollonian view of human culture amounts to a repudiation of nature, repression of instinct, rejection of the body. To the extent that our own contemporary American culture is Apollonian, the revolutionaries among us (Norman O. Brown and Herbert Marcuse included) do well to protest against its repressive establishment. On the other hand, it ought to be equally clear that the Dionysian view of what culture ought to be is really no less a denial of nature, actual nature, than the Apollonian. And in this lies the danger of the revolutionary impulse. For nature is neither as rational as the Apollonians would have it nor as irrational as the Dionysians suppose. Nature is neither cruel nor kind in itself; the Apollonian vision of the ultimate unity of the true, the good, and the beautiful is as illusory as is the Dionysian vision of the primordial One, dancing through time and playing throughout all eternity.

And so it is, I think, that the real resurrection of the body can occur only in and through a culture which neither scorns nor idealizes nature but takes it for what it is. And the key to such a culture is, as Augustine says, the freedom of men to shape their own destiny, to choose their own lives as individuals and as persons, neither blocked by nature nor enslaved to follow it, but freely to make of nature's raw materials a *new* nature, a "second nature." This is what it means, I take it, when the idea of the resurrection of the body is informed by the law of love. The law not of *eros* alone as the Dionysians would have it, nor of *philia* alone, as the Apollonians desire: but the love which the Christians have called *agape*.

8   Death and the Dialogue with the Absurd

MAURICE FRIEDMAN

And if the Wine you drink, the Lip you press,
End in the Nothing all Things end in—Yes—
Then fancy while Thou art, Thou art but what
Thou shalt be—Nothing—Thou shalt not be less.
The Rubaiyat of Omar Khayyam

When you are dead and your body cremated and
your ashes scattered, where are you?

Zen Mondo

Man is the only creature who knows that he will die and who
makes of this knowledge a foundation for his life and even for
his *joie de vivre.*

For the Upanishads the knowledge of death leads to the
choice of the good over the pleasant; for the Buddha it leads to
overcoming the craving for existence and to the eightfold path
to Nirvana; for Greek tragedy it leads to reconcilation with
moira, the qualitative order that includes man, even when, as
with Oedipus, one dare not count his lot as gain until the last

Maurice Friedman is Professor of Religion, Temple University, Philaelphia. He is author of *Martin Buber: The Life of Dialogue; Problematic Rebel: Melville, Dostoievsky, Kafka, Camus; The Worlds of Existentialism: A Critical Reader; To Deny Our Nothingness: Contemporary Images of Man; Touchstones of Reality: An Opening Way;* and the forthcoming *The Hidden Human Image,* of which this essay will be a chapter.

breath is drawn without pain. For Lao-tzu death is no threat to life, since both are a part of the flowing of the Tao. For Psalm 90 the knowledge that all flesh is as the grass which grows up in the morning and withers in the evening leads to a desire not to escape from the mutable to the immutable, as with Plato, but to "number our days so that we may get us a heart of wisdom." For Ecclesiastes the fact of death merges with the passing of all things in time and grows to an impassioned cry to remember your Creator in the days of your youth before desire fails, the grasshopper drags itself along, the silver cord is loosed, the golden bowl broken at the cistern, and all the daughters of song laid low.

Only in the Book of Job does the human condition of death lead to outright rebellion: "Consider that my days are as a breath." "My sons will come to grief, and I will know it not." "Thou wilt seek me, and I shall not be." "It is all one, I despise my life. Therefore, I say, He mocks at the calamity of the guiltless. If it be not He, who then is it?"

Martin Buber planned to have a chapter on death in his philosophical anthropology, *The Knowledge of Man,* but then decided against it because, as he told me, we do not know death in itself as we know the concrete realities of our existence. This is true, but what we do know is the anticipation of death, the imagining of death—one's own and others—and the relationship one brings to this somber and unavoidable future. Buber himself in his early mystical work *Daniel* saw death not just as the movement of past to future but of future to past, and the two so intertwined that death permeated life at every moment:

How could I become death's if I had not already suffered it? My existence . . . was the bed in which two streams, coming from opposite directions, flowed to and in and over each other. There was not only in me a force that moved from the point of birth to the point of death or beyond; there was also a counterforce from death to birth, and each moment that I experienced as a living man had grown out of the mixture of the two. . . . A force bore me toward dying, and its flight I called time; but in my face blew a strange wind, and I did not know what name to give its flight. . . . Coming-to-be and passing-away . . . lay side by side in endless embrace, and each of my moments was their bed. It was foolish to wish to limit death to any particular moments of ceasing to be or of transformation; it was an ever-present might and the mother of being. Life engendered being, death received and bore it; life scattered its fullness, death preserved what it wished to retain.[1]

My own conscious relationship to death began, as I remember, when I was five years old and could not sleep because of the sudden realization that I would die. I cried until my elder sister came up and comforted me with the statement that I would not die for a very long time. That this did not remove the problem for me was evident from the preoccupation with death that I had during my teens, sometimes expressing itself paradoxically in the idea of suicide which would free me from the tyranny of the body —or, as I thought more likely, hand me over to it. At Harvard I often thought of Epictetus, who committed suicide on the basis of reasoning that what would come after death would not be so bad as what we have now. This always seemed to me specious, since I had no way of knowing that the "I" would exist at all after death to be subject to *any* experience, good or bad. When I was in high school, I once said to my girl friend that my whole goal in life was to live long enough to develop a philosophy that would enable me to accept death. Since I have come to know the tales of the Hasidim, I have often been struck by the resemblance between my statement and the Hasidic tale "The Meaning": "When Rabbi Bunam lay dying his wife burst into tears. He said: 'What are you crying for? My whole life was only that I might learn how to die.' "[2]

During my years of immersion in mysticism when I was in the

1. Martin Buber, *Daniel: Dialogues on Realization,* trans. with an In-troductory Essay by Maurice Friedman (New York: McGraw-Hill Paper-backs, 1965), pp. 130–131.
2. Martin Buber, *Tales of the Hasidim: The Later Masters* (New York: Schocken, 1948), p. 268.

camps and units for conscientious objectors during the Second
World War, I seemed to have developed the philosophy I sought
—the belief that consciousness is universal and eternal, that there
is no individual self and that the real self cannot die. But this
belief did not stand the test of time or of encounters that made
me feel that I had gone through a sort of death while still alive.[3]
Once I would have fully accepted the words of comfort that
Rabbi Nahum of Tchernobil gave to several disciples who came
weeping to him, complaining that they had fallen prey to darkness and depression and could not lift up their heads either in
teachings or in prayer:

> "My dear sons," Rabbi Nahum said to them, "do not be distressed
> at this seeming death which has come upon you. . . . Just as on New
> Year's Day life ceases on all the stars and they sink into a deep sleep
> . . . from which they awake with a new power of shining, so those
> men who truly desire to come close to God, must pass through the
> state of cessation of spiritual life, and 'the falling is for the sake of
> the rising.' "[4]

Now I must rebel with Job and Ivan Karamazov and complain
because "nights of weariness and months of emptiness" mean the
passing away in absurdity of our all too mortal life.

Man's attitude toward death has always been bound up in the
closest way with his posture vis-à-vis nature, time, and community. Although he is aware of the seasons, modern man hardly
lives in the time of nature. His time is abstract, calendrical, and
conventional, and his relations to nature are more and more detached—whether nature be the object to be exploited, the scene
to rhapsodize over, the terrain for a holiday from the city, or the
great Earth Goddess that we celebrate once a year to ward off
the threat of pollution and ecological unbalance. As a result, it

---

3. See Maurice Friedman, *Touchstones of Reality: An Opening Way*
(New York: E. P. Dutton, 1971), ch. 3.

4. Martin Buber, *Tales of the Hasidim: The Early Masters* (New York:
Schocken, 1947), p. 173.

is hardly possible for modern man to see his own death as a part of the natural rhythms and cycles of nature, to be accepted with the wisdom of nature itself.

The awareness of past and future is an inextricable part of all living in the present. Man in the age of Jesus already needed to be told to live in the present and not sell it short for the sake of the imagined tomorrow. But only for modern man has present-ness been thoroughly emptied of meaning. Only modern man's relation to the present has become so technicized—so much the effect of a past cause or the means to a future end—that Pascal's dictum that we must be forever unhappy knowing no real present is plain to all who pause for a moment in the unending rush. "The world is too much with us; late and soon,/Getting and spending, we lay waste our powers," wrote Wordsworth, and Emerson's cry still rings out: "Things are in the saddle, and ride mankind." The death of T. S. Eliot's Sweeney is no tragedy because he has never known any meaningful life, and Eliot's Gerontion says, "We have not reached conclusion, when I/Stiffen in a rented house." Time is a meaningless voyage whose haul will not bear examination, wrote Eliot in *The Four Quartets*.

Like K. in Kafka's novel *The Castle*, modern man's attempt to find a foothold in present reality cannot succeed because he is always using the present as a means to some future end. This functional relation to time is caused in turn—and reinforced—by that sense of isolation, rootlessness, and exile which makes modern man feel, in moments of awareness, that he knows no real life. Cut off from the nourishing stream of community, the prospect of his own death takes on an overwhelming importance that robs life itself of meaning. This theme of isolation is end-lessly repeated in modern literature: Hardy's Jude the Obscure dying deserted by everyone with Job's curse on his lips, Camus' "Stranger" aware of that slow wind blowing from the future that destroys all the false ideas of human brotherhood and solidarity that men put forward in the "unreal years" before death,

Kafka's K. attaining a freedom greater than anyone has ever had—and equally meaningless—Sartre's Matthieu unable to belong to any person or group because he cannot commit himself or cherish any value beyond his own freedom.

Certainly, even in the best of communities, death is an individual affair. Even in traditional religions, the journey of the soul to some Hades or Sheol must be facilitated by the community through *rites de passage*. Death *is* that uttermost solitude of which every other abandonment is only a foretaste, as Martin Buber suggests, and time *is* a torrent carrying us irreversibly and inexorably toward "the starkest of all human perspectives"—one's own death. But our obsession with our own deaths, our focus upon them, is in no small part caused by our exile and isolation in the present. This same obsession leads us to use our cults of youth, of having "experiences," of realizing our potentials as ways of not looking at the facts of old age and death. Our culture gives us no support in hearing Hopkins' "leaden echo" of old age in which we give up all the "girl-graces" of youth in favor of that vision in which every future is cut off except death. Yet this fear of time, old age, and death is woven into every moment of our existence so that we have no real present and no real mutual presence for one another.

That which should be the very height of mutual presence—sex and love—has become the opposite. In *Love and Will* Rollo May has vividly shown how our culture uses sex as a way of not facing age or death, of pretending, with Mehitabel, that "there's life in the old gal yet," and that as long as we can go through some more or less adequate sexual functioning (itself endangered by our hurried relationship to time), we are still alive and not threatened by death.

Death is the Absurd precisely as Camus has defined it in *The Myth of Sisyphus*. It cuts us off from meaningful relationship to past and future *and* from meaningful relationship to each other. It is one thing to recognize with "Everyman" that no one else will go for you or that, like Jesus, "You gotta walk that lonesome valley, you gotta walk it by yourself." It is another to carry around one's general expectation and one's specific fears about death as an invisible barrier that gets in the way of any directness of relationship and of any present immediacy. How many of us can really say, with the Song of Songs, "For love is stronger than death," or with Martin Buber that "a great relationship throws a bridge across the abyss of dread of the universe," the abyss of death?

Death has always been the foremost advocate for the absurdity of life. "This too shall pass away." "All things change, all things perish, all things pass away." "Behold all flesh is as the grass, and all the goodliness of man is as the flower of grass." "Vanity of vanities, all is vanity." It is death, as Bergson points out, that makes it necessary to supplement nature by habit and myth so that the depressing contingency which sunders present means and future end can be overlooked. But there is much in our day that has *heightened* the absurdity of death that modern man must confront to the point where it is qualitatively different. The "heartless voids and immensities of the universe" stab modern man "with the thought of annihilation." After the prison chaplain has upset the precarious balance Meursault has attained in the face of the certainty of his guillotining, Meursault hurls back at the priest his real fear beside which the hellfire with which the priest is threatening him pales into insignificance: "It is better to burn than to disappear!"

The assassinations in our day of John F. Kennedy, Martin Luther King, and so many others have brought to the surface that terror and violence that seethes beneath the seemingly most successful civilization in the world's history. Hiroshima, with its sudden death and long years of slow death by radiation, has created, as Robert Jay Lifton has shown, a "death culture" in which even those who live are weighed down by the conviction that they too will be stricken as well as by the "survivor guilt" of those who seem senselessly spared from a common doom. Hiroshima is not an isolated example: the Soviet Union's starvation of three million Kulaks in the vain effort to put through their communizing of agriculture in the 1930's, the bombing of civilian populations during the Second World War, the starvation of the children of Biafra, and the continuing devastation in Indochina of millions of people by napalm, burning, bombing, disease, starvation, and outright murder—all these are illustrations of the readiness of dictatorships and democracies alike in our day to create vast death cultures as instruments of national policy.

More than illustration—prototype—is the Nazi death camp in which six million Jews and one million gypsies were exterminated. "Auschwitz" not only stands for death and death culture, but for a systematic dehumanization such as the world had never known, a scientific undermining of the very foundations of social existence. In the world of Camus' *Plague* social and natural evil are one. In the world of Auschwitz social mistrust and existential mistrust are interwoven into the greatest assault on man as man that human history has known.

If we add to this the ever present threat of a nuclear holocaust that might destroy all life on the planet and the predictions of the ecologists that the conditions for human life may disappear within forty, thirty, or even twenty years, we cannot avoid the conclusion that, however much death has challenged human meaning in the past, death for modern man is preeminently an encounter with the Absurd.

In face of this situation, some men revolt. One type of revolt against death in its aspect of the Absurd is the "Modern Promethean" of whom I speak in my book *Problematic Rebel*. The Modern Promethean rebels against the very order of existence or against the absence of any order, and he does so in terms of the Either/Or of destroying what is over against him or being destroyed himself. This heroic approach toward death is a familiar one—from Browning's "Invictus" ("I would not face death blindfold") to Dylan Thomas' "Do not go gentle into that good night./Rage, rage against the dying of the light." Camus's Sisyphus rejects the possibility of suicide *despite* the absurdity of man's relation to the irrational silence of the universe. Sisyphus' struggle to the heights with his everlasting rock is "enough to fill a man's heart," says the early Camus. This heroic stance takes on greater depth with a character like Tarrou the journalist in Camus' novel *The Plague*—Tarrou who has chosen to be victim rather than executioner, who has vowed never to assist in the murder of another even for the sake of the political party that represents the victims, Tarrou who perseveres in his revolt to the end in an awesome struggle against his own death.

Franz Rosenzweig, the Jewish existentialist, begins his magnum opus, *The Star of Redemption,*[5] by an attack on that "Philosophy of the All" which seeks to gloss over the fact that every creature awaits "the day of its journey into darkness with fear and trembling." Martin Heidegger makes the fact of individual death the cornerstone of his existentialist philosophy. Human existence, or *Dasein,* being-there, is, to Heidegger, *zum Tode sein,* being-toward-death; for it is only the resolute anticipation of one's unutterably unique and nonrelational death which individualizes *Dasein* down to its own potentiality and frees it from the power of *das Man*—the "They" of ambiguity, curiosity, and idle talk.

Jean-Paul Sartre rejects this cornerstone of Heidegger's philosophy on the ground that it is precisely in death that a person is abandoned to the *en-soi,* the objective in-itself, without any appeal left to that subjective personal becoming, or *pour soi,* that during one's lifetime constantly transcends the facticity of what one is. But there is not only our anticipation of being turned into a thing, the revulsion against which filled even the martyr's death of Celia in T. S. Eliot's *Cocktail Party*. There is also our

5. Trans. by William Hallo with an Introduction by Nahum Glatzer (New York: Holt, Rinehart & Winston, 1971).

relationship to our own death, including that fact of finitude that gives concrete meaning to our existence—the precondition, says Tillich in *Courage to Be,* of any enjoyment of positive being. The threat of "nonbeing," of contingency and death, is the given of our existence. But we have freedom in our relationship to that given.

Why then does Martin Buber (with special reference, I suspect, to his emphasis on death) speak of Martin Heidegger's philos= ophy as a "nightmare"? What Heidegger has left out, as Buber has argued in "What Is Man?"[6] is the ultimate reality of the interhuman—the realm between man and man. Similarly the French Catholic existentialist Gabriel Marcel has maintained, in dialogue with Tillich and in explicit critique of Heidegger, that the death of the person who is my *Thou* is more real and more important to me than my own death.

Granting that our anticipation of our death is a present reality that enters into every moment of our existence—and in this sense granting Heidegger's case over Sartre's—I would nonetheless hold that Heidegger seems at times to forget that what is given to us, hence what is *existentially* of importance, is not the actual *future* moment of death but the *present* moment of anticipation. Putting it another way, Heidegger takes the half-truth of separation that the knowledge of our unique and individual death imparts to each of us and makes it into the specious whole truth of our existence being "ultimately nonrelational." If the present moment of anticipation of death often gets in the way of our open presence to others, as I have suggested, it also constitutes the basis for genuine mutual presentness as opposed to any form of symbiotic clinging or ecstatic "unity." At its fullness this present awareness of death is so far from being ultimately nonrelational that it is included within the relationship itself—as the distancing that makes real the relating, the moving apart that

6. Martin Buber, *Between Man and Man,* trans. by Ronald Gregor Smith with an Introduction by Maurice Friedman (New York: Macmillan Paperbacks, 1965).

makes real the moving together. In this sense, I maintain—against both Heidegger and Camus' Meursault—that love *is* stronger than death. The anticipated reality of death is present in love and gives it its special poignancy without—when the love is real —destroying it.

Equally important, our existence is limitation and finitude even without our resolute anticipation of our individual death, as Sartre points out. Nor is its unique potentiality so bound up with this anticipation as Heidegger holds. Our uniqueness is much more importantly connected with what calls us out in each hour and with such reality as we find in responding or failing to respond to that call. Our awareness of our death enters into both the situation and the response, but it does not dominate it. On the contrary, only when we are not *focusing* on the future negation of life by death do we have any presentness and immediacy.

We can understand the problematic of the Modern Promethean revolt against death better if we look at it in its somewhat less heroic and more clearly desperate form—suicide. If man is indeed the only creature that can commit suicide—which is not just the death of the body but the destruction of the self—man is also the only creature of which we know that has a "self" in any fully meaningful sense of that term. What is more, that self comes into being in the meeting with other selves. That self-preoccupation that makes suicide the only philosophical question of importance, as Camus claims in *The Myth of Sisyphus,* is mostly laid to one side in our actual lives, in which what is central is our response to what is not ourselves—our self-realization *as a by-product* of our meeting with other persons and beings in situations that include us rather than we them.

Leslie H. Farber has cogently asserted in *The Ways of the Will*[7] that suicide, or "the life of suicide," is at its most basic a

---

7. Leslie H. Farber, *The Ways of the Will: Essays in the Psychology and Psychopathology of the Will* (New York: Harper Colophon Books, 1967).

"willfulness" which refuses to accept the give and take of life, the fact that we are only on one side of the dialogue. Ippolit Terentyev wants to commit suicide in Dostoevsky's novel *The Idiot* because he had no freedom in his own creation but wants to assert his freedom in his destruction. In the character of Kirilov in Dostoevsky's *The Possessed,* this posture is elevated to that of the "man-god" who proposes to liberate all mankind from the fear of death through his own suicide. Stavrogin's suicide is also a Modern Promethean assertion of willfulness in the face of his inability to discover the genuine will that plays its part in the dialogue of being and being, without trying to control and manipulate existence itself. Meursault is really a willful suicide of this sort in Camus' novel *The Stranger,* and Camus' Caligula, who makes of death the logical conclusion of the absurdity of a world in which men are unhappy and die, is, as Camus himself says, "a superior suicide." But the man who most clearly combines the heroic attitudinizing of the Modern Promethean with the "life of suicide" is Captain Ahab of Melville's *Moby Dick*— the man who identifies himself with a Truth which has no confines, the man who sees his path as laid on iron rails, the man who feels he must destroy the White Whale or be destroyed himself and who destroys his ship, his crew, and himself in the process. "Oh, lonely death on lonely life," Ahab cries out at the end. "Oh, now I feel my topmost greatness lies in my topmost grief!"

Ignoring the absurd, underlining it, heroically revolting against it, or willfully denying it through "the life of suicide" does not exhaust the alternatives of the response of modern man to death. There is also that stance which I have designated in both *Problematic Rebel* and *To Deny Our Nothingness* as the "Dialogue with the Absurd"—a dialogue in which meaning is found in immediacy without any pretense at an overall, comprehensive meaning that would make the Absurd anything less or other other than Absurd.

The first aspect of this stance is the recognition and acceptance of death. Death, Freud points out, is a debt we owe to nature. This does not mean the aesthetic, decadent welcoming of death of Swinburne's "Garden of Proserpine":

> From too much love of living,
>   From hope and fear set free,
> We thank with brief thanksgiving
>   Whatever gods may be
> That no life lives forever;
> That dead men rise up never;
> That even the weariest river
>   Winds somewhere safe to sea.

To a poem such as this one can properly apply the strictures of Nietzsche's Zarathustra against the "preachers of death" who want to get beyond life in one "weary death-leap." Nor is this stance that of T. S. Eliot's Thomas à Becket, eager for martyrdom as part of a divine plan that will give him his place in the heavenly hierarchy. It is perhaps that of Jesus in the Garden of Gethsemane saying, "Father, if it be thy will, may this cup be taken from me. Nonetheless, thy will be done, not mine." It is the stance of the twentieth-century American poet Theodore Roethke, who spent much of his later years in mental hospitals, picking himself up again after each blow that knocked his breath out and disoriented his mind. Roethke writing:

> In a dark time, the eye begins to see,
> I meet my shadow in the deepening shade;
> I hear my echo in the echoing wood—
> A lord of nature weeping to a tree.
> I lie between the heron and the wren.
> Beasts of the hill and serpents of the den.
>
> What's madness but nobility of soul
> At odds with circumstance? The day's on fire!
> I know the purity of pure despair,

> My shadow pinned against a sweating wall.
> That place among the rocks—is it a cave,
> Or winding path?'The edge is what I have.
>
> A steady storm of correspondence!
> A night flowing with birds, a ragged moon,
> And in broad day the midnight come again!
> A man goes far to find out what he is—
> Death of the self in a long, tearless night,
> All natural shapes blazing unnatural light.
>
> Dark, dark my light, and darker my desire.
> My soul, like some heat-maddened summer fly,
> Keeps buzzing at the sill. Which I is *I*?
> A fallen man, I climb out of my fear,
> The mind enters itself, and God the mind,
> And one is One, free in the tearing wind.[8]

There is no slightest admixture of acquiescence or surrender in this stance of the "Modern Job" vis-à-vis absurd death. "If there is a God," says Camus' atheist healer Dr. Rieux in *The Plague,* "I should think as he sits above in silence, he would want us to fight the order of death." If "the plague" teaches that there is more to admire in men than to despise, it is because of the courage to address and respond, not *in spite of* death and the absurd, but precisely *to* and including them. Elie Wiesel speaks in *Night* of never forgetting—even if he lived as long as God himself—how his mother and his sister, and with them his faith in God and in life itself, went up in the smoke of the Nazi crematoria. But in his novel *The Town Beyond the Wall* Wiesel achieves the courage to be human and to resist the Modern Promethean's temptation to madness. In his subsequent novels *The Gates of the Forest* and *A Beggar in Jerusalem* Wiesel shows us how a man who has lived through Auschwitz and Buchenwald can once again, finally, live in the present—bringing with him into

8. Theodore Roethke, "In a Dark Time," from *The Far Field* (Garden City, N.Y.: Doubleday, 1964). Reprinted by permission of Doubleday and Co., Inc.

that present all of the dead for whom he mourns and repeating Job's contending in the very midst of the act of existential trust. This is an unromantic posture, a fight for life without heroics, but it is also the only true courage—the only courage that is equal to life itself. It is this courage that I find in Dylan Thomas' poem on his thirty-fifth birthday:

> Oh, let me midlife mourn by the shrined
>   And druid herons' vows
> The voyage to ruin I must run,
>   Dawn ships clouted aground,
> Yet, though I cry with tumbledown tongue,
>   Count my blessings aloud!
>
> Four elements and five
> Senses, and man a spirit in love
>   Tangling through this spun slime
> To his nimbus bell cool kingdom come
>
> . . . .
>
> And this last blessing most,
>
> That the closer I move
> To death, one man through his sundered hulks,
>   The louder the sun blooms
> And the tusked, ramshackling sea exults;
>   And every wave of the way
> And gale I tackle, the whole world then,
>   With more triumphant faith
> Than ever was since the world was said,
>   Spins its morning of praise,
> And my shining men no more alone
>   As I sail out to die.[9]

Ingmar Bergman's movie *The Seventh Seal* shows Death as the Adversary with whom the hero plays a losing game of chess. The memory of death and the anticipation of death is

9. From "Poems on His Birthday" in *The Poems of Dylan Thomas* (New York: New Directions, 1957). Copyright 1952 by Dylan Thomas. Reprinted by permission of New Directions Publishing Corporation.

often a calling to account, as in Kafka's novel *The Trial* and Tolstoy's "The Death of Ivan Ilych." "This door is meant for you, and now I am going to close it," says the doorkeeper to the dying man in Kafka's "Parable of the Law." We are called to account for the uniqueness of our lives and of the lives of all those with whom we have been intertwined—not in some Last Judgment or moralistic, idealistic, superego standard, but in the simple perspective of that moment when life and death are simultaneously present. "Why is man afraid of dying?" asked the Hasidic rabbi of Ger, and answered, "What man fears is the moment he will survey from the other world everything he has experienced on this earth."

Franz Rosenzweig begins *The Star of Redemption* with the reality of the fear of death and ends it with the phrase, "Into Life." During those weeks when I believed, as my doctors did, that I had cancer, I learned that death is not of the future at all, nor of the past: it is an inescapable reality of the present. It is inescapable because it colors our existence at its far horizons. Yet all we ever know is the present, and all we know in that present is life itself.

When we live with the death of one who was close to us, we know that the mystery of his having existed as a person and being with us no longer cannot be plumbed. It is part of the paradox of personal existence itself, which has no secure or continuous duration in time yet does really exist again and again in moments of present reality. We tend most of the time to think of death as an objective event that we can understand through our categories. But when we truly walk in the valley of the shadow, the imminence of death tells us something that we have really known all along: that life is the only reality that is given to us, that this reality—and not some continuing entity or identity of a personal nature—is all that we actually know. We do not know life without our individual selves, but neither do we know our selves without life. We know death, to be sure, but we know it as death-in-life. Life is the reality in which we share while we are alive. Any existence of the self apart from this shared reality is an abstraction—illicit when reified into a self or soul outside of our common social and historical existence. When our bodies die, our selves die too—though continuing to exist in the memory of others and in that eternity in which all time is present. The heart perishes, but the "rock of the heart," in the language of Psalms, remains.

To say that we once did not exist and again shall not exist is not to make our existence itself nothing, as the quatrain from Omar Khayyam suggests; for this would be to equate reality with immutability. When you are dead and your body cremated and the ashes scattered, where are *you*? This is a question that cannot be answered in objective terms; for it is I myself that ask it of myself and am impelled to respond. I cannot think away my own present existence any more than I can deny "the undeniable clamor of the last annunciation, the bone's prayer to death its god." All I can do is hold the tension of these two existential realities and live in that tension. "In order really to live," said Rabbi Yitzhak the *zaddik* of Vorki, "a man must give himself to death. But when he has done so, he discovers that he is not to die—but to live."

9 Sport, Death, and the Elemental

EDITH WYSCHOGROD

To be human is not merely to know, to enter into social relations with others; it is also to enjoy the world which supports
and nourishes the activity of the living subject. To enjoy the world
is neither to describe nor to represent it in the language either
of science or of lived experience; nor is it the struggle with the
world in the attempt to gain subsistence by wrenching from it
"against the will of the world," so to speak, the necessities of
everyday life. Instead enjoyment is experienced as a giving in
to the world, so that man is at one with it, emphasizing its
quality as world rather than as the backdrop against which
things are organized into the technical ends of a system. To
enjoy is to allow the world to be what it is, to lie fallow so that
even if one takes hold of things one does so with an awareness
not of objects in the world forming a series of references in
terms of their utility but rather in terms of the milieu in which
they are found. Thus the air, the earth, the sky, the sea, light, the
city, the unenclosed spatiality or locale from which things
emerge, a locale which retains its indeterminacy, is the field
from which enjoyment arises. Objects situated within this field
do not belong inherently to it; they are movable, can be trans-

Edith Wyschogrod is Assistant Professor of Philosophy at Queens College
of the City University of New York. She has published in such journals as
The Thomist, Judaism, and *Cross Currents.*

ported elsewhere. But the region of their containment remains fixed, is nonpossessable in its very nature. This field may be designated as "the elemental."[1]

The elemental may be known; that is, it is subject to laws which govern its activities. Thus the pilot learns the atmospheric conditions which govern flight, the navigator the tides through which he must steer his ship, the astronaut the conditions of extraterrestrial space. But the elemental itself "lies escheat," has no fixed limits, is prolonged indefinitely, is unifaceted, has only a single presentable aspect. Lost in depth, it cannot be circumnavigated to obtain a view of its reverse side, since there is only obverse without underside. In the elemental nothing begins and nothing ends. One cannot approach it, for one is always already inside it, steeped in it, bathed in it. Every utilization of things seized from the elemental becomes a source of enjoyment which is purely gratuitous and does not derive from using the thing for the purpose intended. To be in the elemental is to live in the present without concern for the future, to enjoy without referring to a set of utilitarian aims.

It is as a bodily field of sensation and activity that one is inserted into the elemental. One can gain a foothold over it by directing the activities of the body toward building a house, cultivating a field, etc. But such activities separate one from the elemental, from the plethora of sensations which derive from the naked contact of corporeity with the milieu in which it finds itself. While such tasks may provide incidental enjoyment, they are tied to ends which inhibit the immediacy of the body's contact with its world. Being in touch with the elemental involves an immersion of the body in an environment experienced as liquidity which spills over in sensation so that the body

1. I am indebted for this conception of the elemental to Emmanuel Levinas, *Totality and Infinity*, trans. by Alphonso Lingis (Pittsburgh: Duquesne University Press, 1969). Martin Heidegger's view of Being, particularly as it is developed in his later works, and Erwin Straus's notion of the *allon* are comparable phenomenological accounts.

senses itself as being at one with the quality of the milieu, re-turns to a primordial identification with the earth itself.

While the elemental is experienced as a source of pure gratifi-cation, its relation to the separated individual is ambiguous, for to yield to the world is to surrender the identity deriving from the recognition of oneself as other than undifferentiated being. Nor can the elemental be possessed, since it emerges from no-where, is not any *thing;* insofar as it is amorphous it flees from one's grasp. It presents itself as it slips away, sustaining one's enjoyment *en passant.* Moreover, the elemental is indifferent to the gratification which it provides; the same force which sus-tains pleasure turns with alarming suddenness into a power of death and destruction. The destructive potential of sea, sky, wind threatens the very existence which seeks to enjoy them. But more important, the pleasurable loss of identity, of sensed separateness from the world, sublates the sense of responsibility for one's life, the forethought which enables one to take account of the future. Such "taking account" requires separation from rather than a return to the elemental.

The threat of death should not be interpreted, however, as the sublation of pleasure in the elemental, as though once one had obtained knowledge of its destructive potential its hedonic value were destroyed. I shall argue in the analysis which fol-lows that, on the contrary, enjoyment in the elemental is pleasure in the face of death, that in fact, the surrender of the individual to the elemental includes death as an element of the pleasure experienced. The dialectical nature of the process has been lost in the cognitive and utilitarian character of contemporary exist-ence, a character which has been extensively elaborated by existential philosophy and current literature. But contemporary man retains a yearning for identification with the being of the elemental despite its concomitance with the risk of death. His quest for eternal return includes the desire to tempt death. Moreover, he attempts this return by using the sophisticated techniques and gear provided by an advanced technology. The apparatus which he has developed does not preclude the risk of death, a risk which remains genuine, but it offers him a chance to escape in the nick of time, since he provides himself odds heavily weighted on the side of life.

I shall try to show that certain sports fulfill this function, that they represent a grappling with the elemental such that the experience sought is that of the body's identity with the elemental, a riding with it which, at the same time, involves a management and control of the force which the elemental exerts against naked corporeity.[2] The fundamental purpose of such sports is only incidentally competitive, for one's competitor is experienced not only as opponent but also as engaged in an enterprise similar to one's own, as generating a style, an expression of his being-in-the-elemental. It is the elemental itself which is the antagonist and which may exact the penalty of life. It is not only for the sake of this experience that one dares to die, but the risk of death itself is a component in the hedonic quality of these sports. To die is to be divested of consciousness, inert, subject to laws of causal necessity rather than to be as a willing subjectivity. But paradoxically it is consciousness, activity, and will which govern the acquisition of skill in these sports, enabling the body to attain a flexibility which enhances the identity of self with the elemental. The body's activity both

2. Jean-Paul Sartre comes close to conceding this point when he argues that a particular aspect of sport, particularly of open-air sport, "is the conquest of these enormous masses of water, of earth, and of air, which seems *a priori* indomitable and unutilizable; and in each case it is not a question of possessing the element but the type of existence in-itself which is expressed by means of this element." *Being and Nothingness*, trans. by Hazel Barnes (New York: Philosophical Library, 1956), p. 585. But Sartre assumes that sport, like science and art, is an activity of appropriation, thus neglecting the hedonic character of being-in-the-elemental, its intentional structure of sensory inundation. Nor does Sartre's analysis focus on the relationship of death to the sportsman. In his account of skiing, for example, snow and ice both in their actual destructive potential and as conventional symbols of death are absent from his analysis.

masters and mimics the elements in question. The sports which I shall consider (running, auto racing, motorcycling, mountain climbing, and surfing, sports of acute exhilaration and varying degrees of risk) are attempts to acquire for the body and its gear which are circumscribed, have form and limit the being of the *apeiron,* the unlimited, the elemental.

To become one with the elemental one must first conquer the elemental by becoming homologous with it. The drive of the body is to become like a power of nature. One accomplishes this by pushing the body to its limits of endurance, by risking death to achieve the being of an unlimited force. The conquest of the self is the result of intensive training, a rigorous self-discipline canalizing the body's available energies, affective, physical, and cognitive, into mastery of itself and disciplining the volition of the athlete so that it too resembles a force of causal efficacy, viz., a power of nature.

The first impulse of the athlete may be a simple wish to bring the body into rapport with nature. But there is an enormous distance between the immediacy of overwhelming pleasurable sensation in experiencing the body's unison with the elemental and the perfection of the fully developed athletic form. In running, for example, Roger Bannister, perhaps the most significant miler in the history of the sport, speaks of the velleity he perceived as a child just become conscious of the body as the body running in these terms:

I remember a moment when I stood barefoot on firm dry sand by the sea. The air had a special quality as if it had a life of its own. The sound of breakers on the shore shut out all others. . . . I looked down at the regular ripples on the sand and could not absorb so much beauty. . . .

In this supreme moment I leapt in pure joy. I was startled and frightened by the tremendous excitement that so few steps could create. . . .

The earth seemed almost to move with me. . . . I was almost

running now, and a fresh rhythm entered my body. No longer conscious of my movement I discovered a new unity with nature.[3]

The experienced athlete does not lose sight of his initial discovery, of the body and its desire for oneness with nature, but the process of training which must intervene before the body can transmute itself into a force homologous with the elemental becomes a matter of reflective awareness. Thus Bannister:

Improvement in running depends on continuous self-discipline by the athlete himself, on acute observations of his reactions to races and training, and above all on judgment, which he must learn for himself. The runner has to make his own decisions on the track—he has no coach there to help him. If a man coaches himself he has only himself to blame when he is beaten.[4]

The initial sense of unity with the elemental is never lost but is complemented by a sense of struggle and mastery over the body's limitations. The great runner John Landy saw the mile as a fascinating challenge. He considered it the "human struggle artificially contrived." Short races, he declares, "are run without thought"; in longer races one must cover a great deal of territory simply to be present "in the laps that count." But every part of the mile is strategic, for one can lose at any point. "You can never let down, never stop thinking. . . . I suppose you could say it is like life. I had wanted to master it."[5]

To develop a phenomenology of running as the attempt to move from one destination to another with the greatest possible rapidity is to misunderstand the nature of running as enjoyment and leaves the interpreter unable to explain running as sport. The nonutility of running is attested by Bannister, who as a child had no notion of why he wanted to run. "I just ran any-

3. Roger Bannister, "The Joy of Running," *Sports Illustrated* 2 (June 20, 1955): 26.
4. *Ibid.*, p. 48.
5. Paul O'Neil, "A Man Conquers Himself," *Sports Illustrated* (May 21, 1956), p. 52.

where and everywhere—never because it was an end in itself, but because it was easier for me to run than to walk."[6] The sprinter or the long-distance runner has become the wind itself, a burst of air which confers upon the runner a sense of freedom, for the wind "bloweth where it listeth." Thus John Landy, after having achieved the four-minute mile, felt that he had stripped away the "impediments and artifices of civilization," achieved untamed animal power, that he had in fact become a "running animal."[7]

It might be argued that in running the essential thing is to win. There is no doubt that competitive elements belong in a phenomenology of running, for these have become affixed to running, as they have to skiing, swimming, etc. But testimony of runners indicates the fundamental aloneness of the sport without recourse to the team, to others cooperating in the venture. Nor is the fundamental interest victory over an opponent to the extent that speed for its own sake is forgotten. Thus John Landy:

> All the responsibility for making the race rests on the pacer—the hunted. It is an exhausting thing, and you can only attempt to guess what is happening behind you and what is in the minds of the hunters. . . . You can simply sit on your man—stay behind no matter how slow the race goes and wait. It is very comforting to do it— you can draw a bead on him and relax and sooner or later you will find a moment to attack him and if you do it at the right time you will inevitably beat him. *But I don't like slow miles. I wanted to run record times and win.*[8]

What is crucial to my argument, however, is not only the assumption that running represents a human attempt to become one with the elemental through a conquest of the body's own limits of endurance so that the body is converted into an efficient machine for running, but also the notion that the body is

6. Bannister, "The Joy of Running," p. 26.
7. O'Neil, "A Man Conquers Himself," p. 53.
8. *Ibid.*, pp. 52–53. Italics added.

not, cannot in fact, become a force of nature. The attempt to do so, to become one with the elemental, may doom the organism to death in primordial encounters with the elemental, to pain, suffering, and the risk of death in sport. For example, the primordial encounter with the sea in which one immerses oneself, without mastering the element, identifies with the natural force of tide, waves, and water, signifies drowning in it. Such a gesture is suicidal. In sport risk is curtailed; one conquers the element before identifying with its power. But a price in suffering and a degree of risk remain in the attempted conversion of the body, fragile, having form, limited, into what it is not, the inexhaustible, the formless, and the unlimited. Thus Landy concludes that the physical suffering involved in training is very nearly unendurable. In 1951 he cut his running time by thirty seconds from 4:45 to 4:15 by running himself into a state of utter exhaustion. He later went on to top this record by achieving the four-minute mile. Medical records show that he had a huge heart and a pulse rate of 42 as opposed to the average of 60 or 70 per minute.[9] Jim Bailey, who beat John Landy by running the mile in 3:58.6, alleges that in the last 220 he was running on sheer adrenalin. "I always thought a four minute mile would feel like a 4:10 mile but it hurt a lot more. I was just gutting it in the last straight."[10]

Since running is not the simple reinsertion of the body into the elemental but a new identification with its power at a higher level, the art of running generates unique psychological tensions. The technique of "breaking away," for example, is experienced by Roger Bannister as a tension of confidence and the lack of it. Thus the breaker is confident that the speed of his opponents has become too slow and that he can accelerate suddenly, maintaining the newly assumed speed until the finish line.

9. *Ibid.*
10. Paul O'Neil, "The Mile," *Sports Illustrated* (May 14, 1956), p. 14.

But he also lacks confidence, for he assumes that unless he moves at a certain moment his competitors will do so and he will be left behind. In this connection Bannister also claims that the drive forward is costly:

The spurt is extremely wasteful because it is achieved at the cost of relaxation. The athlete's style and mood change completely. His mind suddenly starts driving an unwilling body which only obeys under the stimulus of the excitement. The earlier in the race this extra energy is thrown in, the greater the lead captured, but the less the chance of holding it.[11]

The psychological equivalent of such a break, Bannister declares, is the exposure of one's hand in a game of cards. "You show how much reserve you have left by the speed at which you try to open up a gap and by the point at which you do so."[12]

Clearly the effortless transformation of speed in the elemental requires the development of great stamina for the athlete. Yet the psychological and physical risks of running are not appropriated as reducing the hedonic quality of identification with the elemental. On the contrary, the danger of death is experienced as heightened satiety as though one had appropriated the menacing and destructive force of the elemental itself. Bannister alleges: "It was intensity of living, joy in struggle, freedom in toil, *satisfaction at the mental and physical cost.* . . . I had discovered my gift for running—an unconscious conspiracy of mind and body that made this energy release possible."[13]

In the case of road racing the situation is altered. The machine becomes the extension of the body so that its endurance as well as that of the human frame is at stake. Man no longer runs like the wind but flashes by like a streak of light. In auto racing corporeity attempts to surpass the preliminary rush of speed experienced as wind, storm, a burst of air, while retaining

11. Bannister, "The Joy of Running," p. 47.
12. *Ibid.*
13. *Ibid.*, p. 46. Italics added.

the sensation of motion inherent in these forms. The elemental is experienced as light itself, not as the illumined background of all perception from which things emerge and into which they recede but rather light as motion. Speed becomes so rapid that the sense of distance traversed is nearly lost. Thus the primary question is not: How far have I gone? but: How fast am I going? Auto racing, which appears to be a merely incidental use of the machine, expresses the true purpose of the human intention which developed it: not to get somewhere faster, but simply to go fast.

In road racing the body itself is not subjected to the strains of the natural environment but expresses enjoyment through propelling a vehicle. The abundance of sensation is the consequence of speed experienced not only as the motion of wind but as the speed of light. The attainment of such speed carries with it a corresponding increase of risk so that the enhanced exhilaration is achieved at the price of increased danger. Machines have pushed the limit of speed upward, but when maneuvered at these high speeds they become increasingly difficult for the driver to handle. Thus Jackie Stewart, one of the smoothest drivers of recent years, declares:

Road racing has become a sophisticated art in which the driver must work with his car in an extremely close relationship. With the development of wide tires, delicate suspensions, lighter construction and air-foils, the cars present severe handling problems at very high speeds. The razor's edge has become sharper than ever.[14]

I have argued that in the encounter with the elemental experienced as enjoyment, the risk of death is itself incorporated into the plethora of sensation that constitutes the ecstasy of the body's encounter with the elemental (ecstasy in the sense of

14. Jackie Stewart with Gwilym S. Brown, "Racing's Most Frightening Corners," *Sports Illustrated* (October 12, 1970), p. 38.

standing out as well in the sense of unusual pleasure). It is nowhere more apparent than in auto racing that the moments of greatest peril provide the high points of exhilaration. Cornering is the most difficult maneuver of racing, testing the skill and limits of driver and car. The point in conquering corners is that they must be taken at speeds that seem impossible, an art requiring, as racing driver Jackie Stewart alleges, "natural driving talent, sensitivity, feel and above all mental discipline." And what is crucial to my argument, Stewart adds, "To handle a corner properly at the limit is one of the finest human sensations, one of the ultimate experiences we can have. It brings us right to the edge of life."[15] To become like a force of nature is to immerse oneself in its death-dealing power, a power which provides a great part of the content of the stimulating excitation itself. Thus Jackie Stewart in describing one of the most treacherous corners in road racing, the Karussel at the Nürburgring in Germany, claims:

Well, the Karussel is a blind corner. You approach a steep grade at about 140 mph. . . . You cannot see the corner until you are in it. . . . You simply aim [at a giant fir tree] beyond the track. . . . Then suddenly the road seems to fall away under the car. You shift into second and hold onto the steering wheel like mad as you try to keep the car well down in the turn. As the car drops into the bowl it squashes down under great pressure, hitting the very limits of its suspension. When you exit the suspension rebounds like a tightly coiled spring. If the car comes out too high you will at best skid . . . at worst fly off the track.[16]

This corner is, according to Stweart, held in highest esteem by drivers, for "during the few seconds we spend inside the Karussel we experience something like a real high."[17]

While speed and sensed risk characterize the relationship to

15. *Ibid.*
16. *Ibid.*, p. 39.
17. *Ibid.*

the elemental in road racing, there is still another significant feature which throws light on the relation of corporeity to the elemental. I have already noted the significance of "breaking away" in running. In road racing the excitement of acceleration provides an analogous sensation. To accelerate is to exceed a previously established limit, to hurl one's reserves into pushing body or machine beyond its past achievements, sometimes beyond the edge of what had heretofore been considered plausible limits. In acceleration one has already acquired a degree of momentum, so that one does not need to start but is free to experience the gathering momentum deriving from one's remaining resources as a pure play of power. Acceleration begins from nowhere, that is, it is not a transition from the stationary to motion, but each instant of acceleration begins a new swell of motion. The gradations of acceleration (and its converse deceleration) are the body's graded shifts comparable in quality to the rising and falling of tides or wind, to changes of light moving from day to night. Acceleration is experienced as rapid change in the quality of being as though one were inside being itself. Thus one of the great racing drivers, Stirling Moss:

> But speed itself isn't the great stimulation. After all, speed's a relative thing—you can get as much of a thrill spinning at 20 miles an hour as you can get going a hundred at a straightaway. It's really the acceleration that's important. That's what I call the exhilaration of acceleration.[18]

This feeling is usually at its height in turning corners. Moss claims that one of his most exciting experiences came when he opened the accelerator of his first Mercedes in a major road race in Argentina while cornering. He felt the wheels "at their absolute limit of drift" coming to within a foot of the side of the road. "It is," he alleges, "a fantastic experience, when you feel

18. Paul Deutschman, "Subject Stirling Moss," *Sports Illustrated* (November 14, 1955), p. 30.

you've reached the absolute speed you can get with the absolute wheelspin."[19]

The driver symbolizes his resources, his skill, his victory over death in his appearance and in the appearance of his machine as a vehicle of splendor and power. Thus Stirling Moss patterns himself on Fariña. "When I race I always dress in white . . . white leather boxing boots, white nylon coveralls and nylon socks."[20] Eugenio Castellotti models his style on the movie hero, on Mastroianni or Belmondo. An interviewer declares, "The women of Italy called him Il Bello . . . and they crowded around him as he sat nonchalantly smoking on the tail of his twelve cylinder 3.5 liter Ferrari."[21] He adds that Castellotti's "white helmet sitting loosely on his jet-black hair, his tight fitting blue jacket following every bulge of muscle," made him look "more like a movie idol than Italy's champion driver."[22] Thus attired on the accident-ridden Mille Miglia, Il Bello came in first leading a parade of Ferraris in a race in which five people had died and sixteen were injured.

I have tried to show that in the elemental one is affected by the surface of being while its depths remain concealed, that it cannot be circumnavigated, that one cannot penetrate its depths. The revealed side of the elemental, light, wind, sea, etc., provides the possibility for the enjoyment of the elemental. What is concealed in the elemental is an existence without the possibility of revelation. It is, as Levinas calls it, a "nocturnal prolongation" of the elemental, the unknown *par excellence* in which the elemental is rooted. This underside is expressed in road racing in the mass deaths which frequently ensue as the result of a single accident.

Despite the driver's stance as a demigod emerging from the

19. *Ibid.*
20. *Ibid.*, p. 55.
21. William Rospigliosi, "Five Ferraris and Il Bello," *Sports Illustrated* (May 7, 1956), p. 42.
22. *Ibid.*

elemental, the fragility of the person in his attempt to vanquish human limits is attested in the carnage that is experienced at the great races. Death is the consequence of the driver's loss of control; the derelict machine becomes in fact a force of nature rather than the controlled apparatus which mimics the force and which enables man to be in the world as being-in-the-elemental. The twenty-third Grand Prix of Endurance at Le Mans, for example, produced one of the most spectacular accidents in the history of racing when the Mercedes of veteran driver Pierre Levagh attempted to edge between the Austin-Healy ahead of him and an earthen bulwark to the left. The Mercedes vaulted the bulwark, rolling over three times. "The engine, ripped from its mountings by the almost instantaneous deceleration shot out of the car like a shell from a gun, mowing a lethal path through the crowd which stood five feet deep at that point."[23] The hood of the Mercedes "sheared through the crowd of standees like a guillotine. Its engine followed, parts flying in all directions, like a machine gun spewing dumdum bullets. Some of the people standing directly in the path of the hurtling wreckage were decapitated."[24] Yet not even this disaster stopped the Mercedes team. To attest endurance, death is taken up into the experience of the elemental as part of the flood of sensation. Further testimony is provided by the driver's own willingness to risk his neck over and over again. The case of "Wild Bill" Vukovich illustrates the point. What is often considered the world's most dangerous racecourse runs from Tuxtla to Juarez in Mexico; it is known as the bloody gauntlet. The course is 1,908 miles long, the first 1,200 of which wind through curves covering steep cliffs and ridges as high as 10,000 feet. Twelve persons were killed on the course between 1950 and 1954. It was at the Pan American

23. John Bentley, "Motor Sports, The Firsthand Story of the Grand Prix of Endurance at Le Mans Which Brought Auto Racing's Greatest Tragedy," *Sports Illustrated* (June 20, 1955), p. 40.

24. *Ibid.*, p. 42.

Race held here in 1954 that Vukovich "breasted a hill at 100 miles an hour, coming suddenly into a blind right turn. Helpless as the Lincoln skidded across the road on two wheels . . . [he] plunged over the side of a ravine, turning over five times."[25] Yet Vukovich escaped with his life, only to lose it later at another major race, the Indianapolis 500.

While road racing offers the sense of speed, acceleration, and high risk, it also insulates the driver from direct contact with the surface of the earth itself. The vehicle in which he places his body traverses field, hill, mountain, plain, but the contours of this terrain are not brought into plenary presence as tactile sensation. The world whizzes by, as it were, and the driver responds to it by shifting gear or by swerving his machine, but *he* does not shift or swerve in response, for his body and the machine are distinct entities. In motorcycling the situation changes. The bikie feels the surface of the road as a blind man reads Braille. He knows it through the palpation of its contours; his entire body vibrates to its smallest alteration. Thus: "The slightest irregularity in the surface gets transmitted (rather than absorbed) via plunging springs and Spartan saddle to the rider's kidneys."[26] The cyclist is placed in relation to his machine so that his own body seems motorized as though the bike were an organic extension of himself, a prosthesis which allows him to come and go with incredible speed and which enhances his tactile sensitivity to the earth not with his skin but with his vital organs. Heart, lungs, and kidneys become themselves the sensory apparatus through which the vibrations of the bike transmit the outlines of the surface of the world.

Balance is the key to the cyclist's art, for the earth which is his friend and the source of pleasurable sensation is also geared

25. John Bentley and Coles Phinizy, "Road Race in the Mountains," *Sports Illustrated* (December 6, 1954), p. 14.

26. Melvin Maddocks, "Just Another Face in a Rearview Mirror," *Sports Illustrated* (November 16, 1970), p. 43.

to thwart him. The bikie and his machine can, if properly poised, defeat its thrusts, its outcroppings, and changing surfaces. The use of two wheels rather than four situates him in relation to turf and asphalt as the ballet dancer is situated in relation to the stage when twirling on the forward edge of the toes, remaining upright so long as motion continues. Balance is even more precarious when the cyclist devises techniques which keep him for a time on a single wheel. Thus an interviewer writes of cyclist Colin Newell:

Colin has seen and done it all. . . . The setting: a rough dirt course with treacherous corners and a sort of jump. The only thing motorcyclists love better than two wheels is one wheel or—airborne bliss—no wheels. The technique is to hit the rise fast, go into the air with the front wheel straight and come down hard on the rear wheel, scrambling.[27]

Not only does the bike transmit the message of the earth's surface to the body, but the bike as a medium makes itself felt.

The moment the engine starts . . . a vibration throbs through the handlebars to the hands, the wrists and on up the arms. Only a de Sade could do justice to the way a motorcyclist's back and shoulders can feel at the end of a long day. Just to keep the throttle open, the right wrist has to exert a pressure that makes a foot on the accelerator feel like nature's own position.[28]

Biking necessitates a posture which inhibits blood circulation. The rider experiences "bone-chilling cold" in temperatures below 70 degrees. When he stops he may shiver with teeth chattering for half an hour or so. He frequently lives on coffee to offset this effect.[29] Moreover, the cyclist continues to throb long after vibrations of the machine have ceased. "At night wind-burned and aching, he will go to bed and psychically vibrate.

27. *Ibid.*, p. 47.
28. *Ibid.*, p. 43.
29. *Ibid.*

The stock dream of the motorcyclist is that his throttle has become jammed and an incredible narrow road is winding towards him, like ribbon from a spool."[30]

The great test of biking is hill climbing. Here cycling reaches its "ultimate in self-expression." Writing of Colin Newell, the interviewer declares:

Up the slopes he soars, flying from catastrophe to catastrophe. To drop the revs is to drop the bike. Forced to ride at a speed and at an angle he cannot reasonably control, the hillclimber survives by the tip of his instincts. Somebody's earlier rut can twist the handlebars out of his hands. Or the bike can hit the steep of the grade and flip over backwards.[31]

If the cyclist loses control the accident could be fatal. To die in a cycling accident is to return immediately to the elemental earth while losing the body's tactile awareness in its vital organs of the world's surface. It is to become an inert thing by joining the body's own blood to the elemental. One does not die so that the body is lodged in one's vehicle, hidden from view, but as in a sacrificial ritual through a direct encounter of flesh and earth. The knowledge that in death one becomes the dust that one is produces the feeling of risk in biking. Maddock writes of hill climbing, "To reach the top of the hill is pure absurdity and pure exhilaration. Nothing has been accomplished and everything: the supreme illusion of every sport."[32]

The motorcyclist, like the racing car driver, symbolizes his relation to the elemental in his costume and vehicle:

Down the pike thumps and rolls a motorist's apparition. First the helmet and the goggles vibrate into view, then the leather jacket and cowboy boots—half space traveler, half Daniel Boone and all

30. *Ibid.*
31. *Ibid.*, p. 47.
32. *Ibid.*

alien, alien. Last of all the machine itself: a blur of chrome and noise beneath the aboriginal mask of a face.[33]

Unlike the road racing driver he is not characterized by the futuristic symbols of air and space travel alone, symbols which uncover the realm of the elemental which they designate. The helmet and goggles do in fact belong to air, space, light, but cycling also represents a nostalgia for contact with the earth. Thus the cyclist uses some of the techniques and gear of road racing and flying but in the interest of a quite different repertoire of sensations. His bike hugs the earth, seeking a relation to it not in autochthony, that is, as springing from earth, but in the way, historically speaking, it was last known, as frontier. This is visible in the leather jacket, the cowboy boots. The motorist does not perceive the bikie through his symbols of futurism but as a reminder of the past.

The public's reception of the bikie is also phenomenologically significant. Racing car drivers like Il Bello, Moss, and Fangio are heroic figures, symbols of technical and sexual virtuosity, while the motorcyclist is a semioutcast. The sight of a bikie careening down a turnpike is experienced as a scandal, that is, the motorist, protected by his car as a shield between himself and the surface of the world, is forced in the presence of the bikie to regard the body in its vulnerability. The bikie's lack of cover is apprehended as a kind of public nudity. To be nude in public is not only to be obscene but to be fragile; thus the unprotected character of man's being-in-the-world is announced in the appearance of the cyclist racing down a superhighway at great speed. Furthermore, the bikie's attitude is seen as hubris, for not only is he "naked" vis-à-vis the motorist but he flaunts his nudity through the volume of sound created by his vehicle and the speed at which he travels. To understand mass distrust of the motorcyclist on the basis of the reputation achieved by

33. *Ibid.*, p. 42.

such groups as the Hell's Angels is to misunderstand the phenomenology of motorbiking. The violent cultists of the sport do not make it what it is; rather they choose motorcycling because they recognize it as a scandal, as expressive of the body's right to be seen. This desire to be visible is expressed in the outer symbols used by such bikers. While their regalia may seem futuristic in content, the tight leather jackets, etc., emphasize the body's presence. So-called legitimate bikers as well as the public express resentment at the extremes of style expressed by cultists:

[Colin Newell] is sick . . . of the costume riders, the boys to whom cycling is a kind of pageant. You dress the part—tooled boots, tight leather jacket (with studs), metal flake helmet with leopardskin lining. You customize your bike—chop the fenders; add apehanger handlebars, raked forks . . . and chrome everything in sight. Easy Rider![34]

The scandal of biking is heightened by another factor: the motorist, the pilot, the astronaut, the seaman is in his vehicle; the bikie is on it. This difference is experienced as an obscene reversal of position, the body encompassing the machine rather than sheltering itself within it. This feature is amply demonstrated in Kenneth Anger's movie on motorcycling, *Scorpio Rising*, where shots of the bikie straddling his machine emphasize this relationship. Thus, though his game is speed and acceleration (like the auto racer or the pilot), the bikie remains attached to the elemental earth through the exposure of his body (like the runner or the skier). His death and his sexuality are not symbolically experienced through his vehicle but are visible in his corporeal presence.

The art of mountain climbing does not depend upon the human relationship to a vehicle but upon the organized cooperation of man and gear. "Great things are done when men and

34. *Ibid.*, p. 44.

mountains meet. This is not done by jostling in the street," writes William Blake, expressing the distance between the sociality of civilization and the encounter with the elemental represented by climbing. Wind, weather, altitude, avalanches, and ice are the hazards faced by the climber. Against these obstacles he pits the techniques of mountaineering: the use of rope, the cutting of steps with an ax, the making and breaking of camp, and the evaluation of modes of access and departure that are quick and safe. The intention of climbing is to challenge the mountain's inaccessibility. In 1899 the man who first circled the base of Kanchenjunga, a peak held by many Himalayan experts to be even more forbidding than Everest, wrote: "It is guarded by the Demon of Inaccessibility . . . for the express purpose of defense against human assault, so skillfully is each comparatively weak spot raked by ice and snow batteries."[35]

The elemental of the climber is snow and ice experienced not as a horizontal plane but as the vertical. The Himalayan climber is challenged by a mass of peaks. George C. Band says, "The stupendous faces were daubed with masses of hanging ice which discharged their debris into the high snow basins feeding the great Yalung glacier at our feet."[36] Ice and snow are everywhere. In the trek to the foot of a great Himalayan peak one is steeped in these elements, enveloped by them. The face of the mountain in the case of Kanchenjunga is a "series of contorted icefalls and precipitous snow slopes buttressed by steep walls of rock and gigantic overhanging glaciers which looked as if they might break loose at any moment."[37] Here there is "no semblance of life, but there is ample evidence of death. The frozen bodies of migrating birds, killed while trying to fly high passes during violent storms dot the ice field. Nothing can lead

35. George C. Band, "The Conquest of Kanchenjunga," *Sports Illustrated* (October 3, 1955), p. 46.
36. *Ibid.*, p. 51.
37. *Ibid.*

a mountain climber through this icy graveyard."[38] The mountain climber experiences his world as the world of death itself. No life survives under these conditions unless he pits his own life against them.

The ubiquity of snow symbolizes death. A brief excursus into the sensations of the skier should clarify this point as well as distinguish its intentionality from that of the climber. In speaking of the region into which Hans Castorp, "life's delicate child," had wandered on his newly acquired skis, Thomas Mann writes in *The Magic Mountain:*

> No, this world of limitless silences had nothing hospitable; it received the visitor at his own risk. Or rather it scarcely even received him, it tolerated his penetration into its fastnesses, in a manner that boded no good. It made him aware of the menace of the elemental, a menace not even hostile, but impersonally deadly.[39]

It is clear from Castorp's pleasure that the closer one comes to death, the more exhilarating the contact with the elemental. Yielding to temptation, he courts these deadly forces of nature in "conscious submission to her, the fear of death cast out by irresistible oneness."[40] Castorp is not, however, the usual sportsman, as Mann points out, for the latter, "takes all precautions and prudently yields when he must."[41]

Snow, ice, wind, and altitude are the life world of both skier and climber, but for the climber these elements are more treacherous, corresponding to the difference in the difficulty of the terrain he wishes to explore. Different also is the fact that the skier's motion is sliding, as Sartre has shown. He ascends the mountain only in order to be able to glide down over its surface. He is indifferent to the sensation of ascent; in fact he facilitates

38. Charles S. Huston and William H. White, "The Himalayan Sweepstakes," *Sports Illustrated* (September 13, 1954), pp. 38–39.

39. Thomas Mann, *The Magic Mountain,* trans. by H. T. Lowe-Porter (New York: Random House, 1952), p. 476.

40. *Ibid.,* p. 477.

41. *Ibid.,* p. 481.

his climb by means of lifts and tows. He does not seek to become one with the mountain itself, with its earth, rock, and other inorganic components, but rather to glide over the film which conceals them. The skier is interested in the quality of snow, whether it is fine, powdery, soft, etc., so that he can effect a pleasurable descent. He is selective in his relationship to the snow; he therefore seeks snow that will most readily conform to the needs of his skis. Most important, he senses the snow, contacts its surface, follows trails, slides, leaps, turns, avoids obstacles by means of the skis strapped to his boots.

The climber, on the other hand, has as his objective the ascent of a mountain which presents itself to him as an unassailable vista. His aim is not to derive maximum sensation from the speed and acceleration of his descent but to reach, to explore, to achieve the summit. Snow and ice may be elements with which he is surrounded, but he encounters them as covering rock and ravine which themselves must be traversed. He tackles the mountain in stages, pitting himself against cold, wind, and thinning air which tend to increase with each stage. He selects preliminary objectives, establishes rudimentary habitation along the way, lines his route with the paraphernalia of survival so that the final ascent becomes possible. Unlike the skier, who is interested in the descending trail, the climber's interest in the mountain is, as it were, polymorphous perverse. The entire terrain as it is laid out on the map represents the range of his endeavor. Thus, in conquering Kanchenjunga[42] a plan is drawn, the first objective of which is to reach the Great Shelf, a ledge of ice 24,000 feet long which stretches across the face of the mountain. In order to arrive at this preliminary destination the climber must first make his way through the Lower Icefall, "a 2000-foot barrier of jumbled moving ice, gutted with monstrous crevasses and pocked with shattered blocks of ice."[43] After this he must scale the Upper Icefall, "some 3,500 feet of sheer walls

42. Band, "The Conquest of Kanchenjunga."
43. *Ibid.*, p. 51.

of glistening ice, studded with snow covered ledges."[44] The Lower Icefall proves even more difficult than that of Everest. The art of the climber is to scale the ice while retaining balance. Thus:

Norman and I had reached an impasse; before us loomed an irregular line of overhanging cliffs up to 60 feet in height. Try as we might, we could not find a break in this solid fortress of rock. . . . Taking turns we began cutting away minute bulges of ice so that we could stand in balance. After four hours we had only climbed twenty feet.[45]

The climbers then decide to try another technique called "the artificial": "This is an extremely strenuous technique. . . . The lead man hammers a piton into a crack, attaches a snaplink and slips a rope through the ring. The second man then assists by hauling on the rope much like a primitive pulley system."[46]

Since the purpose of the climber is to ascend a vertical rise, he must sometimes refrain from remaining parallel to the slope he is climbing, widening the angle between self and rise, for only when he is roughly perpendicular to the slope can he make the ascent. Thus on occasion he must treat the vertical rise of the mountain as though it were solid earth and the earth as if he were suspended above it. On an early attempt to scale Kanchenjunga Paul Bauer writes: "We were poised like wild animals, crouching beneath the cornices balancing between earth and sky, sometimes on the party's respective heads to try to avoid a simultaneous fall when the overhang collapsed."[47] These strenuous acrobatics are often undertaken in an environment of utter desolation. Tenzing, the Sherpa who scaled Mount Everest with Edmund Hillary, writes of the South Col of Everest, which he first saw on an earlier Swiss expedition:

I have been in many wild and lonely places in my life but never anywhere like the South Col. Lying 25,850 feet between the final

44. *Ibid.*
45. *Ibid.*, p. 51.
46. *Ibid.*
47. Huston and White, "The Himalayan Sweepstakes," p. 36.

peaks of Everest and Lhotse, it lacks even the softness of snow and is simply a bare frozen plain of rock and ice over which the wind roars with never a stop.[48]

A similar feeling is expressed by Herzog, the leader of the Annapurna expedition of 1950:

This was a different universe—withered, desert, lifeless; a fantastic universe where the presence of man was not foreseen, perhaps not desired. We were braving an interdict, overstepping a boundary and yet we had no fear as we continued upward. I thought of the famous ladder of St. Theresa of Avila.[49]

In addition to the below-zero cold and winds strong enough to knock a man to the ground, the going in the upper reaches is painfully slow because of a lack of oxygen. The body fights suffocation as though buried alive. The need for oxygen is greatest at the point of maximum exertion. Tenzing declares that when he participated in the Swiss expedition the air was so thin that he could take only three steps at a time before stopping to breathe. Every twenty yards he and Lambert, the expedition's chief, changed places to share in the arduous task of trailbreaking and so that one or the other could breathe.[50] Despite its obvious advantages, climbers resisted the use of oxygen, for it diminishes the difficulty of the struggle. In writing of the 1922 Everest expedition Younghusband declares: "But if man wants to know what he can do by himself then he must go by himself. He may take a cylinder of oxygen for medicinal purposes as he would take a bottle of brandy. But he would not depend upon it. He would depend upon himself."[51] To do without despite the difficulty would be, according to Somervell, a member of the same ex-

48. Tenzing Norgay as told to James Ramsey Ullman, "Tenzing: Tiger of Everest," Pt. II, *Sports Illustrated* (May 2, 1955), p. 7.

49. Maurice Herzog, *Annapurna* (New York: Popular Library, 1953), p. 167.

50. *Ibid.*, p. 8.

51. Sir Francis Younghusband, *The Epic of Mount Everest* (London: Edward Arnold & Co., 1926), pp. 167–68.

pedition, "an infinitely preferable, more satisfying and altogether more encouraging feat than an oxygen aided ascent."[52]

In addition to gasping for breath, when the 1922 party attempted the ascent of Everest from the northern face via Tibet, a route now closed to Western climbers, its members experienced a peculiar lassitude in ascending the Rongbuk Glacier, "which evaporated all the energy in them." It was afterwards called "glacier lassitude," a designation due perhaps to the unusually high water vapor content in the air which results from melting ice.[53]

Frostbitten extremities also made climbing difficult as well as presenting a threat of amputation. Herzog, severely frostbitten on the Annapurna expedition, writes:

It was terrible; my wooden feet kept slipping on the ice wall, and I could not grasp the thin line in my hands. Without letting go I endeavored to wind it around my hands but they were swollen and the skin broke in several places. Great strips of it came away and stuck to the rope and the flesh was laid bare.[54]

Snow blindness is still another hazard. In the successful Kanchenjunga expedition one of its members, Jackson, "became snow-blind when he lifted his fogged-up goggles."[55] On the successful expedition to Annapurna, two members of the team suffered from snow blindness: "Rebuffat and Terray were completely blind. . . . It was terrifying to be blind when there was danger all around."[56]

The being of the climber is lived against a backdrop of dazzling whiteness, neither figure nor ground: on the one hand, there is nothing to delineate it as figure, for it is not stretched out against some larger backdrop; on the other, there is no tree,

52. *Ibid.*, p. 168.
53. *Ibid.*, p. 64.
54. Herzog, *Annapurna*, p. 189.
55. Band, "The Conquest of Kanchenjunga," p. 52.
56. Herzog, *Annapurna*, p. 182.

house, or landmark to enrich its surface as ground. To grow blind in such an environment is to be cut off from a scene of incredible brightness, from a milieu in which the brilliance of the sun is reflected, leading one to expect the natural concomitance of light and heat, but finding instead (except at midday) bone-chilling cold. To be cold, to be without air, and in addition to be without sight is to exist as one dead. "Death clutched at me and I gave myself up,"[57] writes Herzog of Annapurna. Yet the excitement of climbing lies in these terrors. Thus Younghusband, in assessing Odell's achievement on Everest in 1924: "One of the great mysteries of existence is that what is most awful and most terrible does not deter man but draws him to it—to his temporary disaster, perhaps, but in the end to an intensity of joy which without the risk he could never have experienced."[58]

To possess the being of the mountain, the climber must first have surmounted it, as though he had its mode of existence in his grasp. The exhilaration of the elemental here is first to seem to subjugate it. Thus "to conquer Mount Everest" has become a cliché in our language to express the overcoming of insurmountable obstacles. Younghusband speaks of the challenge of Everest in these terms:

Both man and mountain have emerged from the same original earth and therefore have something in common between them. . . . Man has that within him which will not let him rest until he has planted his foot on the topmost summit. . . . He will not be content until he has it in subjection under his feet.[59]

But actual subjection implies the power to transform it, to make it do one's bidding as the field does one's bidding in producing a harvest when it is plowed and seeded. But man's being-in-the-elemental does not wish to reduce the mountain so that it is no

57. *Ibid.*, p. 183.
58. Younghusband, *Epic of Mount Everest,* p. 292.
59. *Ibid.*, p. 19.

longer what it was, to flatten it, to radically alter its contours, for to do so would be to destroy the source of his exhilaration. Being-in-the-elemental demands that the mountain remain as it is. The climber wants only to experience its being through the channel of his body, so that his body expresses it. Thus in 1924, speaking of Everest, Somervell remarked, "One seemed to be simply above everything in the world and to have a glimpse of a god's view of things!"[60] To be the god of the mountain is not to subjugate it but to live its freedom as one's own.

It is not the notion that one has conquered the elemental that sustains the climber, for he understands this to be impossible. Conquest was never the expectation of climbers like George Leigh Mallory, who was lost together with Irvine on the 1924 expedition to Everest and of whom Younghusband writes: "To get him away from Everest before Everest itself had hurled him back you would have had to pull him up by the very roots of his being."[61] Mallory, in speaking of Everest, which he called "that jagged excrescence in the jaw of the world," asks: "Have we vanquished an enemy? None but ourselves. Have we gained success? That means nothing here."[62]

The milieu of climbing is one of winter; the environment of surfing is one of unending summer.[63] Surfing "is the endless search for a windless day, an uncrowded beach, the perfect wave."[64] Unlike swimming and diving, surfing is not an immersion, but a contact with the surface of the sea, with the rise and fall of waves. To surf is to recognize the uniqueness of the ocean. One can swim, sail, dive, etc., in any body of water deep enough to accommodate the body or the body and its gear, but one can surf only where there are waves. To surf is to treat the

60. *Ibid.*, p. 267.
61. *Ibid.*, p. 271.
62. Huston and White, "The Himalayan Sweepstakes," p. 45.
63. Bruce Brown's movie *The Endless Summer* documents this point.
64. John Severson, ed., *Great Surfing* (Garden City, N.Y.: Doubleday, 1967), p. 15.

wave as though it were solid, climbing it rather than immersing oneself in its depth. The wave is, as surfers put it, "a mountain that moves." Surfing treats the sea as though one could walk on it. Rather than lying prone, the surfer for the most part walks his board, which is, in effect, to walk on water. Unlike a ship, the board has no sides, and thus it is more like a shoe beneath his feet than habitation which shelters him. The surfer tries to take waves in an upright position, flexing his body to conform to the movements of the wave; he can for example "walk the nose," that is, walk foot over foot in the direction of the nose of the board.

The wave is itself the elemental *par excellence;* it comes from nowhere, goes nowhere. One glides down that which is itself without duration, which is absolutely transient. Hillary's climbing of Everest "because it is there" could not apply to the surfer, for whom the sea endures but for whom each wave is a unique challenge. But the wave is not a discrete entity like the jetty, the reef, the pier; it both is and is not the ocean. Surfer Phil Edwards writes: "That big hollow motherless wave comes crashing down behind you and it vibrates the whole ocean." To experience the wave is to know water as impact. Thus Edwards describes the impact of a giant wave:

The force of a monster wave can pin you right down to the bottom. You lie there on your back—spread-eagled and heavy and helpless— and if you look up you can see those spinning fingers of turbulence reaching down to get you. They scoop you up . . . and for a few seconds you are spinning around crazily in a world that is neither land nor sea nor air.[65]

Not only does the character of the waves change, but their succession is endless. The surfer must time their sequentiality with perfect precision so that after a while he develops a "clock somewhere inside [his] rib cage."[66] Surfing is the experience of

65. Phil Edwards with Bob Ottum, *You Should Have Been Here an Hour Ago* (New York: Harper & Row, 1967), p. 14.
66. *Ibid.,* p. 68.

the elemental as time; it is the body's knowledge that one cannot step into the same stream twice. To miscalculate is to be hurled from one's surfboard—to be "wiped out," in surfing language.

What is sought by the surfer is the upsurge and ebb of water, a surface that is never quiescent. It is an experience not only of local conditions, winds, beach contours, rocks, reefs, and jetties, but of the ocean's remotest depths where waves originate. Sometimes the surf is accompanied by a rush of water moving seaward. For example, at Sunset Beach the waves break over a reef near the shore and surge back, creating a powerful backwash. This is known to surfers as riptide.[67] Surfing in riptide is an experience of the antagonism of land and water. The backwash is the sharp ejection of the tide from the land, the sea returning to itself. To try to swim in this exchange of waters is to exhaust one's resources. The surfer, according to Edwards, stays upright as though treading water and allows the tide to carry him, inching over to the side if he can in order to get out of it.[68] At Makaha in Hawaii a second line of waves breaks over a reef beneath the surface. A shallow spot in the path of a wave forces the wave to break harder and faster and higher than elsewhere, creating a bowl. Such bowls as those at Makaha and Ala Moana create nearly perfect waves.[69] Surfer Phil Edwards alleges that here "you are riding along on the moving, boiling top of the world, attached—only occasionally—to this planet."[70] If the surfer rides straight into the bowl, the impact of the wave comes down directly on his head. To avoid being "wiped out" the surfer turns and "sails along the edge of the bowl."

The art of the surfer cannot be transformed into an act having utility. The runner, the motorcyclist, or the road racer can divert his skill. An activity which is an end in itself can become one

---

67. *Ibid.*, p. 78.
68. *Ibid.*
69. Severson, *Great Surfing*, p. 152.
70. Edwards, *You Should Have Been Here*, p. 64.

whose purpose is different from the activity. Thus these skills can be used to flee a pursuer or to arrive at a destination. But surfing is purely gratuitous. It is *de trop,* for if one wishes to cross the water one swims, rows, sails, etc. To surf is merely to experience the ocean at its outermost edges; it is to arrive nowhere, to pursue nothing. The surfboard is not a vessel; it is a fragment. It cannot take the surfer anywhere. In fact the board itself can rebound against the surfer with lethal force. In the early days of surfing, for example, when boards weighed as much as 95 pounds, "with no lift on the nose, the boards would pearl—which means plunge straightaway into the water. They would ride right to the bottom, and the force of the wave would rifle them up through the back end like a shot, often 15 feet in the air, and they would come down like an ax."[71] To surf is to be thrown, as though shipwrecked with only a plank to which one can cling from wave to beach and seaward again until the surfer is exhausted.

The perfect wave is often found under conditions of greatest danger to the surfer. Sheer height constitutes a major risk. According to Sam Reid, there is a great difference between waves twenty-five feet and those forty feet high. He writes: "I tried to sprint up the face of a forty-foot wall and the board started to slip back while I was paddling furiously. I discovered the technique of zigzagging like a skier herringboning up the face of a mountain and it worked."[72] Coral reefs can constitute an additional hazard. The Banzai Pipeline, a shoreline of perfect waves near Sunset Beach in Hawaii, conceals such a bottom. Phil Edwards writes of it: "The surf was rolling in 15 feet high. Running along the top of each wave was an enormous curl. . . . The curls were bending over to form tubes; Holland Tunnels . . . a man could actually get inside."[73] But if one is wiped out here, one can be cut apart by sharp spires of coral.

71. *Ibid.,* p. 26.
72. Severson, *Great Surfing,* p. 26.
73. Edwards, *You Should Have Been Here,* p. 12.

Existence in the elemental is to be, in Edwards' terms, plugged into the world, deriving from its energy an overflow of sensation:

There is nothing mystical about this. There is a need in all of us for controlled danger; that is a need for an activity that puts us however briefly—on the edge of life. Civilization is breeding it out of us, or breeding it down in us, this go-to-hell trait. The hackers are taking over. . . . The legions of the unjazzed.[74]

Being-in-the-elemental is the hedonic mode of existence which incorporates this go-to-hell trait. Levinas writes: "The element suites me—I enjoy it; the need to which it responds is the very mode of this conformity or of this happiness."[75]

In the sports which I have described death in the elemental is experienced neither as the imminent nihilation of one's being nor as a kind of immortality deriving from a return to the elemental itself. There is another alternative which best suits the case: death in these sports is the adversary, the real opponent in the game of skill. In risking death the sportsman understands the power of death, but it is experienced as the power of an enemy. The elemental is perceived as death's persona which must be vanquished in each encounter and whose power is transferred to the victor. In sport as in suicide death does not choose its victim, but is rather chosen, in the former case as the conquered, in the latter as the conqueror. Seen in this light the sports which I have considered are to be understood as attempts to mitigate fate. The pleasure experienced is the pleasure of freedom, of a struggle with death on man's terms rather than on the terms offered by destiny. If one is reprieved from death it is not a reprieve arbitrarily received, but in part the result of one's choosing. It is true that one might be vanquished, but the occasion and terms of the conflict are stipulated by the human agent. The

74. *Ibid.*, p. 12.
75. Levinas, p. 141.

sportsman seeks to encounter death on the grounds of his own strengths, in surfing, in motorcycling, etc. Each of these sports stresses a unique style and set of skills, a unique mode of engendering exhilaration in the elemental. To engage in sport as a mode of being in the elemental is not merely to *want* to die, but to be *willing* to do so.

10 The Double Apprenticeship: Life and the Process of Dying

ROSETTE LAMONT

To experience every moment of existence as though it were the last breath, to stand at every instant, in joy or sorrow, in pride or modest self-awareness, on the brink of dissolution, to be eternally condemned to capital punishment, reprieved at every second, and condemned again, such is the state of mind of one of the tender clowns of European literature, the contemporary dramatist Eugene Ionesco.

Already as a child of ten or twelve, Ionesco found himself unable to taste the present's full-bodied joy without thinking that it was bound to melt away. He tells of outings to the movies with his family: his parents and grandparents. Pushing the grandmother in her wheelchair—she was an invalid—the group would set off from rue de l'Avre to the avenue Suffren where there was a small cinema. The child Ionesco would be filled with pleasant anticipation, but the moment pleasure invaded his being, his joy was clouded by the realization that the film would come to an end and he would have to go home. Before even entering the movie house, he was struck with the saddening thought that three hours later all would be finished. From that time on he was, as he says, in time, in flight, in finiteness. Ob-

Rosette Lamont is Professor of Comparative Literature of the Doctoral Faculty of the City University of New York and Professor of French at Queens College. She has published widely in such journals as the *Publication of the Modern Language Association* and the *Massachusetts Review*. Her work has also appeared in the Yale French Studies.

jects seemed to stand still, while he was rushing past them. He was chained to a moving train.

Ionesco realizes that the keen longing to live is a neurosis: however, he does not wish to be healed. Nor has Jungian analysis effected a cure. Ionesco realizes that he suffers through dissociation from anima, from the earth, that he must embrace nonbeing, make it the self. The only way out is the creation of living beings, his daughter, his plays. Creative love is divine love, says Ionesco. We may not be entitled to love ourselves, but by loving others we re-create the world and, for a time at least, rescue it from oblivion.

Most of Ionesco's metaphysical farces are based on the awareness of the presence of death in life. This is true of *The Chairs, The Killer, Victims of Duty,* and the most recent of all, *The Death Game.* But it remains for *Exit the King* to make the supreme statement as to the need for a double apprenticeship: the apprenticeship of living, which issues from the knowledge that all is fleeting, and the apprenticeship of renunciation, which is the process of dying.

"We are dying men who do not accept death. This play attempts to define the apprenticeship of death," said Ionesco to Claude Bonnefoy.[1] In *Exit the King,* Queen Marguerite turns to the young and lovely Second Wife of King Bérenger the First and accuses her of having distracted their spouse from the principal occupation of life, that of the contemplation of one's end. "It's your fault if he isn't [prepared]. He's been like one of those travelers who linger at every inn, forgetting each time that the inn is not the end of the journey. When I reminded you that in life we must never forget our ultimate fate, you told me I was a pompous bluestocking."[2] She then sketches a program of apprenticeship: "He ought to have thought about it every day. The

1. Claude Bonnefoy, *Entretiens avec Eugene Ionesco* (Paris: Editions Pierre Belfond, 1966), p. 91.
2. Eugene Ionesco, *Exit the King,* trans. Donald Watson (New York: Grove Press, 1963), p. 13.

time he's wasted." To her husband who refuses to face the reality
of his death she will say:

It's your fault if you've been taken unawares, you ought to have
been prepared. You never took the time. You were condemned and
you should have pondered that fact from the very first day, then
every day, day after day, for some five minutes. It wasn't much. No
big deal. Five minutes a day. Then, ten minutes, a quarter of an
hour, half an hour. That's the way to keep in shape.[3]

Queen Marguerite's *Ars Moriendi* is solidly rooted in St. Augustine's "First Dialogue":

We must picture to ourselves the effect of death on each several
parts of our bodily frame, the cold extremities, the breast in the sweat
of fever, the side throbbing with pain, the vital spirits running slower
and slower as death draws near, the eyes sunken and weeping, every
look filled with tears, the forehead pale and drawn, the cheeks hanging hollow, the teeth staring and discolored, the nostrils shrunk and
sharpened, the lips foaming, the tongue foul and motionless. . . .
This, then, is what is meant by sinking deeply into the soul.

Only after such exercise can one expect to be found, as Montaigne wished, "planting cabbages, indifferent to Death and still
more to the state of one's garden."[4]

For the Christian, death has entered the world as a result of
man's sin, of his Fall. The contemplation of death, therefore, is
an act of repentance, a first step toward salvation. Christ himself
suffered mortality in order to enact for humanity the drama of
resurrection. His body is, according to the great preachers, an
architect's model for that of human being taken as a totality.
Bossuet, the seventeenth-century orator and writer, famous for
his *Oraisons funebres,* urges his listeners to follow him, in
imagination, into a hospital where they will view the effects of

3. *Ibid.,* p. 37.
4. Theodore Spencer, *Death and Elizabethan Tragedy* (New York: Pageant Books, 1936), p. 38.

malady in all their diversity. With characteristic brilliance the author of this sermon "On Resurrection" exclaims: "Chrétiens, c'est la maladie qui se joue comme il lui plait de nos corps, que le péché a abandonnes a ses cruelles bigarreries."[5]

In *Death and Elizabethan Tragedy,* Theodore Spencer states that an unbroken line links the writings of St. Bernard de Clairvaux (1090–1153) through the development of European metaphysical thought to Shakespeare. He says: "The creation of Hamlet may be regarded as a remote consequence of St. Bernard's contemplation of the sufferings of Christ."[6] Using this starting point, we could in turn trace the development of the theme of death from the sermons of St. Bernard through Villon's *Testaments,* Bossuet's *Oraisons,* Donne's *Anniversaries and Sermons,* Hamlet's soliloquies, to Baudelaire's *Spleen* poems and his "Une Charogne," Mallarmé's *Igitur,* right through to Beckett's *Malone Dies* and Ionesco's *Exit the King.* In all of these we would find a similar contemplation of the process of living which is also a process of decay and of dying.

Bérenger's disintegration in *Exit the King* is the visual concretization of the sinful life he has led with the voluptuous young queen. Though she may appear loving, sweet, generous, she is in fact Eve, the temptress. From the start, Marguerite exposes her: "You've led him astray. Oh yes! Life was very sweet. With your fun and games, your dances, your processions, your official dinners, your winning ways and your firework displays, your silver spoons and your honeymoons!"[7] Though bearing the Virgin's name, Queen Marie is in fact the embodiment of Pascal's divertissement. Or is this perhaps the way the Old Queen sees her? For the King she represents a superior form of existence. She is life: that form of life one can enjoy when one is still able to celebrate what Camus calls "the wedding of Man and Earth."

5. Bossuet, *Sermons* (Paris: Librairie Garnise Frères), p. 110.
6. Spencer, *Death,* pp. 15–16.
7. Ionesco, *Exit the King,* p. 11.

Marie is an extension of Bérenger's own senses: his youth, his sensuality, his *eros*. Now that he is dying he finds it difficult to recapture the glorious fullness she describes:

I implore you to remember that morning in June we spent together by the sea, when happiness raced through you and inflamed you. You knew what joy meant then: rich, changeless and undying. If you knew it once, you can know it now. You found that fiery radiance within you. If it was there once, it is still there now. Find it again. Look for it, in yourself.[8]

Ionesco conveys here the ecstasy of a young man in love, the sentiment that death and change do not exist, that he is eternal, beyond contingency. The dying King however, no longer understands what Marie is recalling. Between that young man and the moribund king lies an abyss which cannot be bridged. Indeed, his kingdom reflects his condition as the land cracks, the mountains sink, the seas flood the countryside. The King's malady has infected his kingdom, and we are reminded that our own planet is as mortal as every man living upon it.

There comes a time in the life of each and every one when we realize that we are infected with mortality. For most people this notion does not come early in life. Not so with Ionesco. He himself has often narrated the circumstances which made him realize that there is no escape from death. He was about five years old, and living alone with his mother, his father having had to go back to Rumania. His mother worked hard, and the child noticed that this kind of life was taking its toll. Under the windows of their apartment he could see funeral processions going by. He would question his mother. "Someone died," she would say. "Why?" "He died because he had been ill." The child thought he understood at last that one died when one had suffered some accident or a long illness. Death itself was accidental, and if one were very careful and very good it would stay away. One thing bothered him, however: the process of

8. *Ibid.*, pp. 51–52.

aging. How long could it continue and until what point? A man would grow old; his beard would whiten and continue growing until he would stoop, bending closer and closer to the ground. One day the child ventured: "Mother, does everyone die? Please tell me the truth." "Yes," she answered. Ionesco remembers that he was sitting on the floor, a mere child, and that his mother was standing, her hands behind her back, leaning wearily against the wall. The child burst out crying. She went on looking at him, helpless. There they were. He understood at last there was no place to run. Death sits inside the person, waits. The child's first metaphysical apprehension dates from that moment when he knew he would die, and that this woman he loved and pitied, his mother, would die also. Somehow her death seemed more unbearable than his own. After that knowledge every moment of joy, Ionesco tells us, was tainted. It was as if a gaping hole had opened at the center of things. The most radiant, the most complete events and experiences were irrevocably touched with dismay. This opening is the infinite abyss Pascal described so eloquently in his *Pensées*. The child Ionesco discovered by himself that Man is a middle between Nothing and All, just as Pascal locked in a room had rediscovered Euclidean geometry.

The image of the void is ever present in *Exit the King*. The more Marie proffers the consolations of her love, the keener is Bérenger's realization that it is now too late.

MARIE. Love is mad. And if you're mad with love, if you love blindly, completely, death will steal away. If you love me, if you love everything, love will consume your fear. . . . The universe is one, everything lives again and the cup that was drained is full.

KING. I'm full all right, but full of holes. I'm a honeycomb of cavities that are widening, deepening into bottomless pits. It makes me dizzy to peer into the gaping gulfs inside me.[9]

9. *Ibid.*, p. 68.

Later, Marguerite will echo the King's words when she explains to the maid, Juliette: "We're poised over a gaping chasm. Nothing but a growing void all around us. . . . There's nothing but the crust left. Soon we'll be adrift in space."[10]

Clearly, the shrewish Queen Marguerite assumes here the functions of Ionesco's mother, truth telling. The gentle Marie, mouthing her clichés of love, can do nothing for her husband at the moment of his greatest need. No wonder that, at the end of the play, it is Marguerite who will reveal herself as the great Divinity of the Ultimate Passage.

Written in the space of twenty days interrupted by an illness, dictated to a secretary, *Exit the King* is itself afflicted with a break in the middle, a gaping hole at its very core. Ionesco is well aware of the difficulties this presents, of the necessity to pace the rhythm. If one is not careful the play could appear to be composed of two separate pieces glued together. In point of fact, this break is a positive factor, and in the middle of the play, somewhere between the fear of death and the apprenticeship of dying, Bérenger makes it an apprenticeship for life. Since the play was written as soon as the dramatist recovered from a first bout with his illness, then interrupted by a recurrence of the same malady, and finished after his second recovery, it is infused with the terror at the thought of the ineluctable, and penetrated at the same time with the wonder of life. There is perhaps no other play in the history of dramatic literature in which the dissolution of flesh is so keenly apprehended, and the joys of the most humble activities of life so tenderly rendered.

If Ionesco's universe can be somber, it is because he has not forgotten the dazzling light of his childhood. In his *Entretiens* with Bonnefoy, and in his delightful journal written for Skira and illustrated by himself with childlike drawings, *Découvertes,* Ionesco describes the pure joy he experienced as a child in the

10. *Ibid.,* p. 78.

country, at the Chapelle Anthenaise. Perhaps unable to work and take care of her children at the same time, Madame Ionesco had sent her children to the country, where they lived at a farmhouse and attended the local school. Ionesco has kept intact the memory of these three years when he was eight, nine, and ten. "I lived in the present moment," he says. "Life itself was a state of grace." The village was a microcosm. The old farmhouse, the Mill, stood at the crossroads, and it seemed to the child that he was the center of the universe. Time was a wheel, turning slowly around its fixed point, the boy. The house was a perfect nest, a shelter. Outside stood a lovely village, nestled on a low hill. On Sunday, when the child walked to church, he would see a sky of pure blue, and in it the church steeple. Bells seemed to peel from heaven, celebrating the wedding of sky and earth. The vivid greens and blues of spring, the flowers opening along the road, testified to a kind of transfiguration. Everything was scaled to the size of a small child, everything had a human face, everything was personalized. For Ionesco the Chapelle Anthenaise remains a vision of paradise lost.

When Bérenger realizes fully that his doctor is not lying to him, that his shrewish wife is telling him the truth, he is seized with panic. How dare Death come uninvited, unexpected? This is a *crime de lèse-majesté*. Sure he would have died sometime, when he was ready, when he himself had decided to die. That is *never*. Marguerite reminds him that he is to die in one hour and a half, "at the end of the show." Thus, we, the audience, are reminded that this indeed is a show, a kind of play within the greater drama of life wherein we are all dramatis personae, all doomed to make our exit.

Reviewing the APA production of the play for the *Saturday Review* (January 27, 1968), Henry Hewes writes: "Dying is something we all tend to put off. But in our subconscious minds lies a suppressed awareness that the painful fact of death will have to be met." If Pierre Aimé Touchard is right when he states in his *Dionysos* that the atmosphere of tragedy depends on "human beings recognizing themselves, recognizing one another, reaching that recognition within the realm of the beautiful,"[11] then indeed the comic play Ionesco writes about the King's death is at the same time one of the finest tragedies of our epoch. The actor is he who acts for me, purging me of my fears, my deep-rooted anxieties. Thus, Bérenger dies for me and every one of us. Though we laugh at his childlike longings for a never-ending existence, his absurd desire for immortality, we recognize in him an archetypal character, not very different from the Hamlet who says: "I am dead, Horatio," or Richard II awaiting his end in his cell. As Ionesco himself writes in *Notes and Counter Notes:*

When Richard II dies, it is really the death of all I hold most dear that I am watching; it is I who die with Richard II. Richard II makes me sharply conscious of the eternal truth that we forget in all these stories, the truth we fail to think about, though it is simple and absolutely commonplace: I die, he dies, you die. So it is not history after all Shakespeare is writing, although he makes use of history; it is not history that he shows me, but *my* story and *our* story—*my* truth, which independent of my "times" and in the spectrum of a time that transcends Time, repeats a universal and inexorable truth.[12]

In an essay on the comic in Ionesco, Serge Doubrovsky speaks of catharsis through laughter. We laugh at the King's fears, but it is as though we were laughing off our own. We do not really laugh at him; we burst out laughing, liberating ourselves from the extreme tension of pity and terror. Nor are we spectators at this play. Bérenger is as much our invention as it is that of the author. We participate in the creation, reading into the archetypal, hieroglyphic buffoon upon the stage those characteristics

11. Pierre Aimé Touchard, *Dionysos* (Paris: Editions Montaigner, 1937), p. 39.
12. "Experience of the Theater," *Notes and Counter Notes* (New York: Grove Press, 1964), p. 136.

we call human. Though this play is not in the least didactic, it teaches, it instructs. We learn that all men die a lonely death, that pain is still a form of consciousness and thus of life, that death is a threshold we do not want to cross, that no one can die for us, instead of us. Thus we become what Marguerite accuses her husband of not having been, apprentices of dying.

It is almost beyond the powers of imagination to realize that life was there, and suddenly is gone, that the quick have become the still. Knowing that he will soon feel the stony cold of poison in his body, Hamlet speaks of that paradoxical condition of being still able to speak and yet knowing that the minutes, or seconds, of life are passing: "I am dead." He does not say: "I will die soon. Soon I will be dead." His situation may be more dramatic than that of the patients in a cancer ward, but basically no different. And is it not to remind his people that all men share the same metaphysical condition that Solzhenitsyn wrote a novel in which people from different walks of life, members of different nationalities appropriated by the Soviet Union—former political prisoners, high Soviet officials, peasants, soldiers, students, Uzbeks, Tartars, Georgians—come under one roof, held there by the single factor which unifies even those who do not want to be united, their mortal malady? Writers of tragedies—and we can include among dramatists novelists of tragic, epic novels such as *Cancer Ward*—explore beyond the state of division only too common to human society the fundamental human problems which are revealed when men are alone, or when they feel alone (even in the midst of men), as when they face the unavoidable. It is one of the paradoxes of human nature and human life that human beings are estranged from themselves and one another when they are forced into close contact, but in the state of solitude they are reunited. Camus' Jonah, the artist who lost his individuality when surrounded by friends, and a coterie of admirers, finds himself as soon as he begins a strangely isolated existence, up in a high hatch built on an upper level of the apartment he shares with his family. There he will be found, after his death, having scribbled an ambiguous, richly evocative word, since it might be either "solitaire" or "solidaire." It is obvious that Camus, the great twentieth-century humanist, and Ionesco, one of the creators of the Metaphysical Farce, redefine the concept of solidarity. Both men felt that only when human beings strip off their social personalities, remove their professional levels, their uniforms, their masks, are they confronted with what Ionesco calls in *Notes and Counter Notes* "the immense ocean of the infinite." Interviewed for *Les Cahiers Libres de la Jeunesse,* the dramatist explains: "When I am most profoundly myself, I join a forgotten community. Often society alienates me, that is to say estranges me both from myself and from other people. . . . Ants, bees and birds are sociable. Man, however, is asocial. . . . Being asocial means in the long run being social in a different way."[13] Marxist critics have accused Ionesco of avoiding important political issues. The critic Kenneth Tynan goes so far as to call Ionesco's "neutrality" antisocial, better still "the arch-enemy of art." It is futile to make a case of Brecht against Ionesco. The great plays of Brecht are as concerned with man's vulnerability as those of Beckett and Ionesco. But Beckett and Ionesco are not partisan, and they fear only the ideologue who can and does claim anything, resorts to lies to further his program. The artist cannot lie because, as Ionesco explains, "a work of art is not a reflection, an image of the world; but it is made *in the image of the world.*" Only an ideology that attempts the impossible and grotesque task of abolishing fear, pain, and *caritas* would fail to understand the deeply social significance of *Dr. Zhivago* or *The Cancer Ward.* About the former Ionesco writes:

In the Pasternak Affair, one terrible thing strikes me forcibly. Pasternak has been accused by the official writers of his country of

13. *Ibid.,* p. 111.

being a renegade, a traitor, a bad patriot and a man filled with hatred. Why? Quite simply because he has had and expressed the feeling that the people confronting him, his adversaries, were after all human beings too, as human as their enemies and that, like the others, they had a right to pity, respect, understanding and even love.[14]

Only a society so resolutely ametaphysical as to forbid Jean Louis Barrault—after extending an invitation to his company—to perform Beckett's *Happy Days* could misconstrue the meaning of a novel wherein the contemplation of death becomes a way of looking with love and understanding at friends and "enemies" alike. All have to endure the final humiliation, the absurdity of dissolution. The dream of life and the illusion of the world are irrevocably dispelled by the reality of death. As Ionesco says: "How can I trust in a world that has no stability, that flits away. One moment I can see Camus, I can see Atlan, and suddenly they are gone. It's ridiculous. It almost makes me laugh. Anyway, King Solomon has already exhausted the subject."[15]

As long as men live and die the subject will not be exhausted. But it is true that such awareness cuts through all ambiguities between the real and the unreal. It is with a strange kind of smile that Hamlet says: "I am dead." It almost makes him laugh to feel himself speak, to breathe, and to know, since Laertes has informed him that the poison on the end of the sword will not let him live long, that the one who is saying these words is a living corpse. How strange, how ludicrous! Thus tragicomedy is born. We who watch Bérenger struggle against a set limit of time do not know whether to laugh or cry. He knows his deadline (no pun intended); we are not aware of ours. We are like the prisoners of Pascal's cell. Yet, by watching Hamlet, Richard II, Winnie, and Bérenger we are reminded of our destiny, and can no longer look with proud pity at our neighbor because he is badly dressed, ugly, or old. To this favor we will all come. If we

14. *Ibid.*, p. 160.
15. *Ibid.*, p. 110.

keep this in mind, if we receive the healing lesson of comitragedy, then we will act toward our fellow man as though each meeting were the last encounter, the last chance for flesh to touch other flesh with tender concern, for spirit to contact spirit. In this way the apprentices of death become the apprentices of life.

Ionesco's *Exit the King* is a tragicomedy or a comitragedy about a dying man who discovers the beauty of life. It is a play which teaches us to see, to look. It teaches us not to complain about the weather, about our tiny pains and aches, about poor food, or not quite satisfactory accommodations. It makes us understand that even a tiny ache must be welcome as a sign of being alive.

On the surface Bérenger I seems to be an Ubu devoid of ambition and cruelty. Like Jarry's clown-king he is ruled by his boodle and the nether regions of his person. Both Ubu and Bérenger possess an overwhelming and highly amusing cowardice, and both are imbued with what Roger Shattuck calls an "inverted Dignity." But the nature of this dignity is different in Bérenger. Whereas Ubu is monstrous, a caricature of the primitive soul, the archetype of the dictators of our age, the Savage God made mask, Bérenger is visceral man stripped bare of his epidermis, quivering before our eyes. Jarry's Antichrist said: "When you see your Double you die." Bérenger is our dying Double, and seeing him die we live.

Structurally, *Exit the King* is conceived with the utmost economy: the protagonists, Bérenger I (the Old Wife and Mother Figure, Genitrix and Destroyer) and Marie (Lover, Extension of Self, Daughter), Juliette (Servant, Humanity), the Guard Society, Public Opinion, mass media), and the Doctor, also "Surgeon, Executioner, Bacteriologist and Astrologist" (Science, the Instrument of Death, the Magician). There are three women and three men, which accounts for a certain perfection of form, an architectural equilibrium which makes critics say that this is the most classical of Ionesco's plays. In a sense they are right. The play is as classical as its subject.

As for most of Ionesco's plays, the set, costumes, and vocabulary itself form a time capsule. A single set will be used, as in the French seventeenth-century neoclassical tragedies. This throne room, however, has none of the grandeur of Racine's Nero or Corneille's Augustus. It is frankly seedy, "dilapidated." It echoes the bourgeois, Victorian set for *Hedda Gabler* in which *The Bald Soprano* was given. In fact, Juliette, the maid, does not even call it a throne room. She apologizes to Queen Marguerite at the beginning of the play: "I haven't had time to do the living room." Marguerite corrects her: "This is not the living room. It's the throne room. How often do I have to tell you?" But the Queen protests too much; the tone is set. The throne room is in fact the family room of any bourgeois couple. Nor is there any more bourgeois situation than that of the *ménage à trois* which is presented to us casually from the start. No seraglio this, simply the old-fashioned arrangement of typical *homme sensuel moyen.* The public recognizes at once the elements of boulevard melodrama. Among many things *Exit the King* is a takeoff on Feydeau.

A throne room which is more like a family room, characters straight out of La Belle Époque's boulevard tradition, a most contemporary maid, harassed and grumbling, these are the reassuring, familiar signposts on the road. Lulled by a false sense of ease, the audience relaxes. One can almost hear their sighs of relief as they sink into the red velvet of their seats: "And we thought it would be another Ionesco! Is this about a king? He's like us." They echo Queen Marie's bewildered discovery: "He's just a King. He's just a man." A king is just a man, and Bérenger I is the most human of men, or at least the most frightened. Now, the spectators begin to feel slightly superior to this childlike king, this big baby. "The maid says they don't even have a washing machine! The radiators don't work! He really ought to redecorate this crumbling palace. Wait a minute, guignol, we'll tell you who to call, where to go! We'll teach you *savoir vivre.*" In a moment the audience will be taught *savoir mourir,* but they do not know it yet; they are full of hubris. By making them feel superior to this pitiful king, Ionesco brings each and every one to that stage of the King's life when he is still unaware of the inevitability of death. The intoxication of pride makes them forget their own mortality. By this device the dramatist will capture the audience in the mousetrap of his form and, Hamlet-like, bring them together with his protagonist to the same realization: "What must end one day is ended now."

The thin line which divides health from sickness, life from death, is crossed almost imperceptibly. In everyday life we notice that a friend who is sick is suddenly unable to hold his pen, his handwriting disintegrates, or he will look for words, mumble when he was once a brilliant conversationalist. A vain woman will neglect her hair, become slovenly. We laugh at these signs, content with the humorous surface, unwilling to see them for what they are, signs of the invisible presence of Death.

There are strange goings on in Bérenger's world. All seems familiar, yet everything is touched with weirdness. There are disturbances in the atmosphere which defy rational explanation: the cow is out of milk but the Milky Way is curdling, the earth splits and the streams run dry while clouds are raining frogs. Twenty-five citizens have been liquefied, and the stream in which the ministers were fishing has fallen into a bottomless pit. Above all, the Royal Constellation has vanished from the sky. "This is Ionesco after all," exclaim the spectators inside their heads. They are still laughing, but it is a laughter tinged with unrest. They thought they had their bearings, they thought Ionesco had joined them at last, and now they do not know. Besides there is this Guard who acts as a Greek chorus, and the Doctor-Executioner whose double function suggests primitive rituals, witchcraft, voodoo. No, this is not a divertissement after all, a boulevard melodrama. It is something else, but what?

Death is the invisible actor, the true protagonist of *Exit the King*. If this were a medieval, allegorical mystery play we would be treated to the hooded rider, the grimacing skull. Here the signs are concretized, so that the characters who surround the protagonist reflect the alteration of his state. Like a man who tries to lift a paralyzed arm, Bérenger orders his Guard to arrest all the traitors who wish him dead. It is the Guard, instead, who is arrested in mid-motion, mid-order, turned to stone, the visual symbol of the King's failing will. Beautiful Queen Marie, who would love to prove to the King that he is well, and that love will save him from death itself, finds that she can no longer dance, or even move her head. Loss of libido and loss of will power are thus concretized in dramatis personae who are extensions of the King's persona. Nor are objects or things of nature any more cooperative than people. Bérenger orders trees to sprout from the floor, leaves to grow again. They will not listen, although it is obvious that at one time the King was able to order the impossible and have it happen. Now, even the possible is out of the question. As the Doctor says: "The chef has shut off the gas. He's handing in his apron. He's putting the tablecloths and napkins away in the cupboard, forever." The King will not eat, for he is sick, he is dying, and so is his realm. "Yesterday evening it was spring. . . . Now it's November."

"In one hour and twenty-five minutes, you're going to die," announces Queen Marguerite, and the Doctor echoes: "Yes, Sire. In one hour, twenty-four minutes and fifty seconds." Consubstantial with his role Bérenger I can last only the duration of the spectacle. In that way Ionesco turns his tragicomedy, taken as a whole, into a play within the play. But if this is so, then the play is taking place in the theater itself, in the orchestra and balconies, and the spectators become actors. The sense of unreality which Ionesco creates mirrors the unreality he experiences when he considers that his life will end, that those he loves will no longer be, or have already disappeared. If, as Robert Nelson points out in his *Play within a Play*, "the relationship of the inner play to the outer play prefigures the relationship between the outer play and the reality within which it occurs: life,"[16] then in *Exit the King* it is the final reality which is put to question. The dualism of contradiction and deception, the broken mirror which can reflect only part of a complex society, is now part and parcel of the audience as illusion leaves the stage to seep into the hall. This is a deeply subversive act, since it saps that confidence, that sense of well-being, which spectators experience as they view the "others," the puppets on the stage. No longer sure of their own reality, they are less able to challenge that of the happenings on the stage. They have, in fact, by entering into the magic space of the theater, become participants, worshipers, actors. On the stage we have the play within the play, or ritual; in the theater we have the play. As the ceremony of Death is about to begin it is essential for the audience to go through this *rite de passage,* to leave behind that which belongs to the world. Only by submission to the principle of unreality will the public of *Exit the King* be able to transcend the boundary lines which divide it from the dramatis personae and become true apprentices of life and death.

"The ceremony is about to begin!" announces the Guard. They take up their positions. The King is seated on his throne. Now he knows that there is no escape. The throne takes on aspects of the electric chair, and the King has turned into a sacrificial victim. There is so little time left, and yet it can only move forward. The King hopes for a miracle, a reversal of the time clock. He would even settle for last week, and Marie for yesterday evening. Ionesco echoes Madame Du Barry's famous: "Une minute, Monsieur le Bourreau." Thinking himself back to the schoolboy that he was, Bérenger wishes he could be kept back for a year. Yesteryear's punishment is today's bliss.

As Bérenger wills himself into the past he enters a state of anarchic divagation. By his refusal of our existential situation, he projects himself outward, beyond the rational, into a state of delirium. In that dark zone of the wandering spirit, Bérenger turns, perhaps for the first time, to his people. He is still the King, and thus, not realizing that this time he is on common ground, he hopes that someone will "give his life for the King." This cliché which fostered many deaths on the battlefield is exposed here for the empty thing it is. King that he is, he will have to die his own death. Once he was a hero; he came near death many times. "I only came *near* it," whimpers the dying man. Thus, heroism itself is a cliché. As Giraudoux points out in *Tiger at the Gates*, there are no dead heroes. Heroism is for those who survived. Ionesco goes further still. Between the Grand Illusion of *l'entre deux guerres* and the shameful realities of World War II falls the shadow. The modern hero is not only he who survives, but he who orders assassinations. Modern survival depends on the elimination of one's friends, foes, and relatives. Queen Marguerite accuses Bérenger of having disposed of her family: "I tell you, you had my parents butchered, your own brothers, your rivals, our cousins and great-grandcousins, and all their families, friends and cattle. You massacred the lot and scorched all their lands."[17]

Is this *Richard III, Ubu Roi,* or the history of Ivan the Terrible or Hitler? You learn to die by killing. But killing is also a manifestation of our hatred of our human condition, of our stubborn and absurd refusal of it. In an advance notice for *The Killer* published in *Arts*, March 3, 1959, Ionesco explains:

But are we not all moving toward death? Death is really the end, the goal of existence. Death does not have to be buttressed by any ideology. To live is to die and to kill: every creature defends itself by killing, kills to live. In this hatred of man for man . . . in this inborn instinct for crime . . . is there not something like an underlying hatred of the very condition of man?

17. *Exit the King,* p. 47.

Do we perhaps feel in a confused sort of way, regardless of ideology, that we cannot help being, at one and the same time both killer and killed, governor and governed, the instrument and the victim of all-conquering death?[18]

Marguerite's evocation reveals a Bérenger who was once a ruler in the Promethean tradition of glory through active crime. Though the Old Queen seems to accuse him, she also revels in memories of the past. At that instant, Marguerite and Bérenger, like Père and Mère Ubu, form the figure of the smiling hermaphrodite Shiva, the Great Destroyer. Only by envisioning the inverted aspect of creation can we become apprentices of life. To borrow John Daniel's phrase, Ionesco's "ritual of nihilism" is only a station of Calvary, a void on the eve of Resurrection.

First comes physical dissolution, and Bérenger's mind grapples with this problem endlessly. Immortality, as men define it, is a trap. Humanity itself will die, and the planet wax cold. Monuments will crumble, books turn to dust. The very concept of *gloire* is as ephemeral as man and his universe. All is vanity, yet the King must probe the depths of this illusion before renouncing it. "Let the schoolchildren and the scholars study nothing else but me, my kingdom and my exploits. Let them burn all the other books, destroy all the statues and set mine up in all the public squares. My portrait in every Ministry, my photograph in every office of every Town Hall. . . ."[19] Bérenger-Stalin-Mao is a sad sack. His autocratic dream is deliriously grotesque. "Make them forget all other captains and kings, poets, tenors and philosophers and fill every conscious mind with memories of me. Let them learn to read by spelling out my name: B, E, BE for Bérenger."[20] Not content with leaving his little red book, King Bérenger hopes to become God. That way immortality lies. "Let my likeness be on all ikons, me on the millions of crosses in all our churches. Make them say Mass for me and let

18. *Notes and Counter Notes,* p. 162.
19. *Exit the King,* p. 48.
20. *Ibid.,* p. 49.

me be the Host."[21] Now we know whom Bérenger wishes to rival. Bérenger-Christ hopes to hear his name echoed throughout eternity.

Yet fame, the immortality of glory, cannot efface the horror of physical dissolution. The Doctor suggests that the King's body be embalmed. Bérenger rejects this suggestion, and all other forms of burial. He does not want to have anything to do "with a corpse." He wants to continue to feel, to feel "warm arms, cool arms, soft arms." So long as he feels something, no matter what it is, no matter the quality of the feeling, he will know that he is still among the quick.

The consolations of love will prove to be another illusion. The Young Queen, unable to approach her King, can only mouth clichés of the worst order: "'Exit' and 'die' are just words, figments of our imagination. Once you realize that, nothing can touch you. . . . Dive into an endless maze of wonder and surprise, then you will have no end, and can exist forever."[22] By baring the platitudes with which Eros clothes its magnificent form as it resorts to the inferior expression of speech, Ionesco dispels with anguished humor that men are loath to give us, the idea that love, though it cannot save, will at least reassure and console. The reality of death tears asunder the shimmering words. Underneath their veil, the tender flesh itself dissolves. Later Queen Marie will disappear. At this moment she is calling Bérenger into the past, begging him to recall "that morning in June . . . by the sea." But the "fiery radiance" has turned into the fire within the quivering bowels. "Love's labors lost," puns Watson's Marguerite.

Love's demystification is an essential step in the ritual of purification and renunciation which is the first step in the apprenticeship of dying. Up to this point, the King was an Epicurean whose existence with Marie was all "fun and games, dances, processions and fireworks." Now he will become a stu-

21. *Ibid.*
22. *Ibid.*, p. 51.

dent of the Stoics, those austere instructors in the art of resignation. It is at this point that the characters we had become used
to acquire a new dimension, a new aspect. It begins when the
King is calling on those around him to help him, to pity him:
"All the rest of you, be me, come inside of me, come beneath
my skin." A heart-rending cry of pure terror! We are all prisoners
of our own bodies, and no one can do our dying for us. In that
sense we have no kin; all are strangers, outsiders. Bérenger
comes to this dreadful realization: "I thought they were my
family. They are all strangers." His awareness seems to be the
agent of their metamorphosis. The two wives, the Guard, the
Doctor, even the maid form a solemn chorus. "The Gods have
returned to the bosoms of men," said Schiller. Were these characters humans, or were they all along Olympians costumed as
men? Nietzsche stated that myth is indispensable to the whole
stage world, like the Eleusinian mysteries. As in the case of the
citizens of Athens who lost their civic rank for the brief time
they became members of the dithyrambic chorus, the Guard, the
Doctor, the Maid, and the wives are transformed into the collective conscience, the mother womb which must give birth to
the dying man into the realm of death.

Incantation will be the instrument by which Bérenger will
be brought into contact with the ultimate reality. Like the Zen
archer who must cease to be conscious of himself in order to
hit the bull's eye which confronts him, becoming one with the
flying arrow, the dying man should adhere to the Buddhist epode
which is meant to carry him to the point where the soul "vibrates
of itself in itself" (Eugen Herrigel, *Zen in the Art of Archery*):

JULIETTE. You statues, you dark or shining phantoms, ancients and
          shades . . .
MARIE.   Teach him serenity.
GUARD.   Teach him indifference.
DOCTOR.   Teach him resignation.[23]

23. *Ibid.*, p. 54.

They speak a kind of mantra. Bérenger, however, is not ready to become a Buddha, to lose himself in the egolessness of things. Struggling against the Divinities of Death, he clings to life. Yet, the incantation has brought him closer to the shadowy world, as though song were the ferryman Charon's boat, and he, Aeneas-like, a traveler to the Underworld. Bérenger addresses the Dead, calling on them to help him, since no assistance is forthcoming from the Living. Are not the Dead his kin now, his family?

In Ionesco's *Fragments of a Journal* one finds the entry: "No, no, I want to go on living. To keep on living. I want the company of living men. In a word, I want both to live and to die. To be dead, and yet alive, like everyone else."[24] In the dining room of the nursing home where Ionesco has come for a cure he notices a man "with a blotchy face." He goes on crutches. "His presence is tolerable," says the observer. However, another man, opposite him, a healthy-looking "fine old fellow," is repulsive. Why? Ionesco explains:

He knows, or he believes, that what he eats is giving him life. One mouthful, two hours of life; by the end of the meal he's sure he has won another week of life. But it's chiefly the look in his eyes that is intoerable, the expression of a healthy old man, sharp, cunning and ferocious . . . that dogged determination to live, the way he clings to life and won't let go, seems to me tragic, frightening and immoral. I understand it very well, and it's myself that I hate in him, for I cling to life as much as he does, I shall be just like him in a few years' time; I can't forgive him and I can't forgive myself.[25]

Perhaps Ionesco has misjudged himself; perhaps he is too harsh in judging himself. By having written *Exit the King* he has in a sense exorcised these fears, and by pitying others forgiven in them and in himself this overwhelming anguish. Above all, the

24. Eugene Ionesco, *Fragments of a Journal* (New York: Grove Press, 1969), p. 56.
25. *Ibid.*, pp. 56–57.

most meaningful way of emerging from the Underworld is to glimpse life anew, with the eyes of a child, with the eyes of one who has had the fortune to return to the earth's surface. *Exit the King* is first and foremost a paean to life.

The first stage of the ritual is over. Bérenger knows now that there is no escape. Like an empty puppet the King arises, falls, rises again, and collapses. The Guard punctuates each attempt and failure with: "Long live the King! The King is dead!" The dying man turns to his servant and questions her: Has she mended his cloak? Has she had his shoes resoled? Here Ionesco clearly indulges his taste for *galgen-humor*. Freud's example of the latter is the story of the man who requests a scarf for his neck to walk over to the gallows without catching cold. We had an early example of it in this play when Marguerite scolds her husband for walking barefoot and Marie orders the Maid to give him his slippers. "Hurry up! He'll catch cold!" Marguerite's answer is grimly realistic, and paradoxically severe: "It's no longer of any importance if he catches cold. It's just that it's a bad habit." We laugh because certainly habits are as unimportant as the rest.

As to Bérenger, if he questions Juliette it is simply to gain time, to give himself the illusion that these things still matter, that he still belongs to a world where shoes are worn, buttons are sewn, cloaks are patched. But, by questioning his servant, the King, for the first time in his life, turns with curiosity to the humble existence of this creature everyone takes for granted. Juliette symbolizes life, which we also take for granted, life in its most direct, most primitive aspects. Bérenger asks: "Tell me how you live. What sort of life do you have?"[26] Juliette begins a slow, labored description of day-to-day chores. "A bad life, Sire." Bérenger waves this comment off, impatiently. She does not know what she is saying. "Life can never be bad. It's a contra-

26. *Exit the King*, p. 60.

diction of terms." Juliette answers with the cliché of the simple folk: "Life's not very beautiful." The King: "Life is life." Perhaps he had understood this life for the first time. He speaks in wonder and longing. Now that he is about to lose the most precious of gifts, the most squandered also, he realizes that life is not parades and fireworks, that Queen Marie, or rather his own conviction that he was immortal, has distracted him from the contemplation of the life process. He has never noticed the quality of the light, the riot of colors at an open street market. He has failed to realize the joy it is simply to step on the ground, to walk out of a house, or up the stairs, or down, to turn the key in the lock. If you walk you have feet that can walk, if you turn the key you have fingers that can give this turn. If your back aches from work, you still have a back that can ache. Later the ache will subside, you will rest, peace and life will return into your body. How can we complain about the weather, about having to get up early, about working hard? Everything is an eternal feast, the feast of life. While there is breath, and eyes to see, and hands to feel, all is deep joy and gratitude.

For Ionesco the absurdity of death—and death is the ultimate absurdity and degradation—affects not only the individual, important as he is, but our world as we know it. The eighteenth-century dream of Man's progressive enlightenment is revealed as grotesque. Bérenger invented gunpowder after having stolen fire from the gods. This Prometheus found a way to make steel and designed the Eiffel Tower. He made rails and railways, automobiles and planes. He built large cities—Rome, Paris, Moscow. Nor was he merely Shaw's New Man. He created literature, wrote the *Iliad* and the *Odyssey* and Shakespeare's plays. As the Guard —Chorus of *Exit the King*—recites the list of Bérenger's achievements we are reminded that our planet is doomed to grow cold and die, that immortality is a relative concept, that the greatest inventions, the most beautiful music, the most profound works of philosophy and literature, will be specks upon a dying star, a stone whirling in the abyss of a universe unpeopled by men as we know them.

It is imperative then for the King, and for us, to break free of the supreme illusion of immortality in history. The forms of our invention may seem to bear witness to their own validity. This is a trap. As Pascal said, man and his planet are specks in the void. Ionesco must now teach himself and us the Buddhist acceptance of that void. Emptiness is All.

With the disappearance of Marie a new, a final phase in the ritual begins. Queen Marguerite, the shrewish wife, is revealed at last as a great figure, a divinity of Death who will guide Bérenger toward his resignation. At last he will be able to look beyond the mirror into his entrails, where everything was reflected; he will, at Marguerite's urging, look past her, through her.

Queen Marguerite will be the shaman who will achieve Bérenger's redemption, bringing him to superconsciousness. By following him along the road into death we will follow the hero-path and achieve illumination. It is by listening only to Marguerite's voice that the erstwhile King, a tyrant, like every man, will enter the cosmogonic cycle. As Joseph Campbell tells us in his splendid book *The Hero with a Thousand Faces:* "Transformation, fluidity, not stubborn ponderosity, is the characteristic of the living God."[27]

Bérenger the Clown, the "mistaker of shadow for substance,"[28] will stand face to face with the ultimate reality, the claim of the unseen. By yielding to the Great Master of the Artless Art, by choosing to become egoless, Bérenger will suffer a metamorphosis into the hieratic man, the Bodhisattva. The apprenticeship of death performed by Marguerite is more akin to Oriental philosophy than to any Occidental image of final salvation.

27. Joseph Campbell, *The Hero with a Thousand Faces* (New York: Meridian Books, 1956), p. 337.
28. *Ibid.*

It's all quite safe in a mind that needs no memories. A grain of salt that dissolves in water doesn't disappear: it makes the water salty. . . . Unclasp your fingers! I order you to loosen those fingers! Let go of the plains, let go of the mountains! Like this. They were only dust. . . . It's not the day now or the night, there's no more day and no more night. Try and follow that wheel that's spinning around in front of you! Don't lose sight of it, follow it! But not too close, it's all in flames, you might get burnt.[29]

The fire alluded to here is the light of illumination, the one which breaks into the life of all the mystics Ionesco studies and loves: St. John of the Cross, the Neoplatonists, Plotinus. In *Fragments of a Journal* Ionesco quotes the following story from Martin Buber's *Tales of the Hasidim:* "Rabbi Dob Baer, the Maggid of Mezritch, once begged Heaven to show him a man whose every limb and every fibre was holy. Then they showed him the form of the Baal Shem Tov, and it was all of fire. There was no shred of substance in it. It was nothing but flame."[30]

Thus, the life-eager hero can resist fate and postpone for a short while the time of his death, but as he assumes the character of the Blessed One he will enter the realm of infinite space, infinite consciousness, and nothingness. Perception will leave him and he will abandon the perception of perception. "Smell that flower for the last time, then throw it away! Forget its perfume!" says Marguerite, guiding him along the road to Nirvana. "Now turn and face me! Look right through me! Gaze into my unreflecting mirror and stand up straight! Now you've lost the power of speech, there's no need for your heart to beat, no more need to breathe. It was a lot of fuss about nothing, wasn't it? Now you can take your place."[31]

---

29. *Exit the King*, pp. 91–93. It is interesting to note that the Chandogya Upanisad (VI, xiii, 1–3) speaks of salt dissolved in water as being the same throughout the water in which it is dissolved.

30. Eugene Ionesco, *Fragments of a Journal*, p. 70.

31. *Exit the King*, p. 94.

Ionesco himself acknowledges his "kinship with Oriental thought."[32] Though he writes in French and has become, ironically, an Immortal (a member of the Académie Française), one must not forget that he is by religion an Eastern Christian, a Greek Orthodox. Perhaps also being half Rumanian, rather than wholly French, makes it easier to shake off the shackles of Cartesianism. He would agree with Daisetz T. Suzuki, who says: "Man is a thinking reed but his great works are done when he is not calculating and thinking. 'Childlikeness' has to be restored with long years of training in the art of self-forgetfulness."[33] Thus Bérenger learns to wait, to be breathed rather than breathe. He must indeed become the great Archer, and his arrow will be his own soul. Queen Marguerite is the Zen teacher who instructs him in the technique of letting the arrow fall from the bow toward the goal, rather than aiming the arrow and straining the bow.[34]

Before our eyes, within the brief time of a spectacle, a man has been instructed in the deep meaning of the humble life, and in the process of giving up that life to enter Nirvana. We, the audience, have shared with him this instruction, and have been brought by the dramatist to full human maturity through the ritual enactment of a total initiation. We leave, together with Bérenger, our clown skin, clown faces, clown fears. A place is ready which we must ready ourselves to occupy. Walls, windows, doors, actors disappear. Even the Great Master leaves. Before our eyes a living, frightened man has entered with dignity into the All. We watch him "fade into the mist" wherein our planet, spinning into stillness, must dissolve.

32. *Fragments of a Journal,* p. 59.
33. Eugen Herrigel, *Zen in the Art of Archery* (New York: Pantheon, 1953).
34. This is a summary of the main thesis of the above.

Selected Bibliography

Books

Adlerstein, Arthur M. *The Relationship between Religious Belief and Death Affect.* Princeton: Princeton University Press, 1958.

Alvarez, A. *The Savage God.* New York: Random House, 1972.

Anthony, Sylvia. *The Child's Discovery of Death.* London: K. Paul, Trench, Trubner and Co. Ltd., 1940.

Bakan, David. *Disease, Pain and Sacrifice: Towards a Psychology of Suffering.* Boston: Beacon Press, 1968.

Bell, Thomas. *In the Midst of Life.* New York: Atheneum, 1961.

Bosselman, Beulah. *Self-Destruction: A Study of the Suicidal Impulse.* Springfield, Ill.: Charles C Thomas, 1958.

Bowers, Margaretta K., et al. *Counseling the Dying.* Camden: Thomas Nelson, 1964.

Bowman, Leroy. *The American Funeral.* Washington: Public Affairs Press, 1959.

Carlozzi, Carl G. *Death and Contemporary Man: The Crisis of Terminal Illness.* Grand Rapids: William B. Eerdmans, 1968.

Chesser, Eustace. *Living with Suicide.* London: Hutchinson, 1967.

Choron, Jacques. *Death and Western Thought.* New York: Collier Books, 1963.

————. *Modern Man and Mortality.* New York: Macmillan, 1964.

————. *Suicide.* New York: Scribner, 1971.

Demske, James M. *Being, Man and Death: A Key to Heidegger.* Lexington, Ky.: University Press of Kentucky, 1970.

Dodder, Clyde, and Dodder, Barbara, eds. *Suicide.* Boston: Beacon Press, 1970.

Dublin, Louis I. *Suicide: A Sociological and Statistical Study.* New York: Ronald, 1963.

Dunne, John S. *The City of the Gods, a Study in Myth and Mortality.* New York: Macmillan, 1965.

Durkheim, Emile. *Suicide: A Study in Sociology*. Glencoe, Ill.: Free Press, 1951.

Easson, William M. *The Dying Child: The Management of the Child or Adolescent Who Is Dying*. Springfield, Ill.: Charles C Thomas, 1970.

Eissler, Kurt R. *The Psychiatrist and the Dying Patient*. New York: International Universities Press, 1955.

Farber, M. L. *Theory of Suicide*. New York: Funk and Wagnalls, 1968.

Farberow, N. L. and Shneidman, E. S., eds. *Clues to Suicide*. New York: McGraw-Hill, 1957.

——. *The Cry for Help*. New York: McGraw-Hill, 1961.

Feifel, Herman, ed. *The Meaning of Death*. New York: McGraw-Hill, 1959.

Flew, Antony, ed. *Body, Mind and Death*. New York: Macmillan, 1964.

Freud, Sigmund. *Reflections on War and Death*. Trans. by A. A. Brill. New York: Moffat, Yard and Co., 1918.

Fulton, Robert, ed. *Death and Identity*. New York: Wiley, 1965.

Glaser, Barney G., and Strauss, Anselm. *Awareness of Dying*. Chicago: Aldine Publishing Co., 1965.

——. *Time for Dying*. Chicago: Aldine Publishing Co., 1968.

Grollman, Earl A. *Talking about Death: A Dialogue Between Parent and Child*. Boston: Beacon Press, 1970.

——., ed. *Explaining Death to Children*. Boston: Beacon Press, 1967.

Habenstein, R., and Lamers, William M. *Funeral Customs the World Over*. Milwaukee: Bulfin Printers, 1960.

——. *History of American Funeral Directors*. Milwaukee: Bulfin Printers, 1955.

Hamovitch, Maurice B. *The Parent and the Fatally Ill Child*. Duarte, Cal.: City of Hope Medical Center, 1964.

Harmer, Ruth M. *The High Cost of Dying*. New York: Collier Books, 1963.

Harrington, Alan. *The Immortalist: An Approach to the Engineering of Man's Divinity*. New York: Random House, 1969.

Henderson, Joseph L., and Oakes, Maud. *The Wisdom of the Serpent*, *the Myths of Death, Rebirth and Resurrection.* New York: Braziller, 1958.

Hendin, Herbert. *Black Suicide.* New York: Harper & Row, 1969.

———. *Suicide and Scandinavia.* New York: Grune and Stratton, 1964.

Henry, Andrew F., and Short, James F., Jr. *Suicide and Homicide.* New York: Free Press, 1954.

Hinton, John. *Dying.* Baltimore: Penguin Books, 1967.

Hocking, William Ernest. *The Meaning of Immortality in Human Experience.* New York: Harper, 1957.

Hunsinger, George. *Kierkegaard, Heidegger and the Concept of Death.* Stanford: Stanford University Press, 1969.

Jackson, Edgar N. *Telling a Child about Death.* New York: Hawthorn, 1965.

———. *Understanding Grief.* Nashville: Abingdon Press, 1957.

Kobler, Arthur, and Scotland, Ezra. *The End of Hope: A Social-Clinical Study of Suicide.* New York: Free Press, 1964.

Koestenbaum, Peter. *The Vitality of Death: Essays in Existential Psychology and Philosophy.* Westport, Conn.: Greenwood Pub. Co., 1971.

Kubler-Ross, Elisabeth. *On Death and Dying.* New York: Macmillan, 1970.

Kutscher, Austin, ed. *But Not to Lose.* New York: Frederick Fell, 1969.

———. *Death and Bereavement.* Springfield, Ill.: Charles C Thomas, 1960.

Landsberg, Paul Ludwig. *The Experience of Death: The Moral Problem of Suicide.* Trans. by Cynthia Rowland. New York: Philosophical Library, 1953.

Lepp, Ignace. *Death and Its Mysteries.* New York, Macmillan, 1968.

Levin, Sidney, and Kahana, Ralph, eds. *Psychodynamic Studies on Aging.* New York: International Universities Press, 1967.

Lifton, Robert J. *Boundaries: Psychological Man in Revolution.* New York: Random House, 1970.

McCulloch, J. W., and Philips, A. E. *Suicidal Behavior.* Elmsford, N.Y.: Pergamon, 1972.

Meerloo, Joost A. *Suicide and Mass Suicide.* New York: Dutton, 1962.

Menninger, Karl. *Man against Himself*. New York: Harcourt, Brace, 1938.

Mitford, Jessica. *The American Way of Death*. New York: Fawcett-World, 1969.

Moriarty, David H. *The Loss of Loved Ones*. Springfield, Ill.: Charles C Thomas, 1967.

Osborne, Ernest Glenn. *When You Lose a Loved One*. New York Public Affairs Committee, 1958.

Pearson, Leonard, ed. *Death and Dying: Current Issues in the Treatment of the Dying Person*. Cleveland: Press of Case Western Reserve, 1969.

Quint, Jeanne G. *The Nurse and the Dying Patient*. New York: Macmillan, 1967.

Resnik, Harvey L. *Suicidal Behavior: Diagnosis and Management*. Boston: Little, Brown and Company, 1968.

Shneidman, Edwin S. *Essays in Self-Destruction*. New York: Science, 1967.

————, and Faberow, Norman L., eds. *Clues to Suicide*. New York: McGraw-Hill, 1957.

Stengel, Erwin. *Suicide and Attempted Suicide*. New York: Humanities Press, 1964.

Sudnow, David. *Passing On*. Englewood Cliffs, N.J.: Prentice-Hall, 1967.

Toynbee, Arnold, ed. *Man's Concern with Death*. New York: McGraw-Hill, 1969.

Vernon, Glenn M. *The Sociology of Death: An Analysis of Death Related Behavior*. New York: Ronald Press, 1970.

Weisman, Avery D., and Kestenbaum, R. *The Psychological Autopsy: A Study of the Terminal Phases of Life*. New York Community Mental Health Monograph, 1968.

Journals Concerned Exclusively with Death

Omega—International journal for the psychological study of dying, death, bereavement, suicide and other lethal behaviors. Edited by Richard A. Kalish, Greenwood Periodicals, Westport, Conn.

Bulletin of Suicidology—Prepared jointly by the Center for Studies of

Suicide Prevention and the National Clearing House for Mental Health Information. Chevy Chase, Maryland.

Recent Articles and Unpublished Material

Alvarez, A., "Art of Suicide," *Partisan Review*, 37, no. 3 (1970), 339–58.

Annis, J. W., "The Dying Patient," *Psychosomatics*, 10, no. 5 (1969), 289–92.

Atkinson, J. M., "On the Sociology of Suicide," *Sociological Review*, 16 (March 1968), 83–92.

Barter, James T., Swaback, Dwight O., and Todd, Dorothy, "Adolescent Suicide Attempts: A Follow-up Study of Hospitalized Patients," *Archives of General Psychiatry*, 19, no. 5 (1968), 523–27,

Beberman, A., "Death and My Life," *Review of Metaphysics*, 17 (Sept. 1963), 18–32.

Becker, Diane, and Margolin, Faith, "How Surviving Parents Handled their Young Children's Adaptation to the Crisis of Loss," *American Journal of Orthopsychiatry*, 37, no. 4 (1967), 753–57.

Bennett, A. E., "Recognizing the Potential Suicide," *Geriatrics*, 22 no. 5 (1967), 175–81.

Berardo, Felix M., "Widowhood Status in the United States: Perspective of a Neglected Aspect of the Family Life-Cycle," *Family Coordinator*, 17, no. 3 (1968), 191–203.

Birtchnell, John, "The Possible Consequences of Early Parent Death," *British Journal of Medical Psychology*, 42, no. 1 (1969), 1–12.

Blaine, Graham B., Jr., and Carmen, Lida R., "Causal Factors in Suicidal Attempts by Male and Female College Students," *American Journal of Psychiatry*, 125, no. 6 (1968), 834–37.

Blauner, Robert, "Death and Social Structure," *Psychiatry*, 29, no. 4 (1966), 378–94.

Boreham, John, "The Prediction of Suicide," *Rorschach Newsletter*, 12, no. 2 (1967), 5–7.

Breed, W., "Occupational Mobility and Suicide among White Males," *American Sociological Review*, 28 (April 1963), 179–188.

Brickman, Harry R., "Psychedelic 'Hip Scene,' The Return of the

Death Instinct," *American Journal of Psychiatry,* 125, no. 6 (1968), 766–72.

Bridges, P. K., and Koller, K. M., "Attempted Suicide: A Comparative Study," *Comprehensive Psychiatry,* 7, no. 4 (1966), 240–47.

Brown, Norman O., and Bennis, Warren, "Norman O. Brown's Body— A Conversation," *Psychology Today,* 5, no. 1 (June 1971).

Cain, Albert C., and Fast, Irene, "The Legacy of Suicide: Observations on the Pathogenic Impact of Suicide upon Marital Partners," *Psychiatry,* 29, no. 4 (1966), 406–11.

Chasin, Barbara, "Value-Orientation and Attitudes towards Death," *Dissertation Abstracts,* 29, 6-A (1968), 1963.

Clayton, Paula, Desmaris, Lynn, and Winokur, George, "A Study of Normal Bereavement," *American Journal of Psychiatry,* 125, no. 2 (1968), 168–78.

Darbonne, Allen R., "Suicide and Age: A Suicide Note Analysis," *Journal of Consulting and Clinical Psychology,* 33, no. 1 (1969), 46–50.

Davis, Frederick B., "The Relationship between Suicide and Attempted Suicide: A Review of the Literature," *Psychiatric Quarterly,* 41, no. 4 (1967), 745–65.

Doroff, David R., "Attempted and Gestured Suicide in Adolescent Girls," *Dissertation Abstracts,* 29, 7-B (1969), 2631.

Dorpat, Theodore L., and Ripley, Herbert S., "The Relationship between Attempted Suicide and Committed Suicide," *Comprehensive Psychiatry,* 8, no. 2 (1967), 74–79.

Douglas, Jack D., "The Sociological Study of Suicide: Suicidal Actions as Socially Meaningful Actions," *Dissertation Abstracts,* 28, 2-A (1967), 799.

Ellard, John, "Emotional Reactions Associated with Death," *Medical Journal of Australia,* 1, no. 23 (1968), 979–83.

Farber, Leslie H., "Despair and the Life of Suicide," *Review of Existential Psychology* 2, no. 2 (1962), 125–39.

Faunce, W. A., and Fulton, R. L., "Sociology of Death, a Neglected Area of Research," *Social Forces,* Biblio., 36 (March 1958), 205–9.

Feifel, Herman, "The Function of Attitudes towards Death," *Journal of the Long Island Consultation Center,* 5, no. 1 (1967), 26–32.

————, and Jones, Robert B., "Perception of Death as Related to Nearness of Death," *Proceedings of the 76th Annual Convention of the American Psychological Association,* 3 (1968), 545–46.

Feinstein, Howard M., "Suicide," *Community Mental Health Journal,* 3, no. 3 (1967), 259–61.

Frank, Jerome D., "Breaking the Thought Barrier: Psychological Challenges of the Nuclear Age," *Psychiatry* 23 (1960), 245–66.

Freeman, Walter, "Psychiatrists Who Kill Themselves: A Study in Suicide," *American Journal of Psychiatry,* 124, no. 6 (1967), 846–47.

Ganzler, Sidney, "Some Interpersonal and Social Dimensions of Suicidal Behavior," *Dissertation Abstracts,* 28, 3-B (1967), 1192–93.

Hackett, Thomas P., and Weisman, Avery, "Predilection to Death: Death and Dying as a Psychiatric Problem," *Psychosomatic Medicine* (1961), 232–56.

Haider, Ijaz, "Suicidal Attempts in Children and Adolescents," *British Journal of Psychiatry,* 114, no. 514 (1968), 1133–34.

Harrison, Saul I., Davenport, Charles W., and McDermott, John F., Jr., "Children's Reactions to Bereavement: Adult Confusions and Misperceptions," *Archives of General Psychiatry* 17, no. 5 (1967), 593–97.

Haughton, Anson B., "Planning for the Prevention of Suicide," *American Journal of Orthopsychiatry,* 37, no. 2 (1967), 374–75.

Hicks, William, and Daniels, Robert S., "The Dying Patient, His Physician and the Psychiatric Consultant," *Psychosomatics,* 9, no. 1 (1968), 47–52.

Hippler, A. E., "Fusion and Frustration: Dimensions in the Cross-Cultural Ethnopsychology of Suicide," *American Anthropologist,* 71 (December 1969), 1074–87.

Hortelius, Hans, "A Study of Suicides in Sweden, 1951–1963, Including a Comparison with 1925–1950," *Acta Psychiatrica Scandinavica,* 43, no. 2 (1967), 121–43.

Jacobs, Jerry, "Adolescent Suicide Attempts: The Alienation of Progressive Social Isolation," *Dissertation Abstracts,* 28, 2-A (1967), 801.

————, "A Phenomenological Study of Suicide Notes," *Social Problems,* 15, no. 2 (1967), 60–72.

Jensen, Gordon D., and Wallace, John G., "Family Mourning Process," *Family Process*, 6, no. 1 (1967), 56–66.

Kalish, R. A., "The Aged and the Dying Process: The Inevitable Decisions," *Journal of Social Issues*, 21 (Oct. 1965), 87–96.

Kass, L. K., "Problems in the Meaning of Death, American Association for the Advancement of Science Symposium," *Science*, 170 (Dec. 11, 1970), 1235–36.

Kastenbaum, Robert, "The Mental Life of Dying Geriatric Patients," *Gerontologist*, 7, no. 2 (1967), 97–100.

———, "Multiple Perspectives on a Geriatric 'Death Valley,'" *Community Mental Health Journal*, 3, no. 1 (1967), 21–29.

Klagsbrun, Samuel C., "Cancer, Emotions and Nurses," *American Journal of Psychiatry*, 126, no. 9 (1970), 1237–44.

Koenig, Ronald R., "Fatal Illness: A Survey of Social Service Needs," *Social Work*, 13, no. 4 (1968), 85–90.

Kram, Charles, and Caldwell, John M., "The Dying Patient," *Psychomatics*, 10, no. 5 (1969), 293–95.

Krauss, Herbert H., "A Cross-Cultural Study of Suicide," *Dissertation Abstracts*, 27, 11-B (1967), 4126.

Lanteri-Laura, G., and Pistoria, L. del, "Structural Analysis of Suicidal Behavior," *Social Research*, 37 (Autumn 1970), 324–47.

LeShan, L., "Human Survival of Biological Death," *Main Currents in Modern Thought*, 26, no. 2 (1969), 35–45.

Lester, David, "Attempted Suicide as a Hostile Act," *Journal of Psychology*, 68, no. 2 (1968), 243–48.

———, "Fear of Death of Suicidal Persons," *Psychological Reports*, 20, no. 3 (1967), 1077–78.

———, "Psychology and Death," *Continuum*, 5, no. 3 (1967), 550–59.

———, "Suicidal Behavior: Aggression or Hostility in Social Relationships?" *Dissertation Abstracts*, 29, 1-B (1968), 391–92.

———, "Suicide as an Aggressive Act," *Journal of Psychology*, 66, no. 1 (1967), 47–50.

Maddison, David, and Walker, Wendy L., "Factors Affecting the Outcome of Conjugal Bereavement," *British Journal of Psychiatry*, 113, no. 503 (1967), 1057–67.

———, and Viola, Agnes, "The Health of Widows in the Year Following Bereavement," *Journal of Psychosomatic Research*, 12, no. 4 (1968), 297–306.

Maslow, Abraham, "Abe Maslow Talks about Death," *Psychology Today*, 4, no. 3 (Aug. 1970), 16.

Mattson, A., Seese, Lynne R., and Hawkins, James W., "Suicidal Behavior as a Child Psychiatric Emergency: Clinical Characteristics and Follow-up Results," *Archives of General Psychiatry*, 20, no. 1 (1969), 100–109.

May, Rollo, "The Daemonic: Love and Death," *Psychology Today*, 1, no. 9 (1968), 16–25.

McCulloch, J. W., and Philip, A. E., "Social Variables in Attempted Suicide," *Acta Psychiatrica Scandinavica*, 43, no. 3 (1967), 341–46.

MacLaurin, H., "In the Hour of Their Going Forth," *Social Case Work*, Biblio., 40 (March 1959), 136–41.

Morrissey, J. R., "Note on Interviews with Children Facing Imminent Death," *Social Case Work*, 44 (June 1963), 343–45.

Nettler, Gwynn, "Review Essay: On Death and Dying," *Social Problems*, 14, no. 3 (1967), 335–44.

Nolfi, Mary W., "Families in Grief: The Question of Casework Intervention," *Social Work*, 12, no. 4 (1967), 40–46.

Noyes, Russell, "The Dying Patient," *Diseases of the Nervous System*, 28, no. 12 (1967), 790–97.

O'Connell, Walter E., "Humor and Death," *Psychological Reports*, 22, no. 2 (1968), 391–402.

Parkes, Murray C., and Fitzgerald, R. G., "Broken Heart: A Statistical Study of Increased Mortality among Widowers," *British Medical Journal*, 1, no. 5646 (1969), 740–43.

Pearlman, Joel, Stotsky, Bernard A., and Dominick, Joan R., "Attitudes toward Death among Nursing Home Personnel," *Journal of Genetic Psychology*, 114, no. 1 (1969), 63–75.

Rosenbaum, Milton, and Richman, Joseph, "Suicide, the Role of Hostility and Death Wishes from the Family: A Preliminary Report," *Proceedings of the 77th Annual Convention of the American Psychological Association*, 4, pt. 2 (1969) 551–52.

Rosenblatt, Bernard, "A Young Boy's Reaction on the Death of His Sister: A Report Based on Grief Psychotherapy," *Journal of the*

American Academy of Child Psychiatry, 8, no. 2 (1968), 321–35.

Ross, Matthew, "Death at an Early Age," *Canada's Mental Health,* 18, no. 6 (Nov. 1970), 7–10.

Ross, Roslyn P., "Separation Fear and the Fear of Death in Children," *Dissertation Abstracts,* 27, 8-B (1967), 2878–79.

Schmid, C. F., and Van Arsdol, M. D., "Completed and Attempted Suicide: A Comparative Analysis," *American Sociological Review,* 20 (June 1955), 273–83.

Seiden, Richard H., "Campus Tragedy: A Study of Student Suicide," *Journal of Abnormal Psychology,* 71, no. 6 (1966), 389–99.

————, "We're Driving Young Blacks to Suicide," *Psychology Today,* 4, no. 3 (Aug. 1970), 24–28.

Selvin, H. C., "Durkheim's Suicide and Problems of Empirical Research," *American Journal of Sociology,* 63 (May 1958), 607–19.

Shein, Harvey M., and Stone, Alan A., "Psychotherapy Designed to Detect and Treat Suicide Potential," *American Journal of Psychiatry,* 125, no. 9 (1969), 1247–51.

Shneidman, Edwin S., "The Enemy," *Psychology Today,* 4, no. 3 (Aug. 1970).

————, "Orientations towards Death: A Vital Aspect of the Study of Lives," *International Journal of Psychiatry,* 2, no. 2 (1966), 167–90.

————, "You and Death," *Psychology Today,* 5, no. 1 (June 1971).

Siggins, Lorraine D., "Mourning: A Critical Survey of the Literature," *International Journal of Psychiatry,* 3, no. 5 (1967), 418–38.

Stern, Max M., "Fear of Death and Trauma—Remarks about an Addendum to Psychoanalytic Theory and Technique," *International Journal of Psychoanalysis,* 49, nos. 2–3 (1968), 457–63.

Sugar, Max, "Normal Adolescent Mourning," *American Journal of Psychotherapy,* 22, no. 2 (1968), 258–69.

Switzer, David K., "A Psychodynamic Analysis of Grief in the Context of an Interpersonal Theory of the Self," *Dissertation Abstracts,* 29, 1-B (1968), 381.

Szasz, T. S., "Ethics of Suicide," *Antioch Review,* 31 (Spring 1971), 7–17.

Wahl, Charles W., "The Differential Diagnosis of Normal and Neurotic Grief Following Bereavement," *Psychosomatics,* 11, no. 2 (1970), 104–6.

Wallace, Elspeth, and Townes, Brenda S., "The Dual Role of Comforter and Bereaved," *Mental Hygiene,* 53, no. 3 (1969), 327–32.

Wechter, Eugenia H., "Death Anxiety in Children with Fatal Illness," *Dissertation Abstracts,* 29, 7-B (1969), 2505.

Weiss, Samuel A., "Therapeutic Strategy to Obviate Suicide," *Psychotherapy, Theory, Research and Practice,* 6, no. 1 (1969), 39–42.

Welford, A. T., "Mental Integrity and the Nature of Life," *Medical Journal of Australia,* 1, no. 23 (1970), 1135–38.

Wenkart, Antonia, "Death in Life," *Journal of Existentialism,* 8, no. 29 (1967), 75–90.

Whitt, Hugh P., "The Lethal Aggression Rate and the Suicide-Murder Ratio: A Synthetic Theory of Suicide and Homicide," *Dissertation Abstracts,* 29, 7-B (1969), 2624–25.

Wilkins, J. L., "Producing Suicides," *American Behavioral Sciences,* 14 (Nov. 1970), 185–201.

———, "Suicidal Behavior," *American Sociological Review,* 32, no. 2, 185–201.

Williams, M., "Changing Attitudes to Death: A Survey of Contributions in *Psychological Abstracts* over a Thirty-Year Period," Biblio., *Human Relations,* 19, no. 4 (1966), 405–23.

Wilson, George C., Jr., "Suicide in Psychiatric Patients Who Have Received Hospital Treatment," *American Journal of Psychiatry,* 125, no. 6 (1968), 752–57.

Wolff, Kurt, "Helping Elderly Patients Face the Fear of Death," *Hospital and Community Psychiatry,* 18, no. 5 (1967), 142–44.

COLOPHON BOOKS ON PSYCHOLOGY AND EDUCATION

*In Preparation